Why Can't I Eat That?

Helping Kids Obey Medical Diets

Why Can't I Eat That?

Helping Kids Obey Medical Diets

John F. Taylor, Ph.D.
R. Sharon Latta

R&E Publishers
Saratoga, California

Newly Revised Second Edition

Published by R&E Publishers
P.O. Box 2008
Saratoga, CA 95070
(408) 866-6303

LC# 92-50875
I.S.B.N. 0-88247-981-4

Manufactured in the United States of America

First Edition ©1987
Published by Dodd, Mead & Company, Inc.

9 8 7 6 5 4 3 2 1

*DEDICATED to Gerrik, Gina, Johnn, and Jeremy,
and all children on a special diet, who daily
demonstrate unusual strength and willpower in
order to find health and well-being.*

Contents

Acknowledgments

We wish first of all to express our deep appreciation to the several outstanding dietitians who diligently reviewed this book at all stages of its development. They saw to its technical accuracy and its practical usefulness as a tool to aid dietitians as well as parents in working with diet-restricted children. Elaine Hartsook, Ph.D., R.D., made helpful suggestions, drawing upon her many years of experience with pediatric dietetics and with the Gluten Intolerance Group which she co-founded.

Joan Bleeg, R.D., and Nancy Ludwig-Williams, R.D., added to the information on dietary concerns when a diet-restricted child is hospitalized. Carolyn McGinnis, R.D., gave suggestions based on her experience with the dietetic needs of children in an outpatient setting. We also want to thank Judy Forest, R.D., who gave tirelessly of her vast knowledge of pediatric dietetics.

Consultants and parent educators from several regional and national children's health organizations contributed ideas and suggestions, especially for the chapters involving gaining the child's cooperation. We wish to thank the National Celiac Sprue Society and Debbie Gregg, R.D., of the Cincinnati Celiac Society and Children's Hospital Medical Center, Marge Wett and Linda Beltran of the National Prader-Willi Syndrome Association, Roberta Sich of the Spina Bifida Association of America, Earon Davis of the Human Ecology Action League, Joanne Reynolds of Oregon Diabetes Educators, and Ann Cinquina of the International Association of Cancer Victors and Friends and editor of the *Cancer News Journal*. The interplay of children's diets with exercise and other health concerns was effectively commented upon by Eleanor Houston of the Diet Center, Pamela

ix

Lyons-Nelson of Whole Person Health Services, and Bruce Mac-Farland of the Wellness Center.

We are indebted to the following physicians for their suggestions on dietary needs of hospitalized children, how parents can secure assistance in dietary matters, and the relationship of sound dietary principles to other health concerns: Martin Lorin, M.D., Professor of Clinical Pediatrics at Baylor College of Medicine; Orin Bruton, M.D.; Robert Grimm, M.D.; Roy Hall, M.D.; James Heder, M.D.; Mark Lindau, M.D.; James McDonald, M.D.; William Origer, M.D.; David Sessions, M.D.; and Randolph Stark, M.D.

We also appreciate the expertise of Jill DeVries, R.N., Gail Stockstill, R.N., and Donna Raddatz, L.P.N., pertaining to the parent's role when a diet-restricted child is hospitalized.

We also want to thank the outstanding educators who reviewed the chapter on maintaining children's diets at school: Claude Morgan, Ph.D., Mary Moravec, Lynn Thompson, and Sharon Williams. Drawing on his rich background as a school administrator and consultant on team building, Jerry Stinett gave helpful information for the parent support group chapter.

We also want to thank Mark Weiss of Old Mill School for his insightful analysis of the rights of diet-restricted children in public schools and Gale Roid, Ph.D., for his helpful suggestions on the impact of a child's long-term diet on family relationships.

We want to express our thanks also to the following pharmacists for reviewing the chapters having to do with the relationships of children's diets with other health concerns and with medications: Gary Blevin, James Harrington, Richard Hedges, and Lee Wanke. Eva Cotter researched many of the entries in the medication-nutrition table in the Appendix, along with Richard Hedges. Don Cowles produced the table in its final form, and we are deeply grateful for this excellent contribution.

We wish to thank the following clergymen for their suggestions on family stresses involved with long-term childhood diseases and dietary restrictions: Chaplain Louis Buckley, the Reverend Ed Henderlite, the Reverend Don Sappington, the Reverend Chuck Shorow, the Reverend John Stewart, and the Reverend Christian Thearle.

Expert homemaking advice was supplied by Jana Gunn, Jan

Fuller, and Judy Burridge, home economist. Their contributions were helpful for the chapter on understanding a child's long-term diet.

In the chapter dealing with organizing a parent support group, we sought the combined knowledge and experience of several support group leaders. John and Theda Tawney, who for years have worked on Special Olympics for handicapped children, gave much helpful information. The following parents of diet-restricted children have also been leaders of various parent support organizations and gave helpful suggestions: Jane Hersey, Clark and Marlene Luchau, Judy Origer, Jan and Ken Nolley, Briget Phillips, Ellen Spivack, Don and Marilyn Thompson, and Candy Woodson. We also want to thank Pixie Werner for her helpful comments.

No listing of help received would be complete without mention of the most important help of all—that given by our patient and understanding families. We have the deepest gratitude for their many forms of support during times of pressured activity to produce a book of this magnitude. Their sacrificial support was truly a labor of love.

Foreword

Maintaining a child's prescribed diet is no easy task. At its onset, a diet involves learning its basic principles and initiating it in the home. "Sounds easy!" you may say. The success of any dietary intervention, however, cannot be measured at this point alone. In the initial counseling of patients and their families, dietitians must make an assessment of the parent's and child's understanding of the diet and the anticipated compliance. Do the child and family know enough about the diet actually to follow it?

To initiate a diet, it is necessary to provide thorough teaching about the disease or condition warranting it as well as the rules for following it. Knowing the what and the why forms the basis to a diet plan but does not ensure its success. Once the parents and child learn the concepts and the guidelines of a diet, the challenge of maintaining a dietary change has just begun.

Environmental, behavioral, and emotional factors influence both the child and the family, making even the simplest of diets more difficult than first expected. Disregarding or misunderstanding the roles that situations, behaviors, and feelings play in a child's diet often leads to failure. Awareness and understanding of these factors, however, can minimize their effects when they are negative and can facilitate constructive efforts when they are positive.

This book presents a comprehensive view of any child on any diet. In the limited time of instruction and follow-up, physicians and dietitians rarely have the opportunity to discuss the concepts that the authors so thoroughly analyze. While it does not address specific diets, this book raises questions that are often missed in diet counseling. Dr. Taylor's experience in counseling families is apparent in this book. Not only does he list the factors that affect diet compliance, but he gives advice and examples of how to deal with them. My experience in diet counseling indicates that few parents or children are equipped with the understanding or the skills to meet the demands of long-term dietary intervention effectively without the type of information provided in this book.

The authors' understanding of family dynamics enables them to bring clarity to an otherwise confusing picture of behaviors and emotions. In maintaining their child on a diet, parents need to acknowledge both the child's feelings and their own. The authors encourage parents to ask questions: How does my child feel about this disease or condition? How do I feel about my child's condition, and why? The first section of the book raises these types of questions. Children's typical emotional responses to their diseases and medical conditions are clearly presented. Also included are the parents' possible reactions to their children. The authors present several patterns of emotional states that parents of diet-restricted children often experience. The shame cycle of child abuse, parent's self-abuse cycle, carelessness-nagging cycle, and overindulgence-rejection cycle are discussed in detail. The purpose of acknowledging these cycles is to help parents develop a better understanding and acceptance of their child's situation.

Eating is a very important part of our lives; it has social, economic, emotional, and behavioral demands. Any deviation from a child's normal routine of eating is bound to have effects to which parents may be unable to respond appropriately. If parents expect to carry out a dietary change, they must be able to integrate it into their lives as smoothly as possible. Here lies the strength of this book. The practical information it provides for the transition to a new diet pattern and the recommendations it gives for dealing with the obstacles of an ongoing diet should prove to be invaluable to parents.

The authors stress the multi-disciplinary approach to a child's diet plan. They encourage parents to seek professional help from a variety of health care fields. While physicians and dietitians typically play a central role in children's prescribed diets, other health care specialists may be more helpful in meeting social, physical, emotional, or behavioral needs. Parents should feel comfortable pursuing other sources of information and assistance. In doing so, they are ensuring the meeting not only of dietary requirements, but also of all needs affecting the child's diet.

This book gives parents suggestions for obtaining services from the community. Parent support groups are discussed, including their organization, purposes, and goals. The steps to forming a new support group are listed with procedures and tips for making it an effective one as well. The book also provides suggestions for getting the cooperation of school personnel.

Dr. Taylor and Mrs. Latta have broadened the picture of children's diets. They enable us to look toward a better understanding of what affects the child and the diet. This book should be an invaluable guide to families who may at first lack some of the skills or insights to deal completely with the stresses of a therapeutic diet for a child. The integration of Dr. Taylor's counseling interests and experiences into the field of nutrition and dietetics is encouraging.

There is great challenge in counseling families of children on prescribed diets. I have seen children able to reach and maintain their dietary goals with minimal assistance and very little follow-up. On the other hand, I have seen some children with chronic diseases whose families need to deal not only with dietary restrictions but also with significant medical, social, and financial pressures from their child's condition. As a dietitian, my primary interest is maintaining the nutritional status of my patients. In counseling, I have made every effort to regard each patient as an individual having unique problems and needs.

I am pleased that *Special Diets and Kids: How to Keep Your Child on Any Prescribed Diet* is available to parents of children on diets. Parents should take time to read it carefully, pausing to relate its concepts to their own situation. I also recommend it as a guide for all professionals interested or involved in the care of such children.

Lana D. Peth, R.D.
Clinical Dietitian
Children's Hospital and Medical Center
Seattle, Washington

Introduction

This is a diet book like no others. It contains no recipes, calorie charts, lists of Recommended Daily Allowances of nutrients, foods to be avoided or foods that are recommended. Not a single diet is offered, yet this book contains an important ingredient in every diet that has been prescribed for any child. The absence of this ingredient has led to the failure of the efforts of thousands of parents who have tried to maintain prescribed diets for their children. This ingredient does not come from the fields of dietetics or of medicine, but it is the key to making any child's diet work—without it the diet will almost surely be doomed to failure. The essential ingredient, provided throughout this book, is motivation—getting the child to cooperate and stay on the diet.

Because of the cultural importance attached to the serving and eating of food, any child requiring strict dietary limitations faces complex social and emotional challenges. Most special occasions, for example, are celebrated by the presentation of food as a way of offering love and hospitality. By giving food to their children, parents show their caring for them. By eating the food, the children affirm their parents as providers of that which can fulfill the children's needs.

For parents of children requiring long-term diets, most of the available literature consists of books about specific diseases, allergies, or other conditions. Such books typically give little or no coverage to aspects of dietary maintenance and treatment, other than an occasional list of required foods to feed the child. Even those few books that actually outline dietary treatment tend to gloss over the psychological problems and complexities most likely to undercut the recommended procedures. The remarkable advances in dietary science are often wasted because parents cannot persuade their children to stay on the required diets. Dietitians and physicians have routinely observed that dietary efforts fail more often from psychological factors than from nutritional factors. Solving the problem of staying on a long-term diet is what this book is all about.

The first section addresses the most troublesome psychological factors and sets the stage for effective application of a long-term diet. The initial chapters explain the emotional hurdles most often faced by parents of diet-restricted children. One reason why many children's diets falter at the very beginning is that one or both parents still have not achieved a sufficient amount of emotional acceptance of the child's medical condition or of the necessity for the diet. The first chapter is devoted to this issue because acceptance of these realities is crucially important to successful maintenance of a long-term diet for the child. The issue is a complex one, however, as one parent of a severely handicapped diet-restricted child put it:

As a parent of a handicapped child, I fluctuate between defensive states and acceptance. Further, the fluctuation is dependent upon the current circumstances of my child's life.

Acceptance of what? Accept my child? Yes, I do. Accept the presence of the handicapping condition of my child? As life goes on and the handicap persists, I come to acknowledge and then accept its presence. Accepting the child is easy—striving to accept the handicap is not, and it may not occur. Learning to deal effectively with the handicap and helping my child to do the same are what are important.

The relationship between a parent and that parent's handicapped child is a dynamic one that I believe is constantly changing.

The first section portrays your child's diet as a part of total health care. It focuses on the nitty-gritty of implementing your child's diet and portrays how to support changed household routines as a result of the dietary effort.

The second section gives detailed information on how to get the child to cooperate and share in the maintenance of the diet. The theme in this section is teaching your child to adopt an increasing, appropriately geared share of interest in and responsibility for maintaining the diet.

The third section tells how you and your child can find support from other people, both inside and outside of your family. Professionals from a variety of helping disciplines, siblings and friends of your child, and the parents of other diet-restricted children can all be of great assistance.

The fourth section details what to do when food-related routines are disrupted. These are the most troublesome moments for diet-restricted children and their parents. Holidays, family travel, school, hospitalization, and the lack of support by one parent can undercut a well-planned dietary approach unless the actions portrayed in this section are taken.

Estimates of the incidence of chronic illness or handicapping conditions in children in the United States vary a great deal. It is certainly safe to say that from 5 to 10 percent of all children have a severe chronic illness. The treatments for many of these illnesses include dietary measures. Many conditions for which diets have been generally recommended do not qualify as severe chronic conditions, so that the total percentage of all children who could or should be on some sort of diet is much higher. For example, surveys indicate that three out of ten adolescents are overweight and could profit from dietary measures to reduce weight.

Over sixty symptom complexes and diseases have been identified for which nutritional treatment has been proposed. Many of these complexes are actually clusters of different disorders, so that the total number of specific disorders is much higher.

Some diets are very simple, as when a child with congenital heart disease is required to have low salt intake. Others are quite complex, involving the elimination of whole food groups from a child's allowed food fare. The results of deviating from the diet vary from almost no direct or immediate impact to the risk of imminent death. For some disorders, dietary treatment is still controversial and is not fully accepted by medical or dietetic communities. As knowledge of children's medical conditions advances, dietary approaches will probably become an increasing part of orthodox medical treatment for some and may take a decreasing role for others. Following is a list of most of the symptom complexes and diseases for which long-term diets are currently employed as part of medical treatment for children and adolescents.

Symptom Complexes and Diseases for which diets are sometimes prescribed

Adrenocortical insufficiency
Allergies
Anemia
Anorexia
Asthma
Bronchopulmonary dysplasia
Cancer (childhood)
Celiac sprue disease
Colitis
Collagen disease
Congenital anomalies, multiple
Congenital heart disease
Constipation, chronic
Cystic fibrosis
Dermatitis herpetiformis (DH)
Diabetes, juvenile onset
Diaphragmatic hernia
Diarrhea, chronic
Diverticulitis
Diverticulosis
Enteritis (other than gluten or celiac)
Epilepsy
Esophagitis
Folic acid deficiency
Friedrich's ataxia
Fructosemia
Galactosemia
Glomerulonephritis
Headaches (chronic, migraine)
Hepatitis
Hepatolenticular degeneration (Wilson's disease)
Homocystinuria

Hyperthyroidism
Hypoglycemia
Hypothyroidism
Intestinal lymphangiectasia
Intolerances, food related (e.g., lactose)
Irritable bowel syndrome
Juvenile rheumatoid arthritis
Leukemia
Lupus
Malabsorption (sucrase-isomaltase and glucose-galactase deficiency, a-beta-lipoproteinemia)
Maple syrup urine disease (branched-chain ketoaciduria)
Muscular dystrophy
Nephrosis
Obesity
Pancreatitis
Peptic ulcer
PKU (phenylketonuria)
Prader-Willi syndrome
Reflux
Renal insufficiency, chronic
Renal tubular acidosis
Rheumatic fever
Sensitivities (lactose, sulfite, salicylate, etc.)
Short bowel syndrome
Sickle cell anemia
Spina bifida
Tuberculosis
Tuberous sclerosis
Tyrosinosis

Hyperlipidemia (hyper-
cholesterolemia and
hyperlipoproteinemia)
Hypersplenism
Hypertension

Underweight
Urinary calculi
Vitamin deficiency

This book is meant to supplement but not replace the advice given by a physician or dietitian with regard to your child's diet. We assume that you have either chosen nutritional treatment as one of the available alternatives or that you have been told that there is no choice. Each family situation is unique and calls for a specialized program of diagnosis and treatment, tailored to the child and to the entire family situation. We have provided a chapter to assist you in establishing effective relationships with a physician or dietitian who would be able to comment on the effectiveness of a specific dietary approach for your child.

The focus throughout the book is on general principles that are effective with most children's long-term therapeutic diets. Use this book as a smorgasbord of ideas, as a toolbox from which to select the best tools to help a certain child with a certain diet. But don't assume that all of the ideas will apply to every situation or for every child. A notable exception to many of the trends encouraged in this book, for example, is found in the Prader-Willi syndrome, a congenital syndrome involving short stature, mental retardation, obesity, weak muscle tone, and hormone imbalances. Children with this disorder do not achieve self-sufficiency and personal responsibility for monitoring their diets. They are not encouraged to assist in maintaining their diets as otherwise proposed and encouraged throughout the book. When the right tool is indicated, use it. If an idea or principle in this book does not seem to be the right tool for your child, read on to find a better one, more suited to your specific situation.

This book also represents the additional wisdom, experience, and ideas of many consultants. They have been involved with all phases of children's diets, reflecting a wide range of complexity of dietary needs in the children represented. Additional information in this book was gathered through working with numerous health organizations, examination of current professional literature on various diets and diseases, and reflecting on our years of personal experience in assisting children with long-term diets in a wide variety of family settings. You can rely on the principles and ideas in this book—they come from those who have refined and used them successfully.

It is our hope that this guidebook will become a family reference source, one to be employed often. We also hope that it will be available to the child's siblings, to helping professionals involved with your family, and to friends and relatives who from time to time may be charged with the care of your child. Judicious use of this book can help you become more knowledgeable and effective parents, and your child's siblings can be stimulated to become more loving and responsible brothers and sisters.

Throughout the book, we have referred to the child by feminine pronouns in some chapters and by masculine pronouns in other chapters. Involved adults are usually rendered in the opposite gender within any specific chapter.

There is no help we can offer your family in this book that can remove the struggles and the pain of readjustment regarding menu planning and meal preparation, or magically cure your child of the need for a long-term diet. We have tried to provide sufficient tools to open doors of communication and cooperation within your family. Most importantly, this book focuses uniquely on enhancing your child's self-understanding and willingness to assume a gradually increasing personal responsibility for maintaining the diet. Our hope is that using this book will build a stronger bond of understanding and closeness in your family. At the same time, we trust that it will provide that very important ingredient of successful motivation for your child's long-term diet that up to now may have been missing.

J. F. T.

R. S. L.

Salem, Oregon

1. Understand Your Feelings

No two parents react in exactly the same way to the physical and psychological stresses of raising a child who must be on a special diet. The course of any one child's condition is uniquely affected by a host of factors, many of which may not be controllable by parents. For some parents whose children are on a generous diet for a relatively short period of time, the course is not a difficult one and means only various readjustments of daily routines without any great emotional struggles. The necessity for a very restrictive long-term diet, however, can sometimes send parents on an emotional roller coaster and force them to face trials and challenges far beyond those faced by parents of children who have no dietary restrictions.

Facing the responsibility of helping a child who must be on a special diet can exert severe stress on you, your family, and your child. You face a period of confusion and anxiety as symptoms first appear. Final diagnosis of your child's medical problem takes time. Once your child's condition is identified, you must engineer various treatment programs, including manipulating his diet. All of this effort occurs while you are trying to balance the lives of other family members.

There are numerous new tasks. You must negotiate with helping professionals. You must explain the diet to relatives, friends, and others who may be in charge of supervising your child for periods of time. In addition to probably learning new grocery-shopping and food-preparation routines, you face diet-related decisions while traveling, observing holidays, visiting others, coordinating your child's activities, and juggling a busy family's schedule.

Because you have a child who has a medical disorder, the ordinary events of life may have unusual impact. Events such as a move of the family, a change in job, the birth of a sibling, or even a family vacation can bring stressful problems that may require a great deal of planning.

What Your Emotions Do for You

If you are contented and experience a situation as pleasant, your psychological and physical needs are probably being met at that point. If, on the other hand, you experience feelings that are unpleasant to you, your needs are not being met. The natural response to those signals is to take action to meet your needs better. When you have not had enough to eat, the physical reaction of hunger occurs, and your natural response is to find food and eat. After you eat, the hunger disappears. If you have been deprived of sufficient contact with others, then you are likely to experience the psychological reaction of loneliness. The natural response to loneliness is to seek out the company of others. When you have made sufficient social contact, the loneliness disappears. Emotions that you experience as unpleasant basically defend you by alerting you that you are about to enter a situation in which your needs might not be met.

A defensive emotional state indicates that you are in a high-stress situation. The most common defensive emotional states among parents of diet-restricted children are denial, fear, anger, guilt, and overinvolvement. Your goal should be to progress beyond these defensive states toward emotional acceptance of the situation.

Everyone experiences these defensive emotional states from time to time. When they are brief, no particular harm occurs to family relationships. Under severe and long-standing stress, however, a breakdown of these normal functions of emotions can occur. When these defensive emotional states persist and start to disrupt your functioning as a family leader, you must make the effort to modify them.

Defensive Emotional States Can Disrupt the Diet

The parental habit of nurturing by feeding the family is almost universal. If something goes wrong with the child's ability to use food, the parent must modify her role as food-giver. In this way, part of the parent's role of being the physical sustainer of the family is automatically diminished. This change could affect pre–existing psychological processes and develop into a significant issue. If a parent has defined her role too narrowly—that of the sole food-giver, for example—problems are more likely to occur. The parent may start to feel panicky that somehow her role is threatened because her food is no longer good enough to keep the child in a healthy state.

The parent may have considered the preparation and serving of food to be part of her role of keeping the child dependent. If the child becomes self-sustaining with regard to food preparation and food choices, the parent's ability to make the child dependent is threatened.

There is constant interplay between a parent's emotional needs, a child's emotional needs, and fluctuations in the child's condition. If symptoms decrease because of the diet, the child feels better, becomes less dependent, and is likely to become more assertive. These changes in turn alter the child's relationship with the parent. The decreased dependency can displace the parent and give the parent reason to feel less useful. The parent may even feel as if she is no longer permitted to nurture the child because of the child's increasing self-sufficiency. Sometimes a parent even lures a child into deviating from the diet as a way of strengthening the parent's role as supporter and provider of tasty, off-limits foods to eat.

Another set of important feelings to recognize are those of the parent who does most of the cooking for the family. Time limitations placed on her because of the diet bring significant stresses. She might also need to operate under reduced freedom of food choices and budgetary restrictions while still engineering a special diet.

What if the person responsible for meal planning and preparation hates to cook? This stress is made even worse if this parent is not familiar with cooking as an art and has not developed cooking as an enjoyed skill. There may be a tendency, furthermore, to avoid learning the necessary skills because of a general dislike of kitchen activities.

The parent who has primary cooking responsibility may have an emotional blockage left over from earlier experiences. The mother of the parent who must cook, for example, may not have allowed her children in the kitchen. The current parent who must cook for the diet may have been kept ignorant and helpless about cooking while growing up. Or the kitchen scene may bring in memories of violence or other unpleasantness from the childhood of that parent. Eating might have been a necessary something to get through, accompanied by family arguments or other overwhelming stresses.

The parent who must cook for the diet may feel inferior and have self-doubts about her kitchen skills, or she may feel overwhelmed by the many gadgets and utensils that are available. She might feel obligated to learn to use these things but feel insecure because of her unfamiliarity with recipes. These feelings can have significant impact on her ability to function as the provider of the dietary program, to the extent that the diet involves food cooked at home.

When prolonged, five defensive emotional states—denial, fear, anger, guilt, and overinvolvement—can limit any parent's ability to assist in maintaining a diet for a child. Specifically, these states interfere with the parent's decision-making ability, magnify the problems that must be overcome, and strain the relationships within the family. When the parent is calmer and can better grasp the entire situation, she can make more effective decisions. At calmer times, it is easier for the parent to keep proper perspective on everyday events as well as crisis and emergency happenings.

Directed, assertive action that gets to the heart of the problem does not occur if the parent is experiencing one of these states. Instead, energy is shunted off in useless directions, and the difficulties remain unchallenged or worsen. It is possible for a parent to stay in one of these defensive states for months or even years. Intense personal discouragement is often at the root of these sustained states.

A defensive emotional state becomes even more potent when any sort of neurotic or self-defeating behavior has already existed. In most cases, the parent does not consciously realize that she feels this way. The mother, for example, who cannot admit that her child is chronically ill or is less than perfect in health or behavior may deny aspects of the child's condition for years. The mother's prior inability to admit any imperfections in herself or anyone she is connected to sets the stage for denial. Maintaining a defensive emotional state for an extended period of time magnifies the problems for everyone. Other family members become less able to adjust their actions in a way that would support the diet, because they are less free to discuss the child's dietary needs with the parent. If they try to do so, they risk conflict with the person who is mired in one of the defensive emotional states.

Denial

One of the most common reactions to hearing any unpleasant news is to lessen its impact by minimizing it. Questioning the source of information, insisting that the bearer of the unpleasant news double-check the facts, and making sure that there has not been some mistake are understandable ways to be assured that professionals' findings are accurate. If this kind of double-checking continues for months, however, the parent may have a great need to deny that the child requires the diet. Often accompanying a state of denial is a state that might be best described as numbness or shock. The information, such as a frightening diagnosis or an explanation of the need for a very elaborate and restrictive diet, cannot be addressed directly because of its overwhelming impact.

It is important to differentiate between the natural initial wish to deny, often accompanied by numbness, and the defensive denial itself. "This can't be happening to my child; let's double-check the diagnosis" is a quite normal response and usually passes in a short period. It neither indicates deep-seated psychological complications nor predicts ultimate dietary failure. Sustained denial in the face of numerous pieces of evidence to the contrary is the troublesome form of denial.

Complications caused by the child's medical condition may seem endless. Denials among parents of diet-restricted children commonly center around the following: symptoms—"My child's hives were just a coincidence. . ."; diagnosis—"He can't have that disease; it must be. . ."; severity—"He'll get better quickly; you can't keep him down. . ."; diagnostic procedures—"They just wanted to make money off of us by running all those needless tests. . ."; necessity of treatment—"All he needs is a good long rest. . .''; and suitability of professional help—"These doctors don't know what they are talking about."

The parent may try to dismiss the child's symptoms as reflecting normal behavior. If she recognizes the symptoms as unusual, the parent may try to dismiss them as merely a reflection of the child's uniqueness or of a trait inherited from relatives. The parent may recall having been ill as a child but having "outgrown" the problem. She might try to explain the symptoms away as the result of some minor, temporary, or psychosomatic difficulty, rather than a long-term condition that requires special dietary treatment.

To avoid facing the unpleasant realities, a parent may seek out several specialists in an attempt to find a different diagnosis. Diagnosis shopping can last for years and can have terrible effects for all concerned. Some of the medical conditions that must be treated by special long-term diets merely get worse as time goes on and as treatment is postponed. Seeking a second opinion is wise, but constantly seeking a new diagnosis or emphasis (while the child's condition simply worsens) is harmful. Unfortunately, misdiagnosis can occur; there is a fine line between a legitimate search for competent professional help and a defensive flitting from one practitioner to another.

Even though a parent may recognize the symptoms and accept the diagnosis, she may want to avoid confronting the many aspects of the child's life that are affected by the medical condition. Denial still may occur by assuming that the disorder will be short-term or will have little impact. This form of denial can thrust the child into very difficult situations. Many of the disorders requiring special diets have severe consequences for the child's social life, school adjustment, self-image, and career choices.

A parent may act as if the need for a special diet does not involve significant stress on the family. The parent may pretend that the disorder or the treatment methods do not affect the child's complex relationships with others. She may naively expect the child not to feel "different" when eating with others.

A parent may deny the necessity of treatment. She might maintain that the child will outgrow the disorder. The parent might support the diet for awhile in an offhand manner but in fact intend from the very beginning not to follow through for any considerable length of time.

The parent may claim that the problems will disappear with a simple change in daily routines, alteration of parenting techniques, or quick and easy medical treatments. The parent may claim that the illness is only a phase or that the child is among those who experience spontaneous improvement without needing any medical treatment. As if to guard against psychosomatic problems, the parent may also decide not to pay much attention to the child's symptoms or complaints.

A parent may deny that the child is receiving adequate help from professionals and thus may go treatment shopping for helping professionals who will tell her something more pleasant. This form of denial, of course, makes the parent especially vulnerable to quack schemes, marginal and controversial treatments, fad diet ideas, and questionable medical practices.

What to Do About Denial

To overcome denial and the accompanying emotional numbness and shock, take the following steps:

Avoid the "I don't know" excuse. Sometimes an "I don't know" about any aspect of your child's condition can actually mean "It is hard for me to face. . .," "I don't want to know. . .," or "I can't deal with that thought now." If the issue is one of fact, it can often be found out from a reference work or competent authority. Denial can lie behind the smoke screen of "I don't know."

Learn all you can. Knowledge gained from a searching inquiry into the nature of your child's condition can bolster you against denial. Every family member should understand your child's condition and the principles of effective dietary treatment. Pulling together as a family brings fulfillment and teaches many important lessons about life to your children.

Allow "normal" forgetting. Forgetting aspects of the initial conversations with physicians about diagnosis is not a sign of inadequacy as a parent. It is essential to resolve your first doubts caused by any forgetting or denial in the early stages of diagnosis. Temporary disbelief is understandable, and forgetting is a common defense against emotional pain. Especially if your child's disorder is of a severe nature, a normal reaction is similar to that following the death of a loved one. Immediate acceptance and graceful coping often are not possible. Do not be afraid to ask the physician to repeat what he has already explained to you. Realize that any difficulties you experience in fully understanding your child's situation are probably normal temporary reactions and should not govern your later efforts at engineering treatment for your child.

Avoid being too optimistic. Unrealistic optimism about the situation is a form of denial. Pessimism, of course, should also be avoided. The middle ground of cautious optimism is the best attitude and is supported well by a continuous effort to become more familiar with the need for the diet. Although a completely stress-free situation will not develop, your child can make gradual adjustments to any required diet. Your child and family can learn to adapt to the special challenges posed by the diet, and the experience of doing so can bring psychological growth.

Be aware of your child's changes. While in some cases a prescribed diet brings full restoration of health, some ongoing difficulties may prevail. Your child is continually ready for different responsibilities and new levels of self-sufficiency as time goes on. Allow a changing share of responsibility for the nutritional effort as your child's readiness indicates. As his maturity and understanding increase, be willing to broaden your child's involvement in food choices, meal preparation, and dietary planning.

Fear

Just as blind optimism can stem from denial, blind pessimism can be the product of fear. Fearfulness can deteriorate into a sense of helplessness and panic. The fearful person is saying "I can't cope," which really means "It is hard for me to cope."

When faced with a child on a long-term diet, a parent has plenty to worry about! Many of the worries can be phrased in "what if" questions: What if my child doesn't get better? What if I cannot cook all of the special meals that are needed? What if I cannot afford all of the treatments and diagnostic sessions that are needed? What if my child doesn't like to eat within the guidelines? What if the special diet doesn't work? On and on goes the endless parade of "what if" questions.

Apathy, confusion, disorganization, indecisiveness, and loss of control are frightening. They can arouse questions such as "What lies ahead?" and "Can I safeguard my child?" These types of questions stem from unresolved grief and fears about the child. The sense of helplessness that may be aroused when your child becomes ill is frightening. The child's disorder may seem like a threat to his safety and may seem largely beyond your control. Because you cannot totally protect your child, it is tempting to console yourself with denial: "Those bad things really won't happen to *my* child." Such consolation may have been brutally stripped away from you, leaving you at the mercy of fearing that no matter what you do, or how you do it, your efforts will never be great enough to protect your child again.

At the other extreme is the belief that your child's life is entirely in your hands. Burdened with this logic, you might conclude that it is up to you to monitor treatments, give medication, maintain the diet, protect your child from outside stresses, and perform hundreds of other tasks. Having outlined this course for yourself, you might quickly start wondering whether you can ever be energetic, wise, skillfull, attentive, and protective enough to perform such tasks effectively. It is just as frightening to think that you must do everything for your child as it is to conclude that you can do nothing for him.

What to Do About Fear

The parent who is fearful is looking inward to self rather than outward to the situation. This process makes the parent feel stagnated and helpless. Energy is wasted on endless fretting about the thousands of possibilities constantly confronting the parent, the child, and the family.

Paralyzing fear can be modified into a determined effort to rectify a stressful situation, but only after the fearful person starts taking definitive action. Assertion is the key to overcoming feelings of helplessness. "I can't" needs to be translated into "It's hard for me, but I will try." The action taken can be simple—perhaps initially only one step at a time, but in the right direction.

Use hypothetical thinking wisely. The number of "what if" questions that can be asked in any situation is infinite; therefore, there is no special validity to the hundreds of "what if" questions that you can raise about your child's diet. An endless stream of terrifying questions provides only mental confusion and a sense of being overwhelmed by possibilities. Hypothetical thinking wisely used, however, allows your mind to guide you when you face unknowns and can be helpful in many situations. Asking "what if" prepares you for the various events that could happen in upcoming situations. Just keep in mind that the power of hypothetical thinking must not be allowed to run wild.

Be concerned but not worried. Concern is a warm expression of interest in the child that stimulates you into effective action. Worry, on the other hand, is a weak nonproductive state of anxiety that stagnates you into inactivity. "I am concerned that you stay on your diet" reflects an action-oriented approach. "I worry that you might not stay on your diet" implies criticism and mistrust and creates a sinking feeling in the parent who says it. Make a determined effort to express concern through your actions, while avoiding the helplessness of constant worry.

Be knowledgeable. Like denial, fearfulness stems from ignorance. The more you know about your child's diet, the less fearful you will be. The greatest fear is produced by the unknown and the uncontrollable. Knowledge helps translate fear into effective action.

Realize that you have limits. The best perspective for dealing constructively with any stressful situation is recognizing that there is a problem and that you can take steps to lessen it. Be at peace with what you cannot do and what is beyond the limit of your abilities. Remember that you are not responsible for solving all your child's problems. Set priorities, do what you can, and don't fret about what you have to leave undone. Of course, realizing the limits of your ability should not be used as an excuse for not doing or learning more when the extra effort would be possible and appropriate.

Nurture yourself at every opportunity if you feel under great tension because of your child's condition or the pressures of maintaining the diet. Soaking in a warm bath, choosing favorite food to eat, dressing in comfortable clothes, relaxing in a special chair, reading a magazine, taking breaks, engaging in routine and mild exercise, pursuing an enjoyable hobby, or working part-time in a setting that gives a sense of accomplishment and self-satisfaction are all very wise things to do. Pampering yourself in these ways is not being selfish; it is the opposite. You are replenishing yourself so that you can be more efficient at helping all members of your family in the many ways that a parent must do.

Anger

Anger is one of the most difficult emotional states to handle. It can best be understood as an energizing defensive response to apparent stress from an outside source. Anger readies you for either (1) opposing the outside stress so that it decreases or stops, or (2) removing yourself from the situation.

Your anger at apparent stress is not a reflex. To the contrary, anger is to a large extent controllable. You can consciously aim your anger with a high degree of accuracy. Anger gives you a surge of energy and sheer determination. Furthermore, the amount of anger shown is largely determined by your interpretation of the stress situation. You are not so much at the mercy of your anger as you are its creator and supervisor.

Anger can keep a parent emotionally distant and protected from facing the grief of an oppressive reality. In this sense, anger can be used in the service of denial. Sometimes the anger or the denial is necessary because the parent is already emotionally overburdened and simply would not be able to hold together emotionally if having to face the full complexities of an overwhelming situation.

The three most common ways in which anger is mishandled are to (1) put it back inside; (2) misdirect it outwardly; or (3) overdo its expression. Ideally anger should be (1) expressed rather than hidden; (2) aimed at the stress source; and (3) intense enough to cause either a reduction in stress or removal of the angry person from the situation. Consider this hypothetical situation that could be faced by a parent of a diet-restricted child:

> Mother finds that the price of the special flour that she must buy for her child has suddenly increased by 50 percent. She becomes angry at the increased expense that she must incur from now on. She might misdirect her anger by becoming angry at her child for having the disorder, other stores in the community for not carrying that type of flour at a lower price, the store that carries the flour for raising the price, the government for not managing the economy better, or her husband for not having stocked up on the flour

while it was less expensive. None of these targets for her anger is the actual source of the irritant—the economic inconvenience to the family budget. In her expression of anger, she may conceivably be excessive or violent while misdirecting it.

She could put the anger back inside, do and say nothing, and seethe with resentment over a long period of time. Eventually she would become bitter and pessimistic about the diet. She would likely end up being depressed and stop supporting the diet at all. Her explanation would likely be that she gave up because there were too many obstacles to overcome in order to have kept on supporting the diet. She might thereafter claim that she simply doesn't "care" whether her child gets better.

A constructive use of the energy and determination from her anger would have been to increase her scrutiny of the family budget so that the expense had a minimum impact on the rest of the family's functioning.

An especially dangerous misdirection of anger is allowing the child to become the target of parental frustrations. Most often the real irritants are the inconveniences and stresses incurred because of the child's condition, medical treatment, and dietary requirements. Additional burdens may have been thrust upon the parent: financial stresses, energy drain involved in reassuring the child, having to learn and apply new cooking skills, difficult conversations with helping professionals, problems arising from the siblings, or marital conflict resulting indirectly from these accumulated stresses.

By constantly blaming external sources and others for her anger, the parent can convince herself that anger is always justified. Unfortunately, nobody is ever happy under these conditions. Anger is not easy to hide and quickly contaminates other, more pleasant emotional transactions.

What to Do About Anger

Here are some suggestions for curbing the potential destructiveness in anger and channeling your actions into constructive directions:

Announce your anger. The mere act of identifying the anger helps to defuse it and makes it less likely to be exaggerated. A frank, simple statement that you are feeling angry helps you get control of your feelings. It also clarifies the situation for others who are with you.

Understand your own feelings. Your child senses your feelings even though you might attempt to avoid putting them into words. A frail sickly boy, for example, clearly knows whether his big athletic father views him as less than adequate. He knows from his father's facial expression, voice tone, gestures, and actions. Far better if the father can recognize disappointment, clarify and reduce those feelings by talking with a mental health professional, and find other ways to satisfy his need for feeling masculine. The father needs to set such issues aside and get on with the more important business at hand—learning to love his child for who he is and not just despite who he is.

Separate the child from the condition. Your child's condition is the culprit; your child is not. A useful motto is "I love you; I don't love your illness." You are free to love your child, yet hate the complications and expense of your child's condition. Make sure that you and your child understand this separation of feelings.

Separate anger-at-self from anger-at-others. At times you may sound as if you are angry only at your child, but actually you are angry at yourself for not having dealt more effectively with a situation involving your child. Separate the two types of anger in your mind and deal with each. "I am frustrated because I am confused about what to do now" is more accurate and helpful than "You are frustrating me." Helping your child to understand that you have these feelings, and yet are in control, is good role-modeling and ultimately very comforting for your child.

Own up to your responsibility for your own anger. A common error is to underestimate the extent to which anger is self-generated. This error is indicated by such statements as "*It* makes me angry" or "*You* make me mad." A more accurate statement would be "I feel angry and hurt when. . ." The source of the anger is within you, and it is based on your perception of your own needs in the current situation. As long as you blame the external source entirely for your anger, you feel less in control of it and are less likely to handle it appropriately.

Negotiate only at low-anger moments. The increased energy that anger gives you may make you impatient. The increased focusing of your attention may make you temporarily narrow-minded and stubborn. It will be impossible for you to negotiate and settle issues while you act on these two traits, which are the exact opposites of the patience and open-mindedness needed to negotiate solutions to problems.

It may be best to vent some of your anger before confronting the situation. Common techniques are (1) screaming into a pillow as you pound it; (2) running or walking briskly outside; (3) doing vigorous work; (4) listing your frustrations in a journal or notebook; and (5) taking deep breaths while counting to ten. After you have partially vented your anger, you are in a better position to confront the situation in a rational and effective way.

Identify the primary hurt. Anger always follows a perceived hurt, which can be physical or psychological. Although it is possible to focus on decreasing your anger, it is also very important to focus on decreasing the primary hurt. Identify and label that hurt; then do something to correct the situation so that the hurt does not continue. "I am angry because I am embarrassed" is much more helpful than "You make me mad and embarrass me." Use the increased energy that accompanies your anger for changing the situation so that the source of the stress no longer frustrates your needs. When the initial hurt stops, the anger also stops. Take definitive action that removes you from the scene or that helps you confront the source of the stress directly. Channel your energy into a determined effort to redeem the situation. Recognize ahead of time that there will be hundreds of challenging moments with a child on a long-term diet.

Guilt

The guilt-ridden parent leaves no stone unturned and may try to analyze every moment of planning for the child, every moment during pregnancy, every moment during the child's birth, and every moment thereafter in the search for the causes of the child's condition. The motto of the guilt-ridden parent is "If only I had done this or that, things would have been better." Just as the fearful person projects into the future with "what if. . ."

questions, the guilt-ridden parent relives the past with a discouraging parade of "if only. . ." wish statements.

The potential number of guilt thoughts is infinite. If the pregnancy and birth were not well timed, guilt feelings may be especially strong—"If only I hadn't had this child in the first place!" If the birth processes were complicated or difficult, guilt feelings may occur—"If only I had given birth in a more prepared, natural, or healthful way!" Unstable family situations and marital conflicts are also fertile ground for feelings of guilt—"If only we had not gotten divorced when our child was so young!"

Sometimes guilt feelings develop as a secondary reaction to resentment about having a child who is not lovely, completely healthy, or happy. In the face of this resentment, a parent can feel guilty because she had always been taught that all parents should be completely loving to their children at all times. The guilt-ridden parent might believe the caustic comments of relatives and others that the child's need for the diet stems from inadequate parenting or from some other actions that the parent could have avoided.

The parent might feel guilty about other emotional states, thinking unkind thoughts about the child, or being angry at the frustrations experienced because of the diet. The notion that the parent has produced a defective child is also a cause for guilt. Witnessing the many stresses that siblings go through in response to the child's diet can sustain the parent's feelings of guilt and personal responsibility. If the child is adopted, the haunting notion that he might have been better off if placed elsewhere can help create and sustain a parent's guilt feelings.

What to Do About Guilt

Guilt overstates the parent's role. You are assuming too much personal responsibility for the condition and its effects if you feel guilty. As you dwell on the never-ending possibility that you could have done something else to decrease the severity of the condition or the difficulties of maintaining the diet, you open yourself up to guilt feelings. Here are some suggestions for preventing guilt feelings from interfering with your ability to help your child effectively.

Develop a healthy self-image. Self-confidence about your actions is one of the best insulations against feeling guilty. Guilt feelings tend to haunt parents who have significant self-doubts about their ability to cope with the challenges of maintaining their children's long-term diets.

Recognize the awesome nature of the stresses. You are facing a situation that involves more factors than any one person can possibly control or even influence. Given the complicated state of affairs that you face, it is natural that you would feel inadequate to the task. Of course, you might wish that some of your actions could have been undone or redone in a different way. Allow yourself that wish, but do not extend it to the point of harboring destructive guilt feelings.

Avoid perfectionism. If you have perfection as a goal, you can quickly find hundreds of things to feel guilty about; instead, work for small gains and aim for improvement.

Focus on the here and now. When the emphasis is on the past, guilt misdirects your attention and your energy. Concentrate on helping your child now, rather than thinking hypothetically about how your help could have been different.

Be assured that your love for your child is always there. Love and caring may seem to disappear under the weight of the inconveniences posed by various aspects of your child's disorder, including the diet. You may experience defensive emotional states that may cloud your awareness of your underlying love bond with your child.

Avoid the "if only" trap. Every situation can be analyzed in terms such as "If only this person had done that action in a different way!" There are hundreds of possibilities for every situation. Be determined not to distort and misuse the powers of hypothetical thinking through endless "if only. . ." wish statements.

Overinvolvement

Often maintained by guilt feelings, overinvolvement reflects too tight a meshing of the parent's efforts with the child's arena of life. Out of concern for the child's difficulties, the parent may be tempted to run interference in many settings. The net result can be disastrous for all concerned: The parent can become overworked and physically and emotionally exhausted, while the child becomes increasingly demanding toward the parent and inept at handling the difficulties and decisions of life. Overinvolvement also attacks the child's self-esteem as the child becomes convinced that he cannot cope without having a high degree of parental involvement showered upon him. Overinvolvement is usually shown by one or more of the following patterns:

Overprotection. The child's handicapped condition may tempt the parent into providing excessive shielding from any potential danger or unkind remarks from others. A constant background fear is that bad or overwhelming things might happen to the child. The parent feels a need to intervene so that no misfortunes occur and develops a habit of defending the child automatically, almost without warning.

Shielding the child from any potentially difficult situation, the overprotective parent robs the child of opportunities for growth and challenge. The parent's motto is "Don't do it, because bad things could happen." She supervises the child closely in the kitchen because he might accidentally use the wrong food in the salad he is preparing. The parent forbids him from going outside because it is too cold, discourages him from going for a walk because large dogs are in the neighborhood, and keeps him away from a friend's birthday party to prevent his having to eat special snacks in the company of other children. Convinced that every situation is full of danger or defeat, the child becomes able to cope with only the mildest of situations. Eventually he shrinks from almost any circumstances that involve unknowns or risks, becoming a prisoner of his fears.

Overnurturing. Often as a sequel to overprotection, the parent might lavish nurturing actions onto the child. The child never learns to cope for himself in certain areas and thus remains ignorant and dependent. The parent who spends hours preparing special food, for example, may gain a sense of fulfillment by monopolizing the kitchen. As the child grows older, the parent may deny him the opportunity to learn to prepare the needed food. Because of the child's lack of experience with self-care, the parent always has an excuse for being overinvolved in the act of preparing food.

Spoiling. Spoiling, or overindulgence, is an attempt by the parent to shield the child from every form of frustration. The parent gives excessive attention and service to the child and ends up doing things for him that he ought to be able to do without assistance. One father of a diet-restricted child indicated his tendency to spoil with this motto: "You just breathe; I'll do all the rest for you!" Patronized and overindulged, the child is given too much service and tends to become increasingly demanding. He may also attempt to increase the parents' underlying feelings of guilt, as if the parents *owe* all the excessive service.

Pity. Pity is a discouraging, misdirected, and overstated attempt at sympathy. It conveys the parent's doubt about the child's ability to cope. It is a failed attempt to empathize with the child's experiences of frustration, hurt, or difficulty. Where pity exists, misfortune is exaggerated.

The pitying parent may also feel guilty for not having overprotected sufficiently or not having indulged the child enough. The child's misfortunes may remind the pitying parent of selfassumed responsibilities for having worsened his problems. Motivated by a combined sense of personal guilt and pity, the parent may make exceptions for the child that allow him to deviate from ordinary behavioral or healthful procedures, including following a prescribed diet.

A demonstration of excessive, intense pity has a damaging impact on the child. Trading an occasional small toy or extra privilege for a missed treat at a birthday party reassures a child that the world is reasonably fair and may be a wise move on occasion for the parent of a diet-restricted child. The child who is showered with extra gifts at someone else's birthday as a direct compensation for not being able to indulge in traditional party treats, however, is simply receiving too much pity. He has little choice other than to exaggerate the misfortune of not being able to share traditional party treats with those other children in attendance. The extra favors and gifts may have nothing to do with his physical status, but may have a lot to do with the parent's exaggerated display of caring.

Mutual dependency. The excessive closeness and companionship that may accompany a chronic condition can tempt the child to try to meet a parent's emotional needs, needs that should be met by relationships with other adults or by the marital relationship. Simultaneously, the parent may become the child's best friend and may end up trying to meet many of the child's social needs that other children should be meeting. The result is a tight parent-child bond that severely restricts the social and emotional development of the child. Raised in an overinvolved mutual dependency relationship with a parent, the child delays his emancipation from the home. Although he might keep pace with peers in terms of education, vocational development, or in other areas, the personal side of his life is stunted and underdeveloped.

Nagging. The complications of the dietary program may lead the parent into issuing an endless stream of directives, suggestions, reminders, and commands. The parent may gradually distrust the child's ability to do any diet-related task independently or reliably. Motivated by medical concerns, the parent may want to make sure that the child follows all dietary recommendations on schedule. She might show this concern by frequently asking about what the child is eating and whether he is following other dietary procedures properly.

Reminders and suggestions should generally decrease as time goes on and as the child gains a progressively better understanding of what needs to be done to sustain the diet. The frequency of these reminders from the parent, however, dilutes their importance for the child. If the reminders do not decrease but instead increase, the child is not responding appropriately to them.

A cycle can develop in which the parent feels an obligation to nag because of the apparent need for increased reminders. The more the parent nags, the more sloppy, slow, or forgetful the child may become. The parent feels pressured into having to nag and to remind because the child does not follow through with appropriate diet-supportive actions without the parental reminders.

What to Do About Overinvolvement

The sheer number of concerns surrounding any prescribed long-term diet can easily push a parent in the direction of becoming overinvolved in the child's life. For this reason, overinvolvement is one of the most common types of parental errors and one of the most difficult patterns to change.

Don't exaggerate the difficulties. A diet-related mistake by your child, although temporarily harmful, should not be magnified in importance beyond its true meaning. Consider each event from a larger perspective than the present moment. Your child will have thousands of choice points and stress moments, and any specific event is just one of an endless train of such moments. Ask yourself, "Ten years from now, what difference will this event make?" and realize how little and insignificant this current event is. Or ask yourself, "What is the worst thing that could happen in this situation?" and realize the difference between an unfortunate event and an utterly catastrophic one. Many are unfortunate, but very few are catastrophic.

Encourage your child's efforts. Strength comes from practice and from exerting effort against some sort of resistance. Assist your child in learning to cope with the challenging situations surrounding the prescribed diet. Welcome his attempts to contribute to his own self-care and to the family's well-being. Stand by as an ally and have faith in his abilities to understand and accept his share of responsibility for helping with the diet. Be grateful for each step your child takes toward greater food choice mastery and competence. He has resourcefulness and intelligence; encourage the use of those capabilities in coping with the diet and with the other challenges posed by his medical condition.

Avoid the "I can do it faster" trap. Most parents can do most things faster, better, and more easily than their children. That fact, however, does not justify depriving your child of learning how to do them. The goal should be to teach your child how to make diet-related choices and perform diet-related actions faster, better, or more easily. Allow him direct access to age-appropriate challenges involving dietary as well as other aspects of life.

Be concerned and involved, but don't overdo it. Avoid both extremes of being unconcerned and uninvolved on the one hand and being overconcerned and overinvolved on the other. Express concern without nagging. Give help without excessive service. Reduce stresses without taking away the child's opportunities to learn how to face challenging situations. Show caring and empathy without the discouragement of pitying. The parent who calmly places the diet-appropriate food before the child and conveys a silent expectation that the child eat the food is displaying the correct balance of concern and involvement.

Measure your help. One of the worst things you can do is to shield your child completely from dietary trials and difficulties. In guiding your child through life, it is best to take the position of coach and let your child play the game. Give help from the sidelines rather than do things for him.

Screen out aspects of any new or uncontrolled situation that may be potentially too challenging, overwhelming, or dangerous. When you do not involve your child in dietary choices, in solving food-related difficulties, or in learning to assume responsibility for food choices, you teach him to act even more carelessly and helplessly as challenging situations occur in the future. Your child will be slow to develop personal responsibility if you make all the decisions. As time goes on, he will become increasingly demanding, creating a losing situation for both of you.

Assist only when asked. Don't put your child in an audience position of merely watching you perform various tasks masterfully. Avoid the perfectionistic goal of doing everything for your child and of solving all of life's problems for him. It is far better to give your child a realistic firsthand experience with human limitations than a fictionlike expectation that you are always present to give attention, service, and protection. A child can learn much more by being unsuccessful at mastering a difficult situation than by watching you do it well. At such a moment, be supportive and avoid an "I told you so" attitude.

Give partial help, such as assisting at the beginning of the task, in the middle, or toward the end. Avoid offering the complete solution to a dietary problem or difficulty. Ask your child to figure out the remainder. In these ways your help is available, but it won't suffocate your child.

Refuse to be tricked into guilt-motivated servitude to your child. If you are overinvolved, your child may want to perpetuate the situation, saying things designed to remind you of your own guilt feelings: "If you were nicer, you would prepare this food for me. . ." Be aware of this intended manipulation and purposely do the opposite.

Attend workshops, classes, and seminars in an effort to improve your knowledge about parent-child relationships and family leadership. Seek out and read instructive books and magazine articles about general parenting skills and about the specific talents needed for the situations that occur in your family. As you become more effective in parenting skills, you ensure against becoming overinvolved.

Arrange to have an adequate social life and to spend sufficient time doing things that you enjoy. Arrange periodic times
to be with each child in the family. Build in regular times for
strengthening your marriage relationship. Likewise arrange
visits from friends, peers, classmates, and relatives for your
child and the siblings. A healthy variety of balanced relationships
for all family members helps prevent the entanglements of
overinvolvement.

Patterns of Emotional States

Hope causes a recycling of defensive emotional states. When a
temporary dramatic improvement arouses hope, there is a
natural tendency to revert back to denial. Medical conditions in
which there are alternating periods of hope and then despair
can send a parent back and forth through many defensive emotional states, causing a great deal of emotional turmoil in the
process.

Parents can reexperience many of the defensive emotional
states because they recur with any significant loss. If the child
suffers a major decrease in functioning—such as no longer being able to perform certain physical activities, having a major
operation, or no longer attending school—the parent grieves the
loss of that major function. Accompanying this grieving can be
anger, the temptation to become overinvolved again, and other
related feelings.

In a way, parents sometimes go through a process of
mourning as they face new aspects of the realization that their
child is not normal. During any flare-up of symptoms, parents
are likely to reexperience some of the defensive emotional states
in a condensed form. The most important aspect of these reactions is not that they occur, but that they can be destructive if
they linger for a great while. Eventually they can result in extreme bitterness or even depression.

In their worst form, some patterns of defensive emotional
states result in child abuse. One of the more common patterns
is the shame cycle of child abuse. In this cycle, the parent is embarrassed because of the child's apparent inefficiencies and in-
abilities to function in many life areas, perhaps including food
choices and restrictions. The parent responds to the embarrass-

ment by feeling very angry and venting the anger on the child with verbal, emotional, or physical abuse. The child becomes less functional, becomes more depressed and withdrawn, or shows even more bizarre behavior in reaction to being abused. This deterioration in the child's functioning brings further parental embarrassment, and the cycle is repeated.

Sometimes the defensive emotional states lead to the parent's self-abuse. The sorrowful, grieving parent who is depressed because of feeling overwhelmed at the challenges involved with the diet-restricted child seeks relief in self-abusive ways. She may drink heavily or take illegal drugs, for example. Then the parent may feel very guilty for choosing such an unproductive path. The net result is a lowering of the parent's coping skills, so that the marriage deteriorates further and the parent is even less able to function in the many roles that are required for effective family leadership. In the face of this less efficient helping from the parent, the child simply does not improve and continues, for example, to deviate from dietary guidelines. The parent witnesses the continued lack of improvement and becomes more sorrowful. Saddened and discouraged further by the lack of progress with both her functions as a family leader and the child's ability to care for himself, the parent commits more chemical self-abuse. The cycle is repeated many times. The parent is trapped in a downward spiral of guilt, reduced coping skills, less efficient helping of the child, and further chemical self-abuse.

Patronizing the child sometimes leads to the parent's anger and resentment for all the extra energy and service she has given. The parent first gives too much (spoiling), then resents the amount given and feels guilty about her negative feelings toward the child during the process (resentment). A cycle of alternating periods of spoiling and resentment can develop. This pattern of totally opposite approaches to parenting is particularly confusing and distressing to the child. It becomes, in most cases, a form of emotional child abuse.

Existence of any of these patterns, or a variation on any of them, indicates an urgent need for skilled mental health intervention for the parent and family. Fortunately, these types of patterns are the exception rather than the rule among parents of diet-restricted children.

Acceptance—Your Springboard to Effective Dietary Action

Ideally the child's diet can pull your family together and bring with it the same ingredients that any challenge brings—great opportunity for personal growth among all who are involved. Strive toward emotional acceptance of the need for the diet and its potentially positive challenging effects upon your entire family. Acceptance is a springboard to more effective support of your child's dietary effort and recovery process. Without it, there may be rifts in your marriage, stunted or distorted emotional development among the siblings, and various physical and psychological complications in your child's life. If your care of and attention to your child's situation is choked by anger, distracted by fear and guilt, blocked by denial, or exaggerated by overinvolvement, you are crippled in your ability to help your child.

Giving wholehearted support to a child's dietary efforts depends first of all on the parent's level of emotional acceptance of the need for the long-term diet. Acceptance does not mean that the parent likes the diet or that she welcomes the stresses that it brings; instead, it means acknowledging the diet's necessity and being willing to arrange for its use with the child.

There may be a great deal of grieving to be done in dealing with the loss of the "normal" life style for the child. Taking on a complex, limiting, long-lasting diet ushers in an era that at first can seem overwhelming to the parent. As the parent moves through the emotional stages of processing these stresses, greater and greater acceptance occurs along with its accompanying emotional strengths. There may be doubts, fears, insecurities, guilt, anger, mistakes in dietary management, and a whole host of other potential setbacks. If the parent can remain open and honest with herself and her family, however, her commitment can lead to increased acceptance and the gradual integration of the diet into the family's daily life. The growth pattern is usually two steps forward, one step back; three steps forward, two steps back. As new hope occurs and then is dashed against the hard rocks of reality from time to time, this pattern of slow, frequently backsliding growth perpetuates itself.

The individual who has not approached emotional acceptance will be the weakest link in the effort to bring health and vitality to your child. As a parent gains increasing acceptance, she gradually increases her capacity for emotional growth.

The accepting parent learns to display a firm determination to make the best of the child's situation. Not stunted by denying the need for the diet or by anger or guilt, she can learn to provide calm, balanced leadership for the child. Schooled by a period of confusion while trying to understand symptoms, participating in lengthy diagnostic procedures, and exploring different treatment options, the parent gradually learns to keep going in the face of unknowns and doubts. There is a growing desire to double-check the facts, then improve the situation with whatever methods are available.

The parent gradually learns to appreciate the reasons for the diet. She expects the diet to help her child, and her support of it communicates her caring. Her commitment shows her desire to find more and better ways of improving the situation; it also safeguards her self-esteem.

The accepting parent learns to ask, "What can I learn from this experience?" This useful question facilitates potential growth from the challenges posed by the child's dietary program. The parent uses increasingly more sensitive judgment about the child's condition. The child's confidence in the parent's judgment increases as time goes on.

The parent learns to be flexible and open-minded about entertaining a new idea or exploring a new approach to dietary treatment. She understands the exceptions as well as the rules in life. Increasingly adventurous and brave, the parent becomes willing to try something different or new while applying the diet to suit the child's ever-changing biochemical needs. All such changes and flexibility, of course, must be in concert with sound nutritional principles and the guidance of the physician or dietitian.

The accepting parent learns to understand other people's needs and dilemmas. She becomes more accepting and tolerant of others in general and people with special nutritional needs in particular. The shortcomings and difficulties of parents with diet-restricted children gradually form the bases of bonds of friendship and partnership. This nonjudgmentalness and acceptance of others enriches all the parent's relationships. The parent becomes increasingly willing to lend an empathic ear and a helping hand to others who are facing challenges and unknowns. The parent learns to feel a common bond with other parents and finds wisdom among those who are in a similar plight, wisdom that helps her be a better team member with the professionals caring for her child.

Anger can be constructively channeled in ways that fight for the child against the symptoms that the diet is controlling. Part of usefully fighting is mastering the dietary treatment program. The parent can fight for any of a number of goals to benefit the child.

The parent might want to fight by associating with others. Joining or forming a parent support group is one method. Together with other parents, she might wish to influence medical policies in the community or facilitate care for her child or other children in similar situations.

The parent learns how to wait. She learns that a rash decision, a quick move, or an inappropriate reaction might complicate situations. She slows down the pace with which she expects marked improvements from her child's diet.

The accepting parent recognizes irony, realizes that some things can be taken lightly, and appreciates humor where appropriate. A sense of humor adds balance and sparkle to her relationships inside and outside the family. The parent's optimism doesn't, however, cause her to make light of serious situations or render her silly or clownlike.

There is an increasing appreciation of life. Sensitive to the potential seriousness of the child's condition, the parent gains a renewed appreciation of wholeness, health, and vitality. She might develop a habit of hunting for the good in everything. She learns to appreciate the personal refinement that is occurring in herself, the lessons being learned about life, the patience and resourcefulness that are developing, and the growth that is being stimulated by the challenges she is facing.

The parent's resilience against stress is a constantly growing reflection of her personal strength. Eventually the parent can learn to adjust to a relatively high degree of stress, and she can learn to stay poised and calm even in emergency situations.

Much of the parent's attention toward the child's dietary treatment involves coordinating her efforts with those of the dietitian and physician. She is willing to become an energetic member of a helping team for the child. Relatives and friends without professional credentials who may be involved in the care of the child should also be considered members of the helping team.

The parent learns how best to ration her energy as she decides among various treatment options, copes with side effects of medications the child may be taking, engineers the dietary treatment, manages the child away from home and at other food settings while still encouraging observance of dietary restrictions, protects the child from dietary deviations, and maintains effective relationships with involved helping professionals.

The parent learns new terms having to do with diagnosis and treatment and gradually teaches some of them to the child. She may also want to learn about human biochemistry and nutrition and various interrelationships within those two fields of knowledge, particularly as they apply to the child.

Responding to the broad issues relevant to the child's predicament with an effective value system, philosophy, or religious belief system can reestablish a sense of personal control over otherwise uncontrollable situations. Making sense of the need for the diet helps the parent create an atmosphere of acceptance for her, her family, and the child.

Part of being a good team member is being able to converse effectively and courteously with those who disagree. The accepting parent can learn to admit that everybody has problems. She resists the temptation to pretend that she has no problems managing her child's diet.

In any emotionally charged situation, there are mixed feelings. Love occurs along with unpleasant emotions such as anger, resentment, and guilt. A parent's mixed feelings while maintaining a child on a restrictive diet may result from simultaneously sensing her deep love for the child as well as experiencing various frustrations about the diet. As long as resentment is reasonably under control and countered by love, a state of emotional balance exists.

The parent learns to match her love for others with self-love. She learns to take time to withdraw temporarily for personal renewal, to refresh and recenter herself. To obtain balance in daily life, she allows regular break times for rest.

The parent displays poise and self-confidence as she becomes better informed and more articulate about her child's diet. Faced with an abundance of difficult diet-related choice-making situations, she continually tries to improve her parenting skills. She tries to evaluate and scrutinize the advice she receives and avoids putting helping professionals on pedestals. She isn't intimidated by the credentials or knowledge of helping professionals. The parent learns to trust her own judgment and to rely on common sense while working along with the physician, the dietitian, and any other involved professionals.

The accepting parent becomes a better leader of the children in the household. Except as dictated by the child's need for the diet, the parent doesn't allow behavior that is generally unacceptable in children. She sets the boundaries for behavior and is clear about what types of conduct are expected from the child.

The parent understands the family-wide impact of the disorder and the dietary program. She is especially watchful for imbalances in the family caused by overinvolvement or by other distortions in relationships. She is not surprised, for example, at changes in siblings' feelings and reactions as the child improves in response to the diet.

The parent is also aware that the ripple effect can extend to the marital relationship. Many decisions involved in joint leadership of the family have to take into account the child's dietary treatment program. The parent becomes increasingly interested in stretching marital knowledge by attending classes or reading instructive materials on marriage relationships.

The accepting parent supports the uniqueness of the child, including his tastes and preferences in a variety of areas. Increasingly the parent is able to anticipate how the child will act in various circumstances, and she learns to appreciate the positive qualities in the child's personality.

The child is generally supervised and kept in environments reasonably free from moral, psychological, and physical hazards. The child is protected from outside dangers and influences that might otherwise lead to a dietary deviation or a breakdown in the child's decision-making ability.

Protections are neither overdone nor underdone. If the child has special vulnerabilities, the parent makes decisions about the child's needs for physical and medical protections in consultation with helping professionals. The parent doesn't, however, set the child apart from others more than is medically required.

The parent learns to deliver her love rather than just talk about it. Even though the child may have unpleasant traits, the parent experiences a deep and abiding love that is strengthened by offering her service willingly. She learns to appreciate the sacrificial nature of true love.

The parent appreciates the worth, the very essence of the child, and has little trouble discriminating between a lovable child and the child's unlovable behavior that may occur from time to time. The parent doesn't confuse the frustrations caused by the difficulties of dietary treatment with her appreciation of the infinite worth and innate value of the child.

The parent is supportive of the child's self-esteem and wants to uplift the child's feelings of worth, competence, and confidence. She hunts for activities that are suited to the child's preferences, abilities, and limitations, being especially watchful for opportunities to involve the child in helping to manage the diet, in accord with the child's readiness.

The parent is also concerned about character development because the child's decision making, when not under supervision, is an aspect of moral character. Accordingly, she wants to encourage the development of important traits such as honesty and dependability in the child and in the siblings. The dietary treatment program is used as an arena for strengthening these aspects of character.

The parent supports the child when under stress and defends him when needed. The defense is sufficient to demonstrate that the child is loved, can feel secure, and can trust that the parent is leading. It isn't overdone. The parent learns to help without smothering.

Increasing knowledge brings increasing confidence and relieves the powerful emotional reactions that the parent might otherwise have felt at first. Any sense of failure, self-criticism, or guilt that the parent may have experienced melts away quickly as she becomes more clearly aware that her child's need for the diet is quite unrelated to anything that she ever did, felt, or thought.

The parent gradually becomes more aware of the close connection between physical and psychological health. There is a general growing appreciation of health and wholeness and a concern that all family members achieve a well-rounded life.

The parent tends to become very conscious of food and nutrition. She is willing to learn new methods of cooking, adapt to new utensils, try new foods and recipes, develop food-storage methods, and refine kitchen skills. Food shopping is sometimes modified as a result of maintaining a long-term diet. The parent learns where to find the best prices and selection of ingredients, to comparison shop, and to achieve the best management of time, effort, and expense.

The parent becomes convinced that the diet is a worthwhile endeavor and makes good sense. The *why* of dietary treatment is of continuous importance because it helps motivate her to carry out the diet more enthusiastically. The goals become clear so that she develops neither naively high nor pessimistically low expectations of outcome.

The parent is always willing to read something new and constantly wants to increase knowledge. She wants to make books about the child's diet available to her family and others who care for the child. To expand her knowledge even more, she might consider subscribing to a reputable consumer, paramedical, or medical newsletter or journal. She may not be able to judge whether a new dietary approach has sufficiently been tested or is indeed safe or effective. Being on guard against questionable variations in the dietary program, she learns to discuss any reports of potential dietary modifications with the child's dietitian before making any dietary changes.

A balanced approach to dietary observance that results from a parent's emotional acceptance is, of course, the most desired outcome. Do everything possible to assist everyone in your family in gaining a sense of emotional acceptance of the dietary program. Use the information in this chapter to nurse everyone in the family along in the process toward increasing acceptance. Expect setbacks, and remain encouraging. Just as you can lift any weight if you have the right leverage, acceptance provides almost unlimited leverage to support even the most restrictive and complicated prescribed diet for your child.

As you move from defensive emotional states toward acceptance of your child's disorder, you will find increased optimism and energy. With them you can strengthen the bonds in your marriage, your relationships with the child's siblings, and your supportive role toward your child. You will love yourself more, too, because love of others and love of self go hand in hand. In time you will become more at peace with your unique situation and the dilemmas and unknowns of life in general.

2. Understand Your Child's Feelings

At moments of increased stress, children want to turn somewhere for comfort. Often food becomes a source of solace; children seem to want it to fend off pain and difficulty. Your child's overall reaction to stress in life can become mixed with the handling of issues pertaining to eating.

Your child has a very important choice to make—how to interpret the stresses that her special diet brings. Does the diet present so many difficulties and challenges that she will give it up and regard herself as less of a person for having done so? Her answer to this question determines the psychological course that lies ahead.

Your child needs self-confidence about her ability to make contact with the world, a winning personality in spite of life's difficulties, feelings of being loved and accepted, and realistic integration of the diet into daily life.

If your child becomes discouraged, any number of emotional difficulties can occur, with unfortunate consequences. If she can meet the challenges objectively and follow the diet, trying earnestly to overcome any problems along the way, there is much less emotional drain from the experience. This chapter reviews the most common emotional reactions that diet-restricted children have toward their diets, and it gives specific suggestions for guiding your child to wholehearted cooperation toward accepting the demands of the diet.

Gaining healthy self-esteem provides a source of psychological strength for your child in the present as well as in the future for successful adulthood. Viewing herself as a socially competent and productive person is just as significant as any other factor in determining her level of success at maintaining the diet.

Medical disorders sometimes tend to become mixed with eating problems and child-parent relationships. Even with children who do not have special diets, parental anxiety about the welfare of the family can become related to the issue of eating. For some diet-restricted children, there is little emotional stress to following their dietary programs. On the other hand, difficulties with a diet can have an emotional impact that can, in turn, affect any child's self-esteem and ability to cooperate. If a child feels inferior, embarrassed, or socially isolated because of the need for a restrictive diet, she may gradually become less cooperative about staying on it.

Physical illness requiring dietary measures has wide-ranging implications for any child's adjustment. The specific effect on any particular child depends on a host of factors—medical, psychological, social, and environmental. All these threads weave together to form a complicated net that is unique for each family and each child who must be on a long-term diet.

Medical factors include the severity of the condition, the physical limitations, the child's genetic background, the amount of pain experienced, and the types and amounts of medical procedures experienced. The nature and extent of the child's permitted food choices will affect cooperation. Psychological factors include emotional problems associated with the disorder, the child's understanding of the need for the diet, body-image distortions such as growth stunting or obesity, the level of the child's intellectual ability, and the child's overall resistance to stresses. The age of the child at diagnosis, the child's current age, and geographic and cultural aspects of the child's family are also important. Rounding out the types of influences on a child's cooperation are factors such as the degree of dependence on others for physical care, the degree to which the disorder is socially visible, the types and amounts of emotional support provided by parents, school adjustment and interruptions in school, and the nature of disruptions in peer and sibling relationships.

Certain Emotional States can Lessen Your Child's Cooperation

As children on long-term diets work through the events leading to diagnosis, the actual processes involved in the diagnosis of the disorder, and the methods used for treatment, they are apt to experience one or more of certain emotional states. These states are likely to surface at any age, especially when other life stresses temporarily increase. In order to help your child most effectively, stay alert for signs of the following emotional states and use the suggestions in the latter part of this chapter.

Denial. Denying the need for a long-term diet is a self-protective function that postpones some of the difficult emotional work that a child faces. She might act as if she expects a miraculous cure from a very short-term diet, or she might oppose making realistic plans for following the diet. Denial is often a state of grief over the loss of an idealized body image. It sometimes occurs before healthy psychological functioning takes over in situations involving elaborate treatments, such as long-term diets.

Denial allows a temporary escape from anxiety that would otherwise be overwhelming. It is less likely to occur if the child experiences some sort of pain or other strong physical symptoms as a reminder of the need for the diet. Denial can reappear quickly, however, at moments when symptoms or stresses decrease. Ironically, as long-term diets have their desired effects, some children start to deny the need for continuing on them because of the reduced symptoms. They become lax in following their diets; then symptoms reappear, and a new cycle of dietary effort begins again.

Dependency. A child can become overly dependent as a result of needing a long-term diet. The overdependence can be on the family or on some strong person such as a friend or a physician who symbolizes a parent figure. The child may feel not fully healthy, not fully whole, or insufficiently separated as an individual from parents. The child might feel hesitant to approach situations involving dietary choices. She may seem to require considerable reassurance from parents. She might have difficulty resisting temptations and impulsive choices, such as to deviate from dietary guidelines, when parents are not hovering nearby.

Guilt. How the child perceives the parent's feelings about her is important. Instead of feeling accepted, loved, and supported by her parent's efforts toward the diet, she may conclude that her parent is disappointed. This sense of disappointing her parent can negatively affect her self-confidence.

The child may feel responsible for any inconveniences brought on family members by the necessity of maintaining and supervising the diet. She might conclude that she must have done something to deserve such a "punishment." She might feel guilty that her family is also being "punished" by all the inconveniences attendant to the diet.

Guilt feelings can develop in any child who is on a long-term diet, even though she can't identify the specific actions bringing about the guilt. How the parent portrays the diet and handles the initial explanation of its mechanics and goals are crucial. The child may consider the parent who enforces dietary restrictions to be an oppressor. The continuation of the diet over a long period of time provides further evidence of how "bad" the child must be. This entire process, of course, can do great harm to any child's self-esteem.

Depression. The need for the long-term diet can weaken a child's sense of self-esteem. Low self-esteem is probably a major factor contributing to other emotional difficulties as well. Keeping self-esteem high helps any child alleviate other problems in life and reduce total stress.

If overwhelmed by the restrictiveness of the diet and insufficient opportunities to make food choices, the child might start to feel defeated, then become apathetic, passive, or clingy. Withdrawal can occur if the child remains overly dependent on parents for food choices and other aspects of maintaining the diet.

If the child perceives the diet as testimony to her helplessness and hopelessness, she might start to feel fragile and unsure whether the diet will actually result in a cure or improvement. These concerns can cause her to turn inward and become apathetic or depressed. Her self-confidence can be shaken if she becomes the brunt of jokes, the object of ridicule, or is teased by peers because of obvious dietary differences in social situations. Further social withdrawal can result under such conditions.

Depression can occur if the diet results in too many disruptions of the child's life. When mounting stresses become too great to absorb, depression becomes a possibility. It can be expressed in many ways, such as sadness, restlessness, irritability, boredom, an apparently disorganized way of living, a great need to nibble and snack (often in violation of dietary guidelines), or an apparent need for stimulation from alcohol, marijuana, tobacco, or drugs. Additional signs of depression are faultfinding, whining, pouting, a give-up attitude, failure to follow through on things, and an "I don't care" attitude. These symptoms can result from a child's inability to conform to the dietary requirements.

Excessive concerns about being different. In the child's struggle for acceptance and conformity, any apparent differences from peers may result in uneasiness or embarrassment. The child is, however, constantly reminded of differentness at the school cafeteria, at every birthday party, and at other food-related occasions with friends. Eating with others is a necessary part of normal social life. A birthday party is a serious event in the life of any child. Being labeled as different can become an emotional sore point.

The child's peer group may bring strong pressure to not be "different." To be rejected by peers and siblings because of differentness can be stressful. Instead of following the diet, the child may comply with group wishes in an attempt to gain security in an otherwise insecure world.

Fearfulness. Fear of long-term dietary treatment sometimes results in anger and impatience, excessive self-consciousness, shyness, or excessive apologizing. Another indication of fearfulness is an abnormal concern for other persons or pets who are perceived as being under any sort of threat or danger. A common fear among diet-restricted children is that other family members will be terribly inconvenienced by the diets. Anxiety may also arise about symptom flare-ups despite strict dietary efforts.

Night is generally a time of heightened fears. The child may hesitate to go to bed, stay up rather than go to bed on time, be reluctant to face the dark, make excuses to get up, or want to crawl into bed with parents. This need for closeness can create additional problems, but parental protection is important for the child if fears are prominent.

The precise involvement of various body parts and organs in nutritional treatment; the relationships between the diet and energy, weight, and other observable factors; and many other aspects of the diet can all serve as springboards for fears. If the child lacks sufficient information about these types of factors and relationships, bewilderment and fear of the unknown can occur.

Intense anger. In compensation for the feelings of weakness and helplessness caused by the long-term diet, angry expressions of personal desires can occur. Rebellion against the dietary restrictions and other aspects of the disorder may take the form of reckless disregard for nutritional or medical advice. It may also result in disobedience of authority, as if the child is claiming personal power against the physician, the dietitian, or the parent. Swearing, sarcasm, teasing, and other types of anger-expressing words and actions indicate underlying emotional pain in any child.

Regression. Regression indicates extreme stress. The child should not be criticized for regression; in fact, criticism makes regression worse. Common regressions are bed-wetting, thumb sucking, whining, losing self-control with regard to food choices, and becoming overly dependent. These throwbacks to infantile behavior indicate that the child is wanting magically to get comfort and protection from the stresses of life, possibly including those connected with maintaining the diet.

Not all instances of these common childhood behavior patterns are regressions; consider each on its own merit. An important clue is what is happening in the family scene at the time.

Regressions are more likely when there is a change in the family constellation that suddenly removes the child from special attention. Dietary deviations might suddenly occur, for example, as a temporary regression by an eight-year-old whose sibling is hospitalized and whose parents are spending a great deal of time at the hospital.

The Preschooler's Feelings

The "I want to do it myself" claim is the main theme of life for three- and four-year-olds. Despite their young age, there is a natural tendency among preschoolers to start to decrease their physical dependency on parents. They enjoy feeding themselves, going to the bathroom alone, washing and dressing themselves, and managing other aspects of daily life in a progressively more independent fashion.

Daily activities having to do with eating and food may have some contradictions in them, however. The young child's struggle for independence may lead to resistance about the diet, even though the preschooler longs for comfort and care from parents.

Preschoolers have an oversimplified and almost magical conception of how the body works. They perceive body parts as thinking for themselves and having automatic desires. The stomach wants to be full, and the mouth wants to eat certain food because of taste. Explanations of the need for the diet and the rules for maintaining it should take into account these thinking processes. "Your body doesn't want that food" is a way to explain why certain foods are no longer allowed. Parents should point the child's new-found self-care skills in the direction of preparing and eating diet-appropriate food with lessened help.

Preschool children can sometimes take their parents' directions too literally and show a stubborn strength about what they can and cannot eat. Unashamedly they can quickly learn to ask questions about ingredients and, if necessary, claim "I can't eat that."

The traffic-light system is a handy framework for helping preschoolers conceptualize about appropriate and inappropriate foods. Some foods are "red light" foods and should never be eaten (off-limits because of dietary guidelines). Some are "yellow light" foods and should be eaten only with parents' permission (certain types of snacks, for example). Some foods are "green light" foods, which are the staples of the diet-appropriate foods. This pleasant little reminder, which can easily be illustrated by a picture of a traffic light, reinforces the preschool child's perceptions of food categories relevant to dietary guidelines.

It may be helpful to cut out pictures from magazines depicting representatives of each of the food groupings, then paste them onto construction paper, putting the finished collage on the refrigerator door.

The School-Age Child's Feelings

After the child reaches school-age, contacts with other children become even more significant. The influence of friends needs to be harnessed and supervised. Like any potent force, it can do harm or great good for any child's dietary patterns. Parents can strongly influence the course of events that occur in connection with the school-age child's contacts with other children.

Mastery and power over the environment are also crucial issues. The child may seek answers about how and why the diet works and may want to gain an increased sense of control over the diet. At the same time she probably wants to learn how to handle the inevitable awkward questions from peers during social gatherings and birthday parties. Teaching the school-age child how to cook diet-appropriate food strengthens this basic need for increasing control over her life.

The school-age child can understand more than one dimension of situations. She can comprehend relationships among parts and events, such as those between nutrients in food and overall health. Parts of the body can be understood as both connected and dependent on each other.

Good health can be regarded as something attainable simply by observing the diet and avoiding contact with germs. The school-age child is likely to believe that illness is caused and prevented by specific actions and that following a simple set of rules—such as the dietary guidelines—will help. Unfortunately the school-age child may therefore expect a miracle cure from the diet or may balk at it when the expected cure does not rapidly occur.

The Adolescent's Feelings

The adolescent may be at risk for deviating from the dietary guidelines because it is much harder to start a long-term diet at this age than at an earlier age. Even if cooperation has occurred prior to adolescence, problems sometimes develop after puberty.

An adolescent can act like a child one moment and an adult the next. Dietary deviations are likely to occur when the adolescent loses some self-control and acts childlike. Deviating from dietary guidelines can be an act of self-pampering and a form of consolation for the loss of her close attachment to her parents. It can also serve to brace herself against the turmoil of day-to-day life.

If the adolescent is especially afraid of appearing conspicuous or different from peers, the need for a special diet magnifies this issue. The adolescent may feel a strong need to be like the peer group and may deny the need for the diet in an attempt to avoid appearing different. Any trait that creates apparent differentness from peers can cause significant stress.

The adolescent may wonder about revealing the special diet to friends. There may be fear of losing a friendship, yet also a need to be honest about the necessity for special food at social gatherings. This kind of ambivalent situation happens frequently for the adolescent.

A well-adjusted adolescent gains recognition by being popular, successful, friendly, and productive. An adolescent might try to win peers over by sharing in their food, purposely deviating from dietary guidelines during social occasions.

The adolescent may try to challenge family values concerning such things as life style, cleanliness, hair style, dress, music, and, most important, eating habits. The adolescent may try to rebel against nutrition or principles that symbolize authority, such as by rejecting favorite family dishes that are diet-appropriate. The goal is eventual separation from the family and the establishment of independent self-control and self-identity. Dietary habits run the risk sometimes of getting caught up in this quest for self-determination.

The adolescent wants to gain a sense of mastery and control by making decisions. Supervision of the diet by parents may be interpreted as snooping, prying, and bugging, especially if parents don't allow sufficient dietary choices by the adolescent. Allowable decisions about the diet should be geared to the adolescent's developmental level. For example, parents can encourage meal choices by having the adolescent choose from several allowed food groupings.

One of the special difficulties of a very restrictive long-term diet is that there is little to decide. The adolescent may still want to make decisions anyway, creating food choices where none should be allowed.

The adolescent's attempt at independence does not have to be rebellion, nor does it have to be a process destructive to family bonds. Parents, however, will bear the primary brunt of their adolescent's attempts to create a separate identity. The wish for independence is paralleled, fortunately, with another wish—to retain an emotional connection with the family, specifically with the parents. This simultaneous wish to be independent and yet remain connected to parents results in limit testing.

The testing of limits set by adults is the hallmark of the adolescent's struggle for independence. Adolescents need and oppose limits at the same time. Of course, this battle sets up the adolescent to tamper with dietary guidelines. She might try new foods almost thoughtlessly.

How to Help Your Diet-Restricted Adolescent

Not until the early teens are the majority of diet-restricted children able to learn the abstract ideas necessary to make consistently appropriate judgments about eating. By adolescence, if they have had enough experience with the diet, most diet-restricted children can recognize what reactions to deviations feel like. They can also recognize the value of following the diet in terms of an increased sense of physical well-being.

Adolescence is a time of expanded thinking ability that can aid greatly in maintaining the diet. Your adolescent can generate theories, question values, judge, and critique the imperfect as well as idealize the future. She can understand parts of the whole in their complex relationships. Your adolescent can understand the mechanics of the diet and how it relates to nutritional and medical factors at a greater level of sophistication than when she was younger. Increasingly, the adolescent has the capability to show self-control and more realistic expectations about the results of following the diet.

Some positive features must counterbalance the need for a long-term diet. If the adolescent is to have high self-esteem, she needs to have skills and traits that make her seem more likable, attractive, or skillful. Whether through school work, sports, academic knowledge, or social development and friendliness, an adolescent needs a ticket to acceptability among peers.

Emphasize and enhance the positive aspects of your adolescent and her emerging self-image. Discuss carefully and sensitively how any disruption in the diet might interfere with her life style. Cooperation with the diet is more likely when your adolescent knows that you will do everything you can to minimize the difficulties involved. Let her know that eating right does many good things for her body and is part of a total program of efficient self-care.

The adolescent may scrutinize closely various aspects of the diet and may question any point that does not seem to make complete sense to her. Open communication is an absolute necessity for getting full cooperation on the diet.

Eventually your adolescent should become quite independent of you. Try to influence this stride in growth. As your maturing adolescent shows increasing ability to be trusted, gradually increase privileges and lessen control. Trust is not a gift; it has to be earned. Food privileges should depend on your adolescent's display of increased trustworthiness to make wise dietary choices. Specifically, let her make increasing decisions about options within the dietary limits, based on displayed ability to uphold the diet as a matter of self-control. Clearly state that your goal is for her to become a completely responsible and independent person by the time she reaches adulthood. Make sure she realizes that you want her independence, but at an appropriate rate and time, and that you are for her independence, not against it.

Avoid plunging your adolescent into a situation that presents too many temptations for deviating from the diet. Don't let her attend any occasion that you know nothing about. Call other parents and check on the appropriateness of the event. Ask questions no matter who is sponsoring the event if you suspect the kind of situation that may represent an overwhelming dietary temptation. Do not automatically assume that it is free of challenges for dietary self-control. Beforehand, discuss with your adolescent how she might handle the food situation at the event.

Whereas it is important to maintain dietary guidelines strictly, calmly, and firmly, it is also important to avoid senseless power struggles. At the heart of such struggles, it may be necessary to tolerate less than complete cooperation, recognizing that the short period of limited control is less harmful than risking complete rebellion against the entire dietary effort. While occasional experimentation might lead to dietary excesses and symptom flare-ups, eventually your adolescent can learn from the natural and logical consequences of those mistakes. She will then be likely to return to a more cooperative attitude.

Although you should encourage wholesome expression of her independence, your adolescent will feel frightened if you stop all supervision immediately and entirely. Maintain a firmness and show kindness and empathy if your adolescent tests dietary guidelines and limits. Of course, don't allow any dietary deviations in situations in which the physician or dietitian strictly forbids a deviation because of severe medical consequences.

An occasional adolescent seems to think that the diet is a waste of time now that she is older. She might not comply at all while away from home, and periods spent away from home gradually tend to increase as she gets older. The answer in this type of situation lies in seeking special mental health help to get at the underlying issues. Most often the underlying issues are those of self-esteem and power between the parent and the adolescent.

Be neither a boss nor a buddy. With regard to the diet as well as other aspects of daily life, provide the boundaries and maintain open communication. Reassure of your love often; then remain firm and calm in following disciplinary procedures that are age-appropriate for your adolescent.

How to Help Your Child Feel Good About the Diet

A great many children who are on long-term diets offer no resentment or opposition. They are able to cooperate fully with a minimum of difficulties and accept their diets as part of daily living. A major parental goal is to escort your child to a state of complete cooperation with the dietary restrictions, including an understanding of the need for the diet and how it works. The diet should become smoothly integrated into your child's life and should be considered matter-of-fact not only by you, but by your child.

You as a parent can take many of the actions mentioned elsewhere in this book to support your child's emotional adjustment to the diet. Some actions, however, are so crucial for helping children who are experiencing any of the more troublesome emotional adjustments that they deserve special emphasis.

Keep yourself energetic and refreshed. Try to get adequate sleep and occasionally enjoy some stimulating entertainment. The extra boost that you receive will actually benefit your child and the rest of your family. It is much easier to pull your child out of the quicksand of noncompliance with the diet when you are standing on the solid ground of sufficient energy.

Be calm. You will need to offer much understanding, patience, flexibility, effort, and affection to your child, and you must be emotionally flexible in order to respond to those demands. Strive toward emotional acceptance of the diet, as discussed in Chapter 1.

If you are anxious and overinvolved, your child may be less willing to cooperate. If you overprotect, your child may reflect your attitude by becoming timid and hesitant about trying the foods that you are encouraging. If you express remorse, frustration at inconveniences, or resentment about the diet, your child may feel angry about the restrictions it imposes.

If you have an encouraging attitude, your child can develop a sense of trust and security by being around you. Encourage your child to cooperate in as natural a way as possible, by giving explanations rather than orders. Realistic acceptance of nutritional needs with kind, firm demonstration of appropriate dietary policies are the best approaches.

Treat the diet matter-of-factly. Engineer the diet as you would any other ordinary routine. As much as possible, treat your child like a completely normal child who needs only a few food restrictions beyond the ordinary. Bring her up as though the only things different are a few food choices. Allow your child just as many responsibilities and rights as other children in the family—neither more nor less. The only exceptions would be those necessitated by the medical realities and any dietary restrictions.

While trying to deemphasize the diet, don't downplay it to the point that it seems like a shameful secret. Bring up the topic now and then to show that you are understanding and open to talking about it.

The goal is to escort your child to a smooth integration of the diet into daily life, neither undervaluing or overvaluing its importance. Reality itself gradually brings your child to the correct level of awareness of the diet. Your job is to help your child address the realities. Cushion the blows that come, but make sure that your child understands that realities are what need to be adjusted to, not fantasies of denial.

Show your love for your child. The bottom line of your child's ability to adapt to the diet is her experience of the bond of love between you. You can best show your affirming love by a consistent, calm determination to learn, adapt, and do whatever is needed so that your child can experience optimum health. Helping your child attain her personal best is an important aspect of showing your love. Your child may ask directly: "Are you arranging this diet for me only because you feel obligated, or are you doing it because you love me?" Or your child may ask in a much less direct fashion: "Are you sure you want to cook all that special food?" Make sure that your child receives a reassuring correct answer to her question and that you confirm your love for her.

With no strings attached, give your child love by surprise. Offer a diet-appropriate snack or beverage with "Just because I love you!" as the only explanation.

Words and actions are each more powerful in delivering love if they are combined. An "I love you" will have much more meaning when combined with an action that illustrates it. Have a fun, special time together at least once a week with your child out of the home. Most important, tenderly hold and verbally reassure your child often. Your child should experience from you a daily coming together of enveloping love. Bedtime tuck-in is an ideal time for smaller children. Many families have found that a playtime prior to bedtime provides an excellent opportunity for strengthening their bonds of affection and caring for each other.

Show appreciation for the things your child can do. Encourage your child to help in dietary preparations, selecting food, preparing a menu and snacks, and cooking meals. Start teaching her as early as possible how to read labels for ingredients and shop for appropriate brands of food items. Encourage your child to take the initiative in restaurants about inquiring about menu items as soon as she is able to do so.

Give realistic and understandable information to your child about body processes, medical realities, nutrition, and the mechanics of the diet. Without this help your child will be left to construct personal or magical theories to explain why the diet is needed, and she will be at the mercy of unlimited fears and concerns.

Knowledge can help your child make judgments that can gradually develop into self-care skills and independence about managing her own medical and dietary needs. Knowledge also immunizes her against feeling overwhelmed by others' statements or questions about the diet.

Especially as you introduce the dietary program to your child, try to understand exactly what she is asking. Say, for example: "I'll tell you what I understand about the diet, but you first tell me what you think about. . ." If she indicates readiness to comprehend, proceed further. Consider asking questions such as these: What do you suppose are the reasons for this diet? What kinds of foods do you think would be helpful to you? What foods would be most harmful to you? What do you think will be some of the problems in following this diet? What do you think will happen as you continue to eat this good food?

The answers you receive would indicate your child's current level of medical and dietary understanding. Give her as much knowledge as she can absorb and act on in regard to the diet.

Talk often with your child. The abilities to communicate openly and honestly with loved ones and to ask for help when needed are important parts of any child's adjustment. Can your child bring up concerns related to the diet? Does she have a sense that you are willing to help in dietary matters? Can she be assured that you will not be too restrictive in foods allowed? These questions need to be answered with a confident "yes" if your child is to adjust well to the situation. Any secrecy by parents about the diet is likely to make your child increasingly fearful. Neglecting to answer your child's questions undermines your relationship at a time when she desperately needs to communicate.

Because your child might not immediately want to talk about concerns related to the diet does not prove that she has none. If many aspects of the diet are in fact unpleasant, acknowledge that fact. Expressing unpleasant feelings by discussion with you provides a safety valve for your child. If denied this outlet, she may resort to misbehavior, exhibit stressful psychosomatic symptoms, or display other forms of impaired functioning.

Try to decrease your child's tendency to respond on impulse to tempting situations. Your child may test the dietary restrictions. Unless they are consistent and secure, she may learn to manipulate and intimidate while at the same time becoming resentful, anxious, and insecure about the lack of structure in your home. She needs to outgrow grabbing food, snacking on inappropriate foods, and other forms of socially destructive, impulsive behavior. Clear expectations from you and firm defining of boundaries of appropriate dietary cooperation are very reassuring. Not until she considers the total effort worthwhile is your child ready to develop a genuine desire to master the diet. Demonstrate the diet's effectiveness. Things go much easier after she really wants to participate in the diet. Help your child notice improvements, and help her learn to trust that the diet will bring about the anticipated results.

Teach your child to measure her gains on a personal improvement scale, not by comparison with others. Focus on what she is able to do, not on what she hasn't yet mastered. Help her realize that many improvements can occur, even though there may be a few setbacks along the way. Teach patience for the outcome of the diet by discouraging your child from expecting instantaneous improvements in all symptoms.

Teach positive attitudes about differentness. Being different in food selection can be positive and acceptable. It is important for your child to understand that although there are similarities in people, complete personal uniqueness of all individuals is the reality. Sameness between people is only an illusion, and your child cannot depend on it as the best route to feeling secure. She cannot develop a sense of belonging simply by being exactly like others. She needs to know that it is acceptable to be different and that she can appreciate differentness as a form of strength. After all, your child's sense of belonging is in part a reflection of the contribution that she makes to her peer group. The blending of each person's uniqueness in social situations offers stimulation and enrichment.

It may be interesting and helpful for your child to learn about public figures, historical and current, who have also been on long-term diets of various sorts or have experienced various medical or dietary challenges. Being different can mean being special in a positive way.

Encourage the development of special skills, interests, and hobbies that accommodate any health limitations. Also encourage activities and the development of talents that contribute to popularity and to others' happiness. Friends tend to treat your child better as they notice her unique assets that contribute to their relationships and experiences. Direct your child's interest toward other people or things, so that she doesn't become too engrossed in her own medical and dietary situation.

Develop dietary choice-making skills. Have your child take charge of aspects of dietary management that are age-appropriate. Teach your child to live *with* the diet and not in *opposition* to it. If appropriate, play a game about it. Have your child practice choosing between two types of foods—some that are diet-appropriate and some that would be off-limits. This exercise under your direction will pay rich dividends later as your child makes dietary choices when not under your direct supervision.

Allow choices in other life areas. Dietary treatment is related to your child's need to control what enters and leaves her body. Being on a very restrictive diet seriously interferes with this need. If the struggle for mastery can occur exclusively in other areas, the issue of eating can become less of a psychological sore point. Outline some areas of your child's life in which she can exercise personal discretion and live with the choices that she makes. Examples would be music, hair style, a special hobby, or the decor of her bedroom.

Give your child practical advice on how to talk to peers about the diet. Instruct your child in how to endure or decrease any embarrassment that may occur in social situations where food is served. Teach her to avoid unnecessarily exposing to peers the details of the diet. Rehearse simple explanations that do not arouse undue curiousity or adverse reactions. It is not helpful for your child to blurt out information that makes peers feel uncomfortable or overwhelms them with her apparent needfulness.

Although some peers can accept her simple statements about the diet in a matter-of-fact way, your child should be prepared that others may react with embarrassment, with disgust, or by teasing. If peers tend to avoid or tease your child, reassure her that differences tend to make some children uneasy. If teasing continues for a long period of time, there may be something inappropriate about the way your child presents the issue. Observe what may be wrong and correct the situation by rehearsals with your child.

In some social situations, your child should simply make a bold, firm, and forthright statement about certain food limitations. A comment such as "Weird, isn't it?" can sometimes ensure that peers will be more accepting of an unusual food restriction.

Convey a you-can-do-it attitude. As time proceeds, focus on gradual gains. Be compassionate when improvements in symptoms seem to be slow. Encourage your child that symptom flare-ups will be less frequent, less severe, and recovery time will be shorter after each flare-up. Analyze what may be wrong and use a diet diary (Chapter 3) to double-check and resolve the problem.

Teach your child to look for the positive. Guide your child to be thankful for the gains that are being made and for the setbacks that serve as reminders to eat carefully. Doing so discourages pessimism and maximizes your child's energy and commitment to maintain the diet. Remind your child to notice and appreciate her family for their support and understanding in the dietary effort.

Be empathic. Empathizing with your child's emotions means giving validity to them—agreeing that you understand them, that they are legitimate, that you have had similar feelings in the past, and that you are able to feel something similar at the current moment. State, for example: "I understand that you would like to eat what your friends are eating. I get uncomfortable sometimes when I have to eat food different from what everyone else is eating."

Seemingly small matters do not necessarily appear insignificant to your child. The owner of the mountain determines its size; it is not a molehill if the owner doesn't think it is. Look at the situation from your child's position. Sometimes all your child needs is your acknowledgment of her stated feeling and the awareness that you understand. If, however, your child seems to be asking for more information, your empathic response can help open the door for her to hear explanations from you.

Extreme emotional states interfere with your child's capacity to listen and to understand. Therefore, give empathy before you give explanations. When giving reassurance, follow the same sequence. Reassurance should come after empathy, not before it. For example, say: "I understand how you feel and that is okay—but I want you to realize that I will be there to help you." Attempted encouragements are not as helpful when not preceded by empathy.

You may need to emphasize that feelings are legitimate and that there is no such thing as a bad feeling. When your child experiences an unpleasant emotion about some aspect of the diet, you may want to answer not only with "I know how you feel" but with "It is okay to have those feelings."

Help your child track down the sources of unpleasant feelings. She might not always be able to figure out, for example, why she feels angry or guilty. An individual emotion or awareness that your child may have can often lead to another, such as when embarrassment leads to anger, or when your child's awareness of inconveniences caused to others leads to guilt feelings.

Sometimes if you get a clue that your child is troubled about an aspect of the diet, you may need to take a guess about what she is feeling. For example, you might say: "Are you worried about what will happen next week when you visit your cousin and still have to be on the diet?" Your child will not automatically agree with what you have guessed unless your guess is accurate. Some parents have found it best to give three guesses in a row and then ask the child to indicate which is the closest to her true feelings.

Your child may begin to use irony or frank humor as a way of showing frustration or other feelings. Humor is generally a healthy way to deal with some of the emotional aspects of dietary restrictions, provided that it reflects an underlying acceptance of the realities. You don't have to go to great lengths to empathize—just laugh along with your child.

Be supportive as changes occur. Your child's condition may fluctuate somewhat from time to time. Sometimes new medical knowledge or a switch from one physician or dietitian to another can bring about a change in dietary guidelines. Once your child gets used to a certain dietary routine, to have it suddenly altered can be frightening. Because your child associates her sense of personal safety with the diet, give help in understanding any major changes that occur.

Don't overdo on holidays. Be willing to make special efforts to prevent friends, relatives, or family members from trying to please your child with novel but off-limits holiday treats. Talk to these other people ahead of time to ensure that no out-of-balance attempts to compensate for dietary restrictions occur for your child at holidays.

Seek appropriate professional help. If your child is mired in an emotional state that prevents full cooperation on the diet, don't hesitate to involve the physician, the dietitian, a mental health professional, a parent support group liaison person, or other appropriate resource. Your actions will teach your child an important lesson—that asking for help at appropriate times is a sign of strength, not weakness.

Be alert for signs of emotional constraint that would slow down your child's cooperation on the diet. Be reassuring, and keep your child involved in as many aspects of the diet as possible. Keep your expectations clear, and follow through on maintaining dietary limits while keeping open lines of communication with your child. These steps combined with your reassurance can help your child integrate the diet smoothly into daily life.

3. Understand the Diet

Faced with the need of starting and maintaining a special diet for your child, you may wonder how your dietitian or physician settled on the particular recommendations that went into creating your child's dietary program. No matter what your child's medical condition, maintaining adequate nutrition is important to helping him achieve a better quality of life.

Nutrition consists of the processes by which we take in and use food to promote growth, replace worn or injured body tissues, and provide energy for activity. Good nutrition provides a basis on which medications and medical procedures work. Nutrition is one of the most important factors determining overall health.

Today we know that the food we eat has a long-range effect on our health and that dietary choices are related to preventing and controlling specific diseases.

Health is a positive process, not merely the absence of disease. Improving your child's health means helping him increase capabilities, attain better body functions, and achieve better balance in many aspects of life. Your role involves a constant determination to bring your child to the fullest possible state of bodily and psychological efficiency.

Children's disorders that require long-term dietary measures usually affect several areas of functioning, including social, emotional, and physical, with consequent effects on the entire family. The psychological and social dimensions of disease are seldom more involved than when a parent applies a dietary program for a child over a long period of time.

Your child's diet may complement other forms of treatment. The diet might have a direct relationship to the cause of your child's medical condition, so that it can alleviate the cause and eliminate the condition. Some diets include certain substances for the child's health, such as a substance that is not being made by the child's body or is blocked from being made. Other diets remove something injurious from the child's body or prevent the child from consuming the harmful substance. In some medical disorders, a dietary approach is the only definitive treatment available to ensure a child's very survival.

For those medical conditions not totally treated by following a special diet, nutritional control may soften some of the symptoms. For example, long-term immobilization can cause a child to lose large amounts of certain nutrients and trace minerals. Secretions of hormones are thrown out of balance, and there is an increased need for certain vitamins required to carry out metabolism. Dietary measures are sometimes helpful in compensating for these imbalances.

Many medical procedures are more effective when a nutritional therapy occurs simultaneously. As a supplement to medical treatment, the diet might be able to lessen the symptoms of a progressively worsening or terminal condition. In a child who has not previously been eating a balanced diet, the goals of supportive nutritional therapy might include maintaining the child's overall health status, rehabilitating while the child awaits more definitive medical treatment, improving the child's immune status so that other diseases do not occur, or improving the child's overall metabolism.

The disease process itself may have a profound effect on a child's ability to accept certain foods. Some foods might taste different and might irritate the child's throat or digestive tract, causing changes in a child's preferences for food. Such changes may call for dietary maneuvers in order to adjust food intake.

Long-term medical conditions sometimes lead to abnormal body weight. Control of body weight frequently involves nutritional treatment. To do so, of course, food habit patterns and attitudes must often also change.

Regardless of which goals apply to your child's dietary program, they should be clear to you and to your child. Both of you can then proceed with greater confidence and encouragement.

The Basic Food Categories

Part of the foundation for your child's diet is his specific need for foods from these basic food categories:

Fats. Fats provide calories for energy, help absorb vitamins, and provide essential fatty acids. The body uses these fatty acids for a variety of purposes, such as making cell membranes and myelin, the sheath surrounding nerves. Fat derivatives are involved in the metabolism of cholesterol. Fats enhance food flavor and texture.

Proteins. Important functions of proteins are the building and repairing of body tissue. They are also needed to make enzymes and hormones that regulate body processes. Proteins provide nitrogen and essential amino acids and compose the antibodies that fight disease.

Carbohydrates. Sugars, starches, and cellulose are the three major carbohydrates in foods. In healthy individuals, the simple carbohydrates (sugars such as fructose, sucrose, and glucose) digest quickly and immediately enter the blood stream. Complex carbohydrates (starches) consist of hundreds of molecules of simple carbohydrates. They take longer to break down and digest. All carbohydrates contain four calories per gram, which is the same as protein and about half as much as fat.

The main function of carbohydrates is to supply energy. Carbohydrates assist in a variety of other body functions, however, including digestion and muscle exertion.

Fiber. Most parts of plants that human digestive juices cannot break down are known as fibers. The water-binding effect of fiber prevents constipation. Fiber increases stool bulk and makes the stool soft so that it moves along the intestine quickly.

Water. The majority of body weight consists of water. It provides the medium by which all of the body's reactions take place. It also provides the means of transportation for sending vital materials to cells and for carrying off waste products. All cells in the body are surrounded by a thin film of tissue fluid that is mostly water, and the cells are constantly bathed in a warm fluid that consists mostly of water. Water helps the organs and glands flush out impurities, replaces fluid lost through excretion and perspiration, and helps flush away excess protein and salt.

Vitamins and minerals. Numerous vitamins and minerals occur in a variety of food. Both are essential in maintaining body function.

Success Characteristics of a Long-Term Diet

Frequently a diagnosing professional fails to explain to a child's parents the specific details of the recommended diet. The dietary guidelines must be based on the latest authenticated scientific information rather than on false hopes. Families commit naively to the prescribed diet and yet are unable to follow through because they do not understand what is involved. The successful implementation of a long-term diet is a *major* commitment in terms of time, energy, money, and conviction by the entire family.

Anticipate that your child's eating habits and attitudes are apt to experience transition. Instilling the principle of sound nutrition requires more than just changing what foods are eaten. Your family's increased awareness of nutrition impacts lifelong decisions for their self-care, as well as for your child. Take advantage of the opportunities to teach your family sound nutritional principles.

There is no reason for your child to be malnourished or deprived because of restrictions on certain foods. Eating within dietary guidelines should result in satisfaction of appetite and taste. Even though initially the range of food choices may seem unusually limited, sufficient variety is available by creative food and menu planning. A specific effort to rotate the acceptable foods helps to prevent boredom and disenchantment while your child eats within specified guidelines. No nutritional supplement can compensate for the vitamins, trace minerals, and palatability of a varied diet. Unless your child's medical condition requires otherwise, you can assure sufficient variety by daily offering food from all four of the basic food groups:

1. Fruits and vegetables
2. Cereals, bread, and grains
3. Dairy products
4. Meat, poultry, fish, eggs, nuts, seeds, peas, and beans (protein group)

However, due to your child's dietary guidelines, it might be necessary to limit or eliminate one or more of the four basic food groups. Consulting with a dietitian in this case can offer nutritional alternatives and prevent long-term deficiencies.

Introducing new foods to your child may be a sensitive issue. The medical urgency of your child's diagnosis might compound the situation. With your optimistic spirit, reassure him that his newly adopted eating patterns can easily integrate with his daily routines. If sudden changes in texture or food selection meet with resistance, help your child understand that a gradual retraining of taste and texture preferences occurs in the process of reaching optimum health. Be encouraged by small gains and know that the necessary adjustments can be made.

When medical treatments inflict stresses on a child's body, good nutritional habits are even more important to help in the body's restoration process. Prescribed medications, for example, can affect appetite, interfere with digestion, decrease food absorption, block or destroy vitamins, or alter metabolic processes. A well-designed diet takes these factors into consideration and nutritionally maximizes whatever food choices the child can eat. A comprehensive portrayal of these diet-relevant effects of prescribed medications appears in Appendix I.

An effective therapeutic diet prevents overweight and underweight. Weight control should be orchestrated with the nutritional program.

Most therapeutic diets do not increase the family's food expenses. In fact, your child's diet may prove less expensive to maintain because you as a shopper are no longer subject to impulse buying and can avoid purchasing unnecessary foods. Despite any overall savings, the purchase of specialty items or necessary cooking equipment may increase costs. In some circumstances, there are tax advantages for diet therapy; however, precise record keeping is required. It might be helpful to consult your accountant or the Internal Revenue Service to see whether you qualify for any tax benefits.

To assist further in your child's transition toward accepting, cooperating with, and adhering to the prescribed dietary plan, you may want to consider these practical recommendations shared by parents living with diet-restricted children.

Plan meals and snacks. For many parents, menu planning is a gigantic first hurdle. Planning menus may seem burdensome, but the compensations of easier shopping and always having on hand what you need for food preparations make the extra effort worthwhile.

Once you have developed a clear idea of diet-accepted foods and their nutritional characteristics, you are ready for serious menu planning. The menu can be repeated the second week with adjustments from the first week, so that any mistakes or difficulties encountered are quickly remedied. Include a number of food items that are acceptable not only for your child but also for other family members.

Ordinarily snacks are thought of as being unplanned and spontaneous. Responding to the snack food whim usually represents the greatest time of temptation for the diet-restricted child unless previous plans and preparations have resulted in the availability of acceptable foods. Maintain an easily accessible snack selection in your purse, car, your child's locker at school, or wherever your child might be during the most likely time for needing a snack. Whenever possible, incorporate your child's snacks into the overall daily eating plan.

When emotional or physical energy is at a minimum, the challenge of carefully preparing a meal can be irritating. Take advantage of time-saving foods. Quick access to a mix can save time. Anticipate those occasions when, because of limited time or energy, you need to have available a quick meal or alternative arrangements.

Be realistic about time pressures, schedules of family members, your underlying enjoyment or disdain for being in the kitchen, and other factors that affect the preparation or serving of meals. For instance, avoid a lavish breakfast if everyone is on a tight, early schedule. In this case, a simple breakfast is easier on everyone's digestion and nerves!

Use any leftovers in the next day's lunch, freeze them separately, or create your own frozen dinners; however, it is important for you to become familiar with food safety aspects of leftovers. Watch for adjustments in the shelf-life of any new foods or ingredients that you may be using for the first time.

Set aside time during each week to prepare baked items, if permitted; then freeze them in individual- or family-serving sizes. Whenever possible, double the recipe for baked goods, casseroles, or other foods; serve one portion as planned, then freeze the remainder for another day.

Incorporate variety. Something as simple as garnishing a plate can increase appetite through eye appeal. Vary the color of food and arrange food items attractively. Aim for a variety of tastes and textures. Decorate soup or a soft casserole, for example, with crisp garnishes, or accompany it with crunchy side dishes. Rather than serve two highly spiced foods together, provide a bland food to accompany a spicy food.

In some cases flavor is the prime determinant of whether a child eats diet-appropriate food. Flavor extracts can help some foods taste more palatable for some children. In your attempts to support the diet, avoid sacrificing quality and flavor for the sake of other reasons. Diet-appropriate spices, herbs, and tart juices should enhance the natural flavor of food, but not cover it up or overwhelm it.

Try varying the temperatures of food items to suit your child's taste preferences. Chilling certain food tends to make it more palatable for some children, while warming food works better for other children. Cold food, however, usually tends to taste more bland than warm food.

Shop wisely. Avoid purchasing unnecessary, off-limits foods. If the undesired foods aren't in your cupboards, you avoid risking power struggles. Stock your shelves with what is needed, and don't buy things that represent a temptation for your child. Maintain an ongoing grocery list to avoid depleting an essential cooking ingredient or favorite food item.

Organize your kitchen. Start with what works for you right now—your current kitchen skill, familiar recipes, and an appropriate food supply. Be aware of kitchen machines and appliances that can ease the extra cooking demands. At times it is more economical and less stressful to purchase merchandise from local stores or request mail-order items than to cook from scratch. Your time, energy, and finances greatly influence this crucial aspect of maintaining a special diet.

Develop a collection of favorite recipes. Adjustments are much easier if the foods being served are relatively comparable to what your child already enjoys and associates with family traditions. Think of how to convert an old favorite recipe into compliance with your child's diet. Becoming a flexible and creative cook who is not always governed by past experience ("But that's the way I have always fixed. . .!") makes life much easier. You may want to consider taking a particular cooking class, attending a college or extension seminar on a certain type of food preservation, or broadening your culinary skills and nutritional awareness through other sources.

Not every cookbook is helpful. An easy way to get started is to consult dietitians, home economists, or experienced parents already accustomed to your child's dietary guidelines. Maintain your child's favorite recipes in a card file or a notebook for quick reference as your child increasingly learns to participate in cooking. These accumulated items can later serve as a gift to your child when he leaves home to assume his own cooking responsibilities. This collection of recipes should be easy to send along when your child visits relatives for an extended period of time. Local and national organizations connected with your specific interest may also be able to recommend helpful cookbooks. Appendix II contains a listing of many such resources. A local parent support group might participate in a food co-op in which specialty items as well as staples are available at reduced prices.

Become a label reader. Learn how to recognize ingredients and the expiration dates on product labels. Become acquainted with your child's forbidden foods in all derivatives so that you can become an informed consumer. Taking a list with you of your child's permitted and nonpermitted foods during the early days of adjustment greatly simplifies your grocery shopping efforts.

Nutrition labels provide the following information: calories, protein, carbohydrate, fat, vitamin A, vitamin C, thiamine, riboflavin, niacin, calcium, and iron. Information on cholesterol, fatty acid, and sodium content is optional.

When a primary manufacturer uses ingredients purchased from a secondary company (shortening, for example), the primary manufacturer is not required to list those ingredients. Hidden ingredients can be a stumbling block in some prescribed long-term diets. The ingredient information on any particular label might not be adequate for your needs, and in such a case it is best to forgo using that product until you can obtain further ingredient information.

To help ensure the graceful integration of diet-indicated meals into your family's daily eating routines, use carefully selected recipes, modify some popular food items to keep them within the dietary guidelines, and thoughtfully develop menu and shopping plans.

Involve your child. Children enjoy making choices, so allow them to participate in age-appropriate dietary decisions. To increase enthusiasm for eating and teach specific dietary guidelines, encourage your child to participate in menu development, grocery shopping, label reading, food preparation, recipe gathering, and even cleanup. Novelty meals always bring excitement and anticipation.

Your Child's Appetite Might Sag

Loss of appetite may occur because of fatigue, nausea, side effects of medication, biochemical imbalances, simultaneous acute illness, allergies that may develop, or the direct impact of the medical disorder itself. A distortion or heightened sensitivity in the senses of smell or taste sometimes contributes to a child's decreased appetite. Nausea directly related to the disorder or medical treatments discourages any zeal for food intake. If the child demonstrates digestion difficulties, he may want to reject foods with large amounts of fat. Meals may also be discouraging if the portions seem overwhelming or if emotions upsetting to the child are aroused at mealtime.

The choice of which food to offer your child can sometimes mean the difference between a cooperative eater and one who does not cooperate. If the food still doesn't taste good to your child after you have done everything possible to enhance its taste, texture, and appearance, there is no sense in pretending otherwise. Emphasize instead that the food is healthful and nutritious.

Avoid serving meals when your child is overly fatigued. A short nap before the meal or a readjusted mealtime may better accommodate your child's natural cycles. Exercise that gently stimulates but does not tire your child shortly before a meal can sometimes arouse a sluggish appetite. Some children don't feel sufficiently hungry to eat a full meal, so offering several smaller meals or an occasional snack throughout the day may be a useful consideration. On the other hand, a child who snacks all day is unlikely to take much interest in regular meals.

Mentally and physically prepare your child for the meal. Give a brief notice when the meal is about to occur so that your child is allowed to bring activities to completion and arrive at the table ready to eat. During those few moments before the meal, the shift in attention away from other activities and toward food allows him to anticipate the meal. The child who must eat alone is more likely to succumb to a poor appetite. Children tend to enjoy eating and have better appetites when around others with whom they feel comfortable.

Generally a room that is clean and orderly, with no irritating distractions, provides the best atmosphere. Something as simple as controlling the lighting of the room can affect cooperation when appetite is marginal. An attractively set table with pretty serving dishes, flowers, or a novel centerpiece might help. Use a favorite place mat, cup, drinking straw, or dish set. For a change in routine, eat by candlelight, set up a card table and eat in a different place, have an indoor picnic, prepare a meal of just finger-foods, or use lap trays. A "backward" meal (dessert first, salad last) is an interesting adventure. Cutting or shaping foods into interesting designs brightens up the food selections.

As a rule, limit snacks prior to meals. Avoid foods with high fat content and encourage slow eating. Unless otherwise restricted, save the drinking of liquids for after the meal rather than during the meal, because liquids tend to fill up the stomach.

Medical factors may work against your child's desire to eat. Be willing to negotiate and put your childs' nutritional needs above your desire to avoid temporary inconvenience and frustration.

Avoid emotional barriers between you and your child as you strive together for dietary fulfillment and improved health for your child.

Use A Diet Diary

A diet diary should contain a complete record of the child's food intake and symptoms for each twenty-four-hour period. It aids in monitoring your child's diet with an accurate reading of food intake and symptoms that occur. If you use the format suggested here, a loose-leaf notebook provides the best method for record keeping.

Dietary errors, imbalances, or other concerns are easily discernible when you use a diet diary consistently. Observe which specific foods were consumed, as well as the times of ingestion for the days when your child seemed to be in a good state. Pay special attention to food intake notations when your child's state was questionable. Remember that symptoms in the morning upon awakening can sometimes reflect food eaten the preceding evening. This use of a diet diary applies only for disorders in which a dietary deviation immediately causes an observable symptom of some sort.

Caloric values and the daily pattern of calorie distribution can also be monitored with a diet diary. A well-maintained diet diary provides other important information, such as the overall balance of nutrients and variety of foods.

It is important to assess the effects of dietary manipulations. A diet diary is especially useful when symptoms phase in and out over a period of time. Monitoring the impact of dietary adjustments during a time when symptoms change because of other factors can be misleading. The nutritional adjustment might not have been effective at all but simply might have happened coincidentally during a time when symptoms were declining for other reasons. Diligent use of a diet diary over a period of time eliminates this kind of mistaken assumption about the impact of dietary manipulations.

Another use of the diet diary is to measure the *placebo effect*, which is the extent to which the extra attention your child receives because of the diet motivates him to appear free of symptoms. In other words, symptoms get better even when the diet is not actually applied but when your child *thinks* it is being applied. Use of the diet diary prevents you from assuming that a placebo effect is occurring when in fact it is not.

The testing of foods to be added or eliminated usually requires a carefully maintained diet diary. Occasionally the physician or dietitian may want to test whether to include or exclude a certain food item or ingredient in the dietary guidelines. Some food allergies are such, for example, that individual testing of specific food items is needed. For conditions made worse by certain foods, the diet diary can document all foods that could conceivably cause any type of reaction. Foods to be tested are then reintroduced. If symptoms appear after a certain food is introduced, that food item or food category becomes suspect. It is best that the child be free of symptoms when this challenge testing begins, so that triggering of any symptomatic reaction is cleary the result of the isolated food item.

Adhere strictly to dietary guidelines with respect to all other foods when experimenting with the elimination or addition of particular food items. If other foods are accidentally omitted or added during this same period, changes in symptoms cannot be assumed to result from the intended isolated food. A well-monitored and thorough diet diary, however, also allows you to be aware of additional symptom-causing foods. For many diets, the determination of which foods are allowed and which are off-limits is already made prior to the start of the diet, so this use of the diet diary is not necessary.

A Typical Diet Diary Record Sheet
Date _____

Times: Arise ___ To Bed ___ Asleep ___ Breakfast ___ Lunch ___ Dinner ___

Time Period	Food and Ingredients	Amounts	Notes	Symptoms and Traits
Nighttime before arising				
Arising thru breakfast				
Breakfast thru A.M. snack				
A.M. snack thru lunch				
Lunch thru P.M. snack				
P.M. snack thru dinner				
Dinner thru bedtime				
Bedtime until asleep				

Additional notes:

Understand the role your child's diet plays in overall health Make thoughtful plans for meals and snacks. Plan for variety in food selection through well-selected menus and streamlined shopping methods. Organize your kitchen for efficient meal preparation, and be alert for methods of counteracting any loss in appetite by your child. Finally, use a diet diary under the direction of your child's dietitian or physician to help assess the effects of dietary manipulations. In these ways you can help ensure that the specific dietary effort recommended for your child remains as fully effective as possible.

4. Combine the Diet with Total Health Care

After finally learning the diagnosis of your child's condition, you should establish a primary physician to direct preventive and routine medical care. Your child should receive regularly scheduled immunizations, screening tests, or reassessments for growth and development. Routine health care with periodic visits to the primary physician is important in order to monitor your child's ongoing condition and to evaluate the effectiveness of the diet. Additional aspects of routine health care include exercise, stress management, and sleep.

Exercise

Because it is so intimately involved with overall vigor and with the expenditure of calories, exercise is the natural partner of food intake in helping determine your child's energy level and weight. Physical activity brings a great deal of pleasure, and children are attracted to it. In addition it brings grace, agility, and skill at coordinated body movement, and it increases strength and physical appearance by enhancing the firmness of muscles.

Exercise is not limited to team sports and competitive activity. Your child does not have to go to a recreation center, purchase expensive equipment, or invest in lessons. Most exercise can be self-initiated and very pleasurable without bringing exhaustion. Good exercise does not have to be grueling to be effective, and the activities of daily living can often be done in such a way as to provide meaningful exercise.

In addition to its many health benefits, regular exercise also provides mental distraction. Exercise done in a recreational frame of mind promotes relaxation. It also helps build up endurance and self–confidence. Your child can learn through regular exercise to have the confidence necessary to face difficulties and surmount lengthy periods of physical challenge.

Exercises that require greater-than-normal amounts of oxygen by cells, especially muscle cells, and that involve continuous large muscle movement are commonly called *aerobic exercises.* Deep breathing tones the child's respiratory system and increases its efficiency. Muscular exertion during aerobic exercises increases the rate of blood flow, keeps blood moving through the circulatory system, and strengthens the heart.

Aerobic exercises include long-distance hiking, swimming, running, jogging, dancing, cross-country skiing, speed bicycling, and fast walking.

Before involving your diet-restricted child in any type of consistent exercise, consult a physician. Some aerobic exercises may be too strenuous for some children with the types of health problems necessitating a long-term diet.

Most children get enough exercise and are not in need of a strictly regimented exercise program. If you would like to encourage additional exercise for your child, here is a checklist of important questions you should ask that will help you decide. For maximum benefit to your child, try to arrange exercise that fulfills as many of these conditions as possible:

Is the exercise self-regulatory? Can your child help determine how long or how fast to exercise? Can your child avoid comparing performance with that of other children, particularly children who do not have medical conditions? Can your child avoid comparing performance with children who are thinner or who weigh less? Can the activity be done alone if desired? Can your child happily participate before he has built up a high degree of skill? Can he accomplish the exercise one step at a time?

Is it interesting? Is it fun, and does your child enjoy participating? Is your child able to avoid boredom while doing it? Does your child develop a desire to continue exercising in this same way? Will your child be able to use the exercise as a release of tension? Will it improve your child's mental state? Will it have a soothing effect to break up the monotony of daily life? Can your child sense improvement in such areas as vigor, appearance, strength, stamina, sleep, appetite, or attitude? Does the exercise give your child something to be proud about? Will your child's self-image improve because of a sense of accomplishment? Can other types of exercise be performed simultaneously for variety?

Is it convenient? Can your child do the activity at or near home without the need for a gymnasium, a spa, or public areas? Can he do it at times of day and in locations that are not too restrictive? Can your child do the exercise on a regular basis? Can he conveniently rotate it with other exercises? Can he perform the exercise without the purchase of expensive equipment, uniforms, lessons, or memberships?

Is it appropriate to your child's needs? Do the demands of the exercise parallel the frequency and the amount of exertion that your child wishes to devote to it? Is the activity in concert with your child's age, state of health, physical condition, and activity preferences? Does the activity improve physical appearance? Does the activity improve your child's overall physical condition? Does it emphasize major organ systems, such as heart and lungs? Is it physically invigorating to a pleasant degree without exhaustion?

The physician, physical therapist, or other involved helping professional may be able to give guidance about the factors that would be appropriate to consider when selecting exercises for your child. A sensible diet, adequate activity, proper exercise, sufficient rest and relaxation, and good habits of personal hygiene are key ingredients to any successful physical fitness program.

Unless your child's dietary program indicates otherwise, it is acceptable, and in most cases highly advisable, for your child to drink fluids during a workout. Solid foods, however, are to be avoided. Children in general should avoid eating during or immediately after a period of exercise and should not eat anything for at least two hours prior to a major workout.

Almost any time of day is acceptable for exercising except within two hours after a meal. Afternoon and evenings are generally preferred by children, but there is no ironclad rule. Brief exercise is more stimulating and should be avoided just before bedtime. Exceptions to this rule may occur with some medical conditions, however, so consult your child's physician if there is any doubt about when your child should exercise.

A warm-up period should generally precede vigorous exercise. The session should be brief because children are eager to get right to the main event. Warm-up exercises prepare muscles for action and decrease discomfort during and after strenuous activity. The more strenuous the activity to be undertaken, the longer and more vigorous the warm-up period should be. Here is a simple warm-up routine:

> Relax arms.
> Let hands hang limp; shake hands.
> Rotate arms, leading with the elbows.
> Rotate the head (jaw slightly open).
> Rotate just the shoulders, together.
> Rotate shoulders separately.
> Jog in place.

A warm-up needn't be extensive for an occasional, casual exercise experience; simple muscle stretching may do in such a case.

After an extended exercise period, it is also important to allow a gradual return to a normal rate of body processes, including heartbeat and breathing. The cool-down period should involve walking along with easy relaxed stretching. It should last approximately the same length of time as the warm-up period. Some children pace their own cool-down but want to skip the warm-up if not instructed otherwise.

A question facing parents is how frequently exercise should be done—daily, three times a week, once a week, or at some other frequency. The length of each exercise period also needs to be determined. Parents need to know how much is enough, how much would be too little, and how much would be too much. For the best solution to these questions, seek professional counsel geared to your child's individual needs and medical condition.

It is important not to enroll your child in too many scheduled classes or exercise programs. Activities like these could tire a child to the point that he feels worn out and loses enthusiasm for other important responsibilities, like home chores and homework.

If you wish to enroll your child in a regular exercise program, carefully select the type, the length of exercise periods, and the frequency of exercise sessions. Encourage activity that is suitable to your child's age, body size, and body build.

A cardinal principle is to begin slowly. Even very limited steps toward exercise can be rewarding. The biggest danger to a child is getting involved in complex exercises too early. Your child should stay loose and playful; the simpler the exercise, the better. Make sure that your child is having fun. Gradually build up to more demanding activities. With a properly guided program of vigorous physical conditioning, a healthy but unconditioned child significantly improves physical fitness in six to twelve weeks.

For some diet-restricted children, exercises must be brief and tightly monitored to avoid overstressing. Train your child to identify and respect the fatigue point. The point is probably being reached and your child should stop immediately if there is pain in any body parts, labored breathing, extremely fast heartbeat, or discomfort from cold, cramps, or sore feet. The goal is always to help your child develop a positive attitude toward physical activity. Encourage your child to have fun and be vigorous while not going beyond the fatigue point.

Avoid forcing your child to join any regular group-exercise program. Your child might prefer calisthenics or weight lifting at first because privacy would be assured. As your child's confidence increases, he might become interested in progressively more social or more public exercises. Concentrate on adding variations. Exposure to several options not only keeps interest high but also provides activity for different sets of muscles and strengthens your child in various ways.

Stress Management

Feeling overwhelmed and out of control frequently results in a child's attitude of "I don't care" or "I give up"—and dietary defeat. Training your child in how to react to stress in constructive ways and providing avenues by which your child can adapt to stresses can help to ensure better cooperation. Stress reduction is an important part of overall management of your child's diet.

The meaning of stress depends on individualized interpretation of each life circumstance. What is stressful for other
children may not be stressful for your child. The opposite is also
true: What is stressful for your child may not be for other
children. Stress is also very situation-specific. What is stressful
for your child at one time or circumstance may not be stressful
under a different set of conditions.

Your child may initially experience stress by fearing that
the dietary treatment won't work, that it won't be enjoyable, or
that the guidelines are too rigid to follow. Anxiety may be evi-
dent as your child anticipates comments from friends regarding
his changes in eating habits.

Your child is likely to need your direction in developing
the activites that will eventually become habits of stress reduction. To help your child reduce and adapt to stress, arrange for
these forms of support:

Suitable goals. Goals that are too simplistic and too easily
attainable offer no challenge; reaching them would be only
hollow victories for your child because no growth is necessary
to attain them. On the other hand, goals that are too challenging usually demand excessive energy and are rarely accomplished. The result is a discouraged child. Help your child set
dietary and other types of personal goals that are challenging
but attainable. These goals can be in various areas of life on
which you and your child agree, such as social, educational,
health and diet, or athletic.

Pinpointed pressures. Your child must identify and understand which stresses are occurring. Inventory your child's feelings, paying special attention to unpleasant ones. If you suspect
that your child is having a particularly difficult day, suggest
possible sources of stress that have occurred. Ask your child to
confirm the accuracy of your ideas. Follow this same procedure
with suspected pressures that may be diet-related. When
awareness of a specific stressor is identified, the first step has
been taken toward reducing it.

Outside interests. A life characterized by balance and fulfillment renders your child less likely to object to the inconveniences of a restricted range of food choices. Shifting your
child's focus from self onto something or someone else generally improves resilience against stress. Your child can invest

energy in the family, a special project, helping another person, a favorite pet, social or character-building organizations, or a longed-for experience. On occasion, try to provide an item or an experience that your child has wanted. In this way a birthday or a holiday celebration can be turned into a therapeutic maneuver that will decrease the total stress that your child experiences. Because overcommitment may produce a separate additional stress, outside interests must be balanced carefully with the other aspects of your child's daily life. Make sure that outside interests serve to support the dietary effort and do not provide significant temptations to disrupt it.

Hobbies. Being engaged in quiet play with small objects that form a hobby, such as collectables, needlecraft, and models, helps to develop feelings of comfort and success. The mild, gentle stimulation of tinkering with a hobby can distract your child from the pressures of day-to-day living. It can also distract from the restrictiveness of the nutritional program and result in a more cooperative effort toward the diet. Keeping busy and occupied also helps make your child more interesting to other children and decreases the likelihood of isolation or social difficulties. Although your child might not participate in certain vigorous sports, for example, familiarity with the rules or players may provide a source of joy and improve relationships with peers. A hobby also provides opportunity for interaction with you, as a parent, in a way that can strengthen your love bond with your child.

Rest breaks. Fatigue tends to decrease your child's ability to cope with stress. Weariness may make your child more subject to temptations to deviate from the diet. Teach your child to leave stressful situations for awhile in order to refresh and gain a new perspective. You might encourage your older child, for example, to limit work time to no more than sixty minutes at a time on a difficult task or on homework assignments from school.

A time-out place. Periods of rest and being by one's self are essential tools of health, in balance with periods of activity and social interaction. Provide a location at home (not to be confused with a time-out place as an aspect of discipline) where your child can have refuge from stressful events and situations. A bedroom may be the best choice. A time-out place should afford peace and quiet, and it should not be barren or unpleasantly sterile. Encourage a quiet activity, one that your child enjoys, such as reading or listening to music.

Deep breathing. Breathing is a key to successful relaxation and stress reduction. A quick and simple way to reduce tension when other means are not available is to take three very long, slow, deep breaths. Teach your child this simple maneuver and suggest the types of circumstances in which it can be applied.

Music. Make provision for music that your child enjoys and for a comfortable place for your child to sit or lie while listening to it. Headphones may be helpful in blocking out distractions and in confining the music to your child.

Gentle stimulation. Gentle stimulation to the skin reduces tension. Examples include taking a leisurely bath, washing and combing hair, sitting in a rocking chair, sipping a beverage while sitting in a relaxed position, and taking a long shower.

Stress-reducing imagery. Teach your child how to relax. Find a place that is free from distractions and get your child to assume a loose, comfortable position. Have your child tense various muscles, one at a time, and then relax them in order to gain a total sense of relaxation. If high blood pressure is a problem, teach the child to think "let go" and feel the muscles becoming heavy, imagining only the force of gravity pulling on them.

Encourage your child when relaxing to focus on some simple and encouraging scenes, such as a pleasant memory, a delightful fantasy, or a beautiful picture. Your child should be able to relax intentionally with just a little practice. Your child can make or purchase a tape of stress-reducing imagery and listen to it for a pleasant experience to aid in visualization. Instructing your child "Don't think about..." only forces the thought of the very thing you mention. In controlling imagery, your child should focus on what *to* think about, not on what *not* to think about.

Sleep

Sleep provides a period during which body cells are continuously repaired. Of course those processes occur at all times, but they increase greatly during periods of restful sleep.

Regular sleep also aids in maintaining psychological and emotional balance. Inadequate sleep creates irritability and impatience that can render your child more likely to deviate from the diet. By age four, most children sleep continuously through the night. When your child is an adolescent, the sleep requirement may be as much as ten hours a night.

To ensure the maximum benefits of sleep as they relate to your child's observance of the diet, provide the following aids:

A pleasant room. Adjust the physical aspects of your child's room to encourage physical comfort, assurance of safety, and calmness. Adjust night light, window blinds, position of the door, bedding, and room temperature in accord with your child's wishes.

An active day. Sleep is easier when some amount of physical exertion has occurred during the day. The assistance in sleeping is another advantage of regular physical exercise. A short nap during the day can interfere with that night's rest.

A prelude to sleep. Your child needs time to unwind from daily stresses. It is important that he be calm and not overly stimulated during the hour prior to bedtime. He should avoid physical exertion. Taking a bath may bring relaxation and encourage a smooth entry into sleep.

An elaborate tuck-in. Especially when your child is young, an elaborate tuck-in procedure is well worth the effort and develops a calm and reassured state. Rubbing and touching in an affectionate way, praying together, playing simple games such as writing letters or numbers on your child's back, telling a bedtime story, or fetching a favorite doll can provide rich and rewarding moments of togetherness to close the day. Bedtime tuck-in should be pleasant but should come to an end at a reasonable time without exhausting or frustrating you. When the tuck-in is over, give a good-night kiss or hug as your last expression to your child for the night, and depart quickly.

A day's review. Bedtime is an excellent time to express love and to talk tenderly with your child. Review the day's events with a focus on those that were pleasant and fulfilling. During this moment, express your love in a frank and honest way. This exchange at the close of the day is an excellent form of tuck-in procedure for the older child or adolescent. The last awareness that your child has upon going to sleep is a reassurance of your love.

In response to this type of daily bedtime closeness, your child is more likely to cooperate on the diet and accept it as a joint effort with you.

Just as your child's condition affects virtually all aspects of life, your addressing of that condition should involve solutions for your child's overall health, exercise, stress management, and sleep. By maintaining a global approach and keeping in mind the needs of the total situation for your child, you can become an even more effective guide for your child and supervisor of the dietary program.

5. Encourage Your Child's Self-Care

Teaching self-care habits may require changes in daily routines, but the energy and effort that you put into the task is likely to be very well invested. Developing skill at various aspects of self-care can become a source of deep personal encouragement for your child and bring a lasting sense of competence, health, and achievement.

Self-care involves eliminating unhealthy life-style habits; being in partnership with helping professionals for diagnosis and treatment; remaining informed about changes in the medical condition; identifying new changes in symptoms; refusing diet-inappropriate food and requesting diet-appropriate food; and observing basic principles of health such as regular exercise and sufficient sleep.

Just as in any other area of personal functioning, such as learning to dress one's self, the goal is gradually to increase the child's share of personal responsibility. The parent sets up the structure, starts by doing most of the activity for the child, then gradually decreases his share while increasing the child's participation.

When the diet starts, be very actively involved and in complete control. Gradually, as your child becomes ready, hand over increasing responsibilities for carrying out the various aspects of self-care to your child. Stand by to supervise and encourage during this process. You have a greater responsibility for maintaining the diet than your child does, but you must determine the increasingly larger share to be given to her as time goes on. Maintaining the diet should be part of a total self-improvement program that includes eliminating eating habits that would be unsatisfactory even if your child did not need a restricted diet. The more choices your child is able to make safely and within dietary guidelines, the greater the total share of responsibility she should ultimately have for dietary self-care.

This gradual increase in your child's share of responsibility for maintaining the diet may be difficult. Sometimes parents are reluctant to give up control or supervision, and some children are reluctant to accept the responsibilities of increasing self-care. If you run too much interference, you risk overprotection on your part. You also risk creating excessive dependency, helplessness, and avoidance of responsibility on your child's part.

Your child should have less responsibility, and you should retain more under the following circumstances: if your child is young; if your child's condition involves impaired judgment and decision-making ability or other impairment of mental processes; if severe physical distress would occur with the slightest exposure to diet-inappropriate foods; or if there is an extremely narrow range of acceptable food choices.

Encourage your child to make small choices within the limits you set. The limits help prevent dietary excesses while the choices you allow facilitate your child's decision-making skills. For example, you might offer several permitted food items and then ask your child to choose those for the upcoming week's menu.

Build Toward Emotional Maturity

Self-sufficiency in food choices is a reflection of overall maturity. Your child can gradually take responsibility to observe a long-term diet more easily when traits such as these develop:

Encouragement and optimism. Your child can become increasingly self-caring as she develops the ability to tolerate dysfunction, disability, and frustrations while still feeling encouraged and optimistic about herself and about life. She can learn to develop positive self-regard and to accept love and affection from others.

Ability to accommodate to the handicap. Your child can become increasingly able to limit the impact of the medical condition so that it does not affect any more aspects of her life than necessary. She can continue to participate well in areas not directly affected by the condition. If she can't button her clothes because of difficulties with movement of her hands and fingers, for example, she can use pullover shirts or shirts that zip.

Adaptability. Flexibility can increasingly occur in the face of disrupted routines or lowered expectations of gains from the diet. As new experiences occur, your child can integrate them and grow from them. She can become increasingly able to adapt to new dietary demands and situations.

Assertiveness. Your child can work toward recognizing personal needs and asking for what she needs from others. She can gradually learn to wait to have her needs met, rather than insist on instant gratification.

A sense of humor. Your child can gradually learn to find pleasure in the ironic, the unexpected, and the unaccustomed, and she can learn to see the silver lining in the dark clouds that life sometimes presents. Particularly for very severe disorders or very restrictive diets, a sense of humor is extremely helpful to the child.

Changing personal habits can be a difficult task. Getting commitment to the diet from your child and cooperation in carrying it out are important goals. She has won half the battle when she has successfully started the diet. Shaking off old habits of eating is a giant step forward.

Eating within the limits of a special diet when everyone else is eating unrestricted foods requires a high degree of self-control. The temptations can be great, and your child might need to have a very high level of motivation to maintain the diet.

Offer food to your child neither as a reward nor as a punishment. Your child should be able to accept it as an aspect of joy in life and as something to appreciate for its own sake.

Your child may experience decreased energy for a number of reasons, including the possibility that some body cells have been changing and repairing from previous inadequate nutritional support. In general, there is an energy lag that goes along with any healing process. You and your child must expect that a higher level of activity is likely to develop as new, healthier eating habits replace the former ones.

Keep Your Child's Life in Balance

A crucial aspect of developing your child's ability for self-care is to encourage balance in life. Aspects of life that are out of balance can come back to haunt your child and may threaten the diet. In similar fashion, a dietary deviation can upset other facets of your child's life. Work with your child toward a balance of age-appropriate physical, psychological, and social experiences. When your child is leading a balanced life, fewer obstacles to the diet are likely to occur.

Parents receive pressure to cram many extracurricular activities into their children's lives—play groups, sports, lessons, and similar activities. Sometimes the children's own wants get lost in the shuffle. Let your child be the ultimate judge of the activities and the levels of participation that she prefers. Because each person is unique, your child will have her own specific ways of staying healthy and achieving balance.

Conspicuous misbehavior, chronic tiredness, or other obvious signs tend to indicate an out-of-balance life. A life that is well-balanced for your child, on the other hand, is likely to result in sufficient energy and enthusiasm to tackle all of life's major tasks, including gradually increasing responsibility for dietary self-care.

Explain the Diet Thoroughly

Your support of your child's diet is absolutely necessary. You are the primary source of information about the diet. Many persons who require nutritional treatment simply do not understand their diets. Make sure that your child is not one of the victims of this common and unfortunate occurrence. Explain everything you have to at the appropriate times.

Don't let your child diet from the mouth down only. Her brain must be involved; she must understand what she is eating and why. Instruction should occur before the diet starts. No age is too young to begin instruction in the diet. To the extent that you can increase her knowledge and familiarity with the diet, she can be less intimidated by its demands and more willing to follow it. A physician or dietitian may be able to provide educational materials for helping to explain the diet to your child.

Follow your child's interest and awareness. Tell her only as much as she seems ready to understand. As she shows increased understanding of the mechanics of the diet, provide additional information. When she asks about the diet, use words that are appropriate for her age. Use the correct scientific words when your child is ready to understand them.

Stress what your child can have, not just what the dietary guidelines disallow. Explain that she is on a special program, but avoid the word "diet" if its use would be frightening. Eventually you are probably going to label the program as a diet, but be sure to clarify that it has more to do with nutrition or relative health than with deprivation.

Be realistic in helping your child come to terms with any difficulties in maintaining the diet. Express confidence that she can learn to adjust. Help her understand the diet's role in sustaining health without understating the problems involved. Acknowledge that it may be stressful; then stand by to help. Point out the expected benefits and the absolute necessity of her cooperation.

Children who are starting long-term diets tend to ask their parents some basic questions. No child asks all of them, and a very young child may want only the barest minimum of information on one or two of these topics. If necessary, prepare yourself for answering your child's questions by consulting your physician, dietitian, or parent support group on these issues. Be prepared to give your child reassuring answers to these types of questions:

Need for diet. What are the reasons for the diet? What relationship does the diet have to the causes of the disorder? Why is this particular diet an effective one? What changes in symptoms can result from it? What happens to the child's body if she ignores the dietary guidelines? Why is this diet more wholesome than the previous food selections customarily eaten by the child? What are the beneficial results of an increased emphasis on wholesome food?

Allowed and disallowed foods. Which foods that the child is accustomed to eating does the diet still permit? Which foods are a regular part of the menu? Which kinds and what amounts of new foods does the diet include? What favorite foods does the diet no longer allow? What changes in food habits can result from the exclusion of certain foods? Are there new flavors because of the way the diet-appropriate food is prepared?

Monitoring for nutrition. Does the child need to keep track of nutrients, calories, or both? Does the child need to keep track of food high in certain nutrients? Is a diet diary to be maintained as part of the monitoring process? For how long? By whom? In what phases of the diet (menu development, shopping, food preparation, and so on) is the child to participate? What is the schedule of regular meetings with the child to discuss aspects of the diet?

Duration. How long does the diet have to be followed? What factors might cause this estimate to be inaccurate? How might this estimate change as symptoms change over time?

Consistency when routines are disrupted. Do the dietary guidelines require special arrangements during travel and for holidays? How is the child or parent to inform friends and relatives during visits or social occasions where food is served? What activities are involved in maintaining the diet at school? What temptations might occur when adults are not directly supervising the child? Why are such moments especially important? In what ways can self-control and a self-caring attitude develop to help the child resist temptations?

Realistic anticipated effects of the diet should form the basis of the expectations that you give to your child. Typical expectations might be reduction in symptoms, increased energy, controlled weight gain or loss, or decreased gastrointestinal problems. When you explain expected results, be specific and concrete rather than vague. For example, instead of "feel better," the expectation should be "feel strong throughout the entire day at school."

Confine the stated expectations to improvement rather than cure. Avoid making exaggerated promises, such as that your child will feel perfect. Be cautious about giving the impression that the diet cures the medical disorder or changes something terrible into something wonderful overnight.

Establish Orderly Routines

Good use of routines is an extremely important principle in getting cooperation at mealtime. Because your child expects your family to do things at a certain time and in a certain way, routines reduce the likelihood of power struggles. For example, place supplements or pills on the kitchen counter or next to the plate as a matter of routine. If your child is to eat supplementary food or a snack at a certain time each day, have a special place set aside so that she can rely on its presence. These matters should have a very low profile.

Children need the security of predictable and orderly environments. Be as punctual and efficient as possible; then make your child responsible for observing the routines surrounding the diet. Your child must develop the expectation that routine happenings occur as promised.

It is better to avoid personal confrontations that appear to be challenges or invitations to power struggle. For example, say "It is time for your snack" rather than "Eat your snack now." The first statement addresses the flow of time, while the second is a direct confrontation.

By careful wording and timing, you can keep a gentle mention that it is time for something to occur even less personal and thus less likely to trigger resistance. However, don't let your child maintain that a deviation from the diet is your fault because you did not remind her.

You can structure and organize to provide more than one simultaneous reminder. For example, some parents of diet-restricted children display a chart listing when to eat certain items or when to take pills along with a check-off sheet that the child writes on when the pill is taken. A note taped to the child's bedroom door can serve as an additional reminder when to take pills. Using such impersonal reminders prevents nagging, which becomes tiresome for you and for your child. Notes and charts are neutral and effective substitutes for your memory and your tongue!

Once you develop effective routines, guard against becoming so rigid that you risk insensitivity to your child's special needs. You may sometimes need to play dietary adjustments by ear. When your child receives an invitation to a party, when the family is traveling, or under circumstances that permit food choices within dietary limits, allow your child to exercise judgment. These circumstances provide excellent demonstrations that rules, guidelines, and routines must have a certain amount of built-in flexibility to be most helpful. Of course, all dietary choices should remain within the bounds set by the dietitian and physician.

Your child has three viable choices within dietary restrictions when invited to a social event or when your family travels: (1) take along a special assortment of diet-appropriate food; (2) eat nothing at all; or (3) eat permitted food in common with others but turn down diet-inappropriate food although others may be eating it.

To assist your child in making these types of choices, consider developing a trade-off list. For example, if your child should not have chocolate, consider substituting baked goods flavored with carob, a substitute for chocolate. Your child might also take acceptable ingredients to the social event in a small container, as when making pizza at a birthday party. Also consider keeping an acceptable snack at any frequented location (school or a friend's house, for example) for unexpected get-togethers or parties.

Gently Encourage Your Child

Build on strength, never on weakness. Focus on success. Although the ultimate motivation must come from within your child to eat appropriate food and to resist inappropriate food, your consistent encouragement is crucial. Be patient, understanding, and supportive. Of primary importance is your affirmation of your child as a person of worth and credibility.

Nurture your child's capacity for self-discipline, patience, and perseverance. Point out how far your child has come rather than how much further she needs to go in applying the diet. Because all growth proceeds in gradual fashion, reassure that you do not expect perfection. Make sure that your child learns to define dietary success as "any forward progress." She must learn to be patient and to expect gradual improvement. Your child needs encouragement when progress is slow. Compassion without pity is one of the most useful tools for helping your child at these times.

Strengthen self-reliance by nurturing your child. While very young, your child starts out feeling safe in dependency. If you are sufficiently nurturant during the early years, your child is likely to graduate smoothly into a period of increased self-reliance later. She cannot evolve past dependency if problems of self-esteem prevent the process.

Insecurity from feeling insufficiently loved is a common stumbling block. Another is insecurity from being overnurtured and concluding that she can't fend for herself. These types of insecurities can cause any child to remain clingy and dependent and to shrink from challenges such as a long-term diet. As your child becomes more capable of self-care and more involved in the diet, stay emotionally close while gradually lessening any need to have your child remain dependent on you.

Sustain your child's hope by reassurance. Explain that you are using the diet because you believe it works. Have a "you can do it!" philosophy. Express faith that your child can cope with the challenges of the diet and that she can become competent in managing it. Indicate that you expect some difficulties, but show your intention that your child can learn to manage the diet in a calm, matter-of-fact way.

Treat your child with dignity; she must maintain self-esteem. Do not threaten with exaggerated consequences for deviating slightly from the guidelines. Outlandish predictions lower your credibility and seriously weaken the bond of love and trust that is needed in order to win your child's consistent cooperation.

Your child needs to visualize the improvements that are likely to occur as the diet is observed. Help her visualize in detail the improvements that should take place over a long period of time. This visualized set of final outcomes can strengthen your child's willpower to maintain the diet.

Visualization is daydreaming focused on a specific goal and reviewed in detail. Sit down with your child and ask her to close her eyes and play the "imagination game" with you. Tell a story that helps her visualize being successful on the diet through eating and enjoying proper food. Have her imagine feeling the joys of increased energy, reduced symptom annoyances, weight control, appetite control, ability to resist harmful foods, deep enjoyment of diet-appropriate foods, more nutritious and better balanced meals, a better-balanced life, increased confidence in social settings, feeling less uncomfortably "different" from peers, radiance of complexion, improved body processes and senses, or any other likely realistic long-range outcomes of the diet.

Cause-and-effect relationships are very important for understanding how a diet works. Trace the chain of interconnected events so your child understands that most or all of these benefits can be accomplished. Let her know that the whole process rests on her determination to stay within the dietary guidelines. A clear understanding of the expected improvements can lessen any tendency to deviate from those guidelines.

Like anything valuable, these visualized improvements have a price; that price is the habit of staying within the dietary guidelines. When your child is at peace with that fact, she will be much more willing to cooperate on the diet.

There are many times when the most effective leadership response from you should occur immediately after a deviation from dietary guidelines in order to get your child back onto the right track. Discussing with your child the dangers of dietary deviations while the matter is fresh in your mind is often the most effective approach.

Sometimes it is better, however, to step back and take a broader view of the factors that may be influencing your child when dietary excesses occur. Hold regular brief meetings with your child, weekly at first. During these "personal, private interviews"—sometimes know as PPIs—assess her feelings about the diet and about changes in household structure, organization, and routines that would support it better. Parents of diet-related children who use this method tend to be very pleased with its simplicity and effectiveness.

Assess your child's readiness for increased responsibility during these regular meetings and by observations between meetings. Make it clear that you are still standing by to assist, encourage, and help arrange things so that the diet will be less difficult to follow. The majority of the effort still rests with you. Uphold your parts of the total responsibility for the diet but indicate clearly that you expect your child to assume a gradually increasing responsibility for dietary self-care.

Provide whatever help your child asks for. To have the strength to admit the need for your help is a sign of expanding maturity in your child. Negotiate with her about the types of support that you are able to give toward helping her maintain the diet.

Help your child appreciate prior gains. Although symptoms may not have disappeared, you can still recognize and acknowledge your child's progress. Teach her to expect occasional setbacks. One of the most important things your child can do with a mistake is to learn from it. Encourage your child to examine the sources of the setback and to explore changes in attitude or routines that would prevent a repeat of the dietary deviations. The regular PPI meetings provide an excellent arena for this discussion.

At the first sign of a dietary deviation, see that your child gets back on the right track. Employ professional help if needed. Scolding your child for being weak-willed or self-indulgent does not help and only undermines cooperativeness and trust in you.

Challenge your child with "What should you do now?" In this way you can help her to develop conscience and exercise decision-making powers.

If you insist that your child follow the diet, she may try to make you feel guilty. Attempts to ignore the dietary guidelines may accompany tearful pleas for this or that food or privilege. If you allow your child to manipulate you in this fashion, you will feel even more guilty. Set the limit firmly; don't allow the questionable food choice; then stand by as an empathic friend. For example, say "I understand how you feel, and I want what is best for you. That means staying on the diet."

For some diet-restricted children, forgetting reflects a need to remain dependent as well as ambivalent feelings about their diets. Provide the necessary firmness without nagging. Your firmness is demonstrated by your consistent efforts to maintain the diet and by your expectation that your child is capable of following the dietary guidelines. A child who excuses a dietary deviation by "I forgot" is usually not fully convinced of the need for the diet.

Don't make your child completely responsible for what she eats unless she is ready to assume that responsibility. Give whatever help seems needed, check for compliance periodically, and gently lead your child to take an increasing share of responsibility that is tailored to her readiness.

As you adjust the diet, do so in concert with your child's physician or dietitian. Use professional guidance to help decide which aspects of the dietary program to leave to your child's personal judgment and which aspects you must simply define and maintain.

There may be times when you are not able to uphold your share of responsibilities completely. You might, for example, accidentally run out of the required food or prepare it improperly. You and your child need to have previously arranged plans for maintaining the diet despite these minor inconveniences. The best back-up system is to store diet-appropriate food in the freezer for emergency use when ordinary food preparation procedures break down for any reason. It is not legitimate for your child to blame you or use your mistakes as excuses for deviating from the diet.

Help the Diet Become More Child-Centered

As you reduce your direct supervision of the diet, your child can assume increasing responsibility for it. The physician and dietitian should address your child directly when talking about the diet and should avoid talking to you about the diet when your child is present. In this way they can reinforce your child's participation in the diet.

Encourage your child to be aware of changes in her physical state and of any symptoms that may occur as a result of accidental deviation from dietary guidelines. A diet diary is useful for this purpose.

Strengthen your child's ability to screen out undesirable food choices. Menu planning is an ideal arena for developing this skill under your supervision.

Effort spent in training her to shop for desired food items is well invested because wise shopping skills are useful in many aspects of life. Involve your child in the purchase of desired items. If possible, have her also make choices between brands. Her involvement in these types of food choices is likely to bring greater willingness to eat the food that she has selected.

Involve your child in preparing food. Take advantage of opportunities to teach kitchen skills, such as using cookbooks and utensils. Your child's desire to eat the food can increase because she already has a sense of participation in its purchase and its preparation.

Set up the structure, tell your child what has to be done, win your child's cooperation, establish routines and impersonal reminders to sustain her efforts, monitor progress, encourage her in regular PPI meetings, routinely inspect for compliance, and alert your child to the dangers of noncompliance. Your guidance, cushioned with empathic love and sufficient structure to support the routines surrounding the diet, can facilitate a smooth transition in your child from dependency to a confident sharing of dietary responsibilities with you.

6. Provide Effective Dietary Discipline

To help ensure cooperation on the diet, it is vital that your child feel the love and support of everyone in your immediate family. All family members should learn what is correct for your child to eat and why your child must eat only those items. Family members need to learn how to help your child deal with the dietary restrictions.

There should be a team spirit and a sense of partnership between you and your child. In general, try to avoid actions that tend to set up divisions between you and your child or put you into the role of an adversary in conflict with him.

Gaining effective cooperation from your child involves a balance of love and discipline. Cooperation should result mostly from talking with and guiding your child, rather than forcing things by a harsh technique. You can integrate this whole process into your pattern of daily living, and the steps you take along these lines also serve to enrich the bond of love with your child. Everyone wins when there is an effective partnership for making the diet work for your child.

A critical part of creating an effective diet is to encourage helpful attitudes toward it. Encouraging your child to talk with you about things other than the diet can often reveal the underlying connection between other issues and any compliance problems that exist.

Complications and disturbances in family relationships can upset your child's ability to follow the diet. His behavior as eater and your functions as preparer of the food carry inherent psychological implications. The providing of food can sometimes develop into a larger issue that affects your relationship with him. Your child may complain, for example, of insufficient hunger, of bad-tasting food, of food not cooked just right, or of being full too soon. If you have tracked down these complaints and followed the measures outlined in Chapter 3, but cooperation still hasn't improved, you may discover that psychological problems are the basis for those complaints.

Every dietary deviation can become a learning experience for both of you. Routines and processes change as a result, so that the frequency of instances in which your child eats off-limits food decreases and he can become more enthusiastic about maintaining the diet.

Why Your Child Might Oppose the Diet

Most children's long-term therapeutic diets involve an acceptable group of food choices as well as another group that is not to be eaten. Some diets, however, have few or no specific items that are labeled as incorrect; diets designed to increase caloric intake are typical of these types of diets. Such a diet encourages foods that are relatively high in calories but considers few foods as strictly off-limits. If your child's diet involves a considerable restriction in acceptable food choices so that many foods become off-limits, his desire to eat diet-disallowed foods or hesitancy to eat diet-appropriate foods can become an area of conflict.

Here are some of the most common reasons why children oppose long-term dietary restrictions:

Fear of change. Trying many new foods is psychologically similar to having to adjust to a long series of new situations with challenging and constantly changing unknowns. As it begins, the diet either narrows or broadens the child's customary range of food preferences. In reaction, he may literally act as if the dietary guidelines are suddenly removing an important aspect of daily security.

Too much distraction. Sometimes eating a meal is something to do while some other activity such as television watching occupies the child's focus of attention. If parents consistently present food in this manner, the child may learn to head for the kitchen every time he starts to participate in the other activity. The end result can be overeating of the wrong kinds of food.

Too much temptation. The child, like most people, may feel more satisfied about one-half hour after the meal than while still at the table. During this after-meal period before he actually feels full, he may be tempted to snack on any available off-limits food. The practice of serving highly tempting off-limits food at the meal is risky and puts a great deal of pressure on the child's ability to resist temptation. The situation is made even worse if others cannot quite finish all the off-limits food, which might "go to waste" unless the child were to eat it.

Eating for avoidance. While occupied by eating, the child may feel justified in putting off responsibilities. He may ask for a snack before doing homework or household chores, for example. Over a period of time he may end up exceeding dietary guidelines often as a way of postponing tasks. He might regard the off-limits food as his deserved pay or his emotional bracer to help him face the task or responsibility.

Pressure from peers. Peer pressure is troublesome to the extent that the child feels different in a negative way from his friends because of the diet. This pressure has even greater impact for a child with low self-esteem. An insecure child who feels uncomfortably different from peers and who envisions sharing food with them as a way to bridge the gap of differentness is especially susceptible.

Pressure from parents. Is the parent willing to give up a favorite snack food if some of the ingredients are off-limits for the child? Can the parent resist eating a favorite candy or pastry in front of the child if such sweets are not approved for the diet? Can the parent be positive and flexible with new recipes and serving portions? Is the parent willing to introduce new main dishes and side dishes to the family and discontinue others, for the sake of minimizing temptations and difficulties for the diet-restricted child? Is the parent willing to work with the child to gain the siblings' cooperation on such changes? These are crucial questions to which the answer must be an unqualified "yes" if the parent is to support the child effectively.

Any parental concern, for example, that the child eat a great deal of food should reflect the health of the child, not the parent's own unmet psychological needs. If the parent has become preoccupied with food for any reason in the past, making sure that everyone in the family has enough food may seem especially important. If the child protests about being expected to eat too much food, the parent's first impulse might be to lecture on the children starving in under-developed countries. Eventually the child may opt to overeat to avoid having to hear the lecture.

The parent may attempt to fulfill an unusual need for status by fixing elaborate meals and having a great deal of food available. Keeping children dependent on her may be very important to the parent, and providing food may seem like an avenue for attaining that goal. The next step is insisting that everyone eat the food that she has worked so hard to prepare.

Because the giving of food is a way of expressing love, withholding it is a way of saying "Love will come only when you do what I want." The child may resent having food withheld by the parent for the purpose of gaining power over him. This apparently manipulative aspect of the bestowing of food may bring about rebellious eating of off-limits food.

If the parent associated eating with solving problems and emotional hurts in childhood, she may crave food when she is feeling down. When the child is unhappy, afraid, or bored, the parent might likewise project her own past or present tendencies onto the child and try to comfort with a tasty but off-limits treat.

For lack of a better response to the child's stressful day, the parent's first impulse may be to offer the child some food as a way to bring comfort. Offering food as consolation can lead to many problems, even though given in the spirit of love and help.

The presence of a simultaneous acute illness when a child already has another chronic medical condition can cause severe anxiety for any parent. Any increase in symptoms that the child may experience because of the double burden of a simultaneous illness also adds to a parent's worry. Concerned about the child's increased physical vulnerability, the parent may be excessive in urging the child to eat, including off-limits but tasty food.

The parent may be especially concerned about the child's apparently weakened or complicated physical status. Feeding the child may seem like a way to safeguard a child who is perceived as being vulnerable and in danger. Guilt feelings may persist to the point that the parent concludes that she is somehow failing the child. Feeding offers one channel through which the parent may be able to feel some tangible impact on the child's life. This impact is in contrast to other aspects of the child's life, including the medical condition, about which the parent may feel almost helpless. This urge to feed the child can extend to off-limits or questionable food items. The parent might try to compensate by overemphasizing the diet and allowing it to dominate her relationship with the child.

Insufficient variety. If there is simply not enough diet-acceptable food conveniently available to the child, the temptation to eat off-limits food is much greater. Sometimes the desire to eat foods outside the dietary guidelines is a way of claiming that the restrictiveness of the diet is unpleasant and hard to bear. In some cases, diet-appropriate food is available but must be prepared or cooked, while off-limits food is more accessible and therefore is much more convenient and tempting.

Opposition to get attention. One way to be special is through illness. The diet is one potential claim to fame and thus becomes a possible tool to affect social standing in the family. Children sometimes enlist parents' help in emphasizing their own weaknesses. The child might welcome special consolation, sympathy, and help from parents with regard to treating the medical disorder and maintaining the diet.

Because of their perceived weakness and vulnerability, diet-restricted children sometimes use whatever is available to influence their lives in a way that helps them feel more in control of things. They interpret their diets as a form of deprivation and so have an urge to compensate by pampering themselves. Symptoms have a great deal of power potential, because when they flare up, everybody gets excited. Parents start paying a great amount of attention to the child, who feels powerful because of it. This entire mechanism may not be a conscious or intentional act.

Another mechanism that gains extra attention and service from parents is passive opposition. The child may be sloppy or irresponsible and might appear to be lazy, negligent, or ignorant about the diet. The child may appear to be helpless by either covertly or openly asking others to serve him excessively: "You select the food for me. I can't remember which one I'm not supposed to have." Parents usually dislike being treated like slaves and resent being tricked into having to nag and remind so often. They become disgusted with the child's apparent helplessness, but all the while they have given unwarranted and unnecessary attention to the apparently helpless child.

Opposition to express power. One way for the child to gain a sense of control is to determine what he eats. No one can make the child swallow or keep him from spitting out what he has just taken into his mouth. At the extreme, he may try to eat almost nothing and then only the things that are liked, keeping parents in a state of constant anxiety as they try to devise new ways to get him to eat diet-appropriate food.

A defiant or contrary nature is the hallmark of this misbehavior pattern. The child may appear stubborn, rebellious, sneaky, or argumentative about dietary directions. There might be a "you can't make me" attitude and a tendency to resist everything about the diet. The child experiences power by the act of opposing; winning isn't necessarily important. All he wants to accomplish is to put up a good fight.

In its early stages, this type of misbehavior may be a testing process in which simple, calm firmness from the parent is quite adequate to stop the pattern. In a fully developed power display pattern, parents usually feel provoked, attacked, and challenged by the child. Then they conclude that their ability to guide the child is threatened.

A common first impulse is to force the child to conform and not allow him to get away with such a challenge. By responding in this way, the parent duplicates the child's display of the need to control and sometimes makes the situation worse. When this process occurs, a power struggle between parent and child begins. When the parent responds with stop-gap discipline techniques, the child retaliates by dietary stubbornness: "Punish me all you like; you still can't make me eat that stuff!" The child digs in his heels, argues more energetically, and does almost the opposite of what the parent wants when it comes to observing the diet.

Opposition to get revenge. The child who has the goal of getting revenge appears bitter and negative, openly criticizes parents, and tries to make them feel hurt and guilty for beginning the diet. The child is trying to get even with the world by harming and punishing. He may even claim that he hates his parents or that he believes that the world owes him a favor in return for the dietary restrictions that he is having to tolerate.

Parents usually feel rejected and confused about this kind of bitterness. If the child becomes a target for the parents' revenge as they punish, scold, and criticize, their actions become a mirror image of what the child is doing to them. The child's response to these kinds of stop-gap discipline techniques is simply to increase the misbehavior and attempt to get greater revenge on the parents, verbally and by outright opposition to the diet. The child knows that the one sure way of hurting parents is to deviate from the diet, because the parents have such a deep emotional investment that he keep following the diet.

Opposition to avoid responsibility. The child may lose the desire to try any more, having concluded that he is unable to meet parental expectations about staying on the diet. He may try to maintain the role of complete helplessness as a way of saying: "I can't do it—it's too hard." The child may display an "I don't care" attitude about almost every aspect of the diet.

Dietary Deviation Cycles

Two self-perpetuating cycles tend to occur in children who consistently deviate from their diets. One involves continuous discouragement, while the other involves alternating periods of discouragement and complacent self-confidence.

The discouragement cycle. Feelings of discouragement, guilt, and defeat may follow the eating of off-limits food. The child might feel unsuccessful, might feel like a failure, or might experience increased anxiety and self-doubt. To make matters worse, he may wish to be coddled and may want to pamper himself by eating pleasurable foods. The food that is the most nurturing may be off-limits, so that a continuing cycle of discouragement, dietary deviation, and further discouragement develops.

The complacency cycle. A different cycle, but one that is equally self-defeating for the child, occurs after he cooperates and complies with the diet. Symptoms decrease and self-confidence increases. Self-confidence can lead to complacency and decreased diligence about following the diet. Feeling better and starting to invest his attention on other aspects of life, the child eases up on the dietary restrictions and eventually eats off-limits food. Symptoms or difficulties increase, and the child has a sudden sense of desperation to adhere to the diet once more. In this cycle, the child weaves in and out of dietary restrictions, first obeying them, then disobeying them.

How to Win Your Child Over

Your child must learn to be responsible for his dietary choices. Here are some methods to help him make better choices of foods in order to stay within dietary guidelines.

Avoid excess pressure. The suggestions to act casual and avoid overurging about feeding children are wise ones in general, and they are certainly true for a long-term diet. Your feelings of urgency to maximize your child's nutrition, however, may overshadow your desires to use discretion and to be calm. Be extra careful not to force things or overwhelm your child. As you back off and reduce pressure about eating, your child is more likely to stop struggling against you and the diet.

If you provide all the energy, as with punishment or excessive coaxing, your child has no reason to contribute very much to the dietary effort. Motivation from sources other than those within your child is effective only when you are there to exert influence. The ultimate goal is to develop sufficient self-motivation in your child to make decisions about when, how much, and what to eat. As he learns to respond to body rhythms, including hunger, and what triggers symptoms, self-motivation can gradually take over. He can then make dietary choices in a more sensible, self-respectful fashion. His diet-related decisions can gradually become less influenced by psychological factors pertaining to family relationships.

Do not force foods or promise food rewards. Both of these methods should be last resorts. Your child must face a difficult task of accepting a dietary situation that may not be completely to his liking. Show that you understand his plight and his potential dislike of some of the prescribed food. Then reassure him that the food is healthful and needed and that you expect his cooperation.

Provide choices. Your child simply wants to be able to control and influence things more; encourage him to develop non-dietary areas of his life in order to meet this need. Your child can display self-expression in many constructive ways, such as through hobbies, academic work, sports, participating in family meetings and discussions, and developing skills and talents. The key will be the opportunity of making many choices—the more the better. Children who do not feel the right to make choices often misbehave as a way to assert their natural desire to influence things.

Promote harmony. Reinforce your child's uniqueness and specialness. Avoid comparing siblings with each other: "Look how well your brother eats; don't you want to eat as he does?" Drawing comparisons and stirring up competition will only complicate matters. Remember that you are aiming at a unified team approach—not divisions, rivalries, and factions within your family.

Mealtimes should provide a relaxing experience, not a courtroom drama. Allow no arguments or debates among family members. Do everything you can to ensure harmony and goodwill among all persons at the table.

Teach dangers of pleasure-of-the-moment. Your child may want to think only of the momentary pleasure of eating the off-limits food. As with any destructive habit, the temptation for the pleasure of the moment has long-term consequences. Help your child develop this awareness. At the very moment of temptation, he can remind himself: "Short-term gain—long-term pain!"

Don't let unfairness be an excuse. Some children deviate from their diets with the excuse that their food restrictions are unfair. Teach your child to accept that not all things in life are fair and that dietary restrictions are sometimes among the most unfair. It may seem to your child that life is treating those who can enjoy any food preferences more fairly; however, those same other people may experience difficulties or inadequacies in other areas. Therefore, they have their own share of restrictions, just as your child has his. Although one of your child's friends does not have a restricted diet, for example, the friend may have other struggles in life—at school, in the neighborhood, or in a non-dietary aspect of health. Teach your child that his burdens are similar to those of others because everyone has problems. Point out the strengths and advantages that your child has experienced, in contrast with less fortunate children in some other families. Help your child realize that complete fairness in all aspects of life is unlikely to occur for anybody.

Make the right foods available. Be sure to have diet-acceptable food choices available and teach your child how to prepare the food for himself, if he is old enough to do so. Don't buy food that you want your child to avoid eating or that he has trouble resisting. If you must have it available for others, keep it out of sight, out of easy reach, and try not to serve it at mealtimes.

Plan meals and snacks ahead of time. Eating on a schedule may be very helpful in controlling your child's appetite. If your child is going to be in a situation where eating is impossible for several hours, for example, consider allowing an appropriate snack beforehand to help maintain self-control during the period of temptation.

Although you may want to train your child to avoid wasting food and to eat all that you serve him, it is important that the size of portions be geared to his appetite and needs. Be conservative in the amount of food customarily eaten in your family. Rather than piling plates high, offer small servings and provide second portions when indicated. Better yet, have your children determine their own portion sizes, within reasonable limits. Set an example of eating slowly, selecting appropriate portions, and appreciating the meals.

Help your child compensate. Avoid making excuses for your child when symptoms occur after a deviation from the diet. One way to help your child learn to be accountable for the functions of the body is to teach the importance of compensating after dietary deviations occur. Help him understand that self-hurt has just occurred and that deviations from the diet are always destructive: "Eating that food will cause some changes in your body. Now you will need to . . . (eat other food, or rest, for example) in order to make up for those changes." Additionally urge your child to decide not to inflict further self-hurt by any more deviations.

If you know in advance that your child will be eating off-limits food, consider arranging compensation in the preceding meal. Vary the meal in order to keep total food intake that day as balanced as possible. Your child can also compensate by making the portions of food larger or smaller.

If your child's condition warrants a prompt dietary compensation, going to elaborate lengths to make the subsequent meal especially nutritious can be a wise strategy. Point out that the subsequent meal requires extra attention in order to compensate for the body imbalances caused by the off-limits food. This form of compensation trains your child to be constantly alert about nutrition and teaches the responsibility of dealing promptly with the consequences of dietary deviations.

Develop after-meal routines. When the meal is over, it should end abruptly. Take away all the food as part of table clearing. Plan activities that your child can do immediately upon completion of the meal instead of sitting at the table and watching people eat off-limits food. Just about any routine activity will work; washing dishes, doing homework, participating in recreation, and taking care of pets are common choices.

Teach responsibility for food choices. Teach your child responsibility for his own dietary choices. Your child may be entertaining the belief that he literally cannot prevent himself from making poor food choices. A related belief is that outside forces require him to eat improperly: "The candy was too good to resist. My hands just put the food in my mouth." This logic places the burden of the decision to eat improperly on the shoulders of someone else, or on mysterious external forces such as the alluring nature of the food or peer pressure. Denying the fact that he makes the choice about what and when to eat allows your child a would-be escape from the responsibility of making wiser choices.

Being around tempting food does not automatically mean that your child must yield to the temptation. The food has no lure in and of itself. Your child's thoughts about the food create the lure. Point out that external forces do not make his mouth open and shut to swallow the off-limits food—your child is still in control. External forces never make him deviate from the diet.

Point out that liking something does not necessarily provide justification to have it. Your child may like an expensive item in the store, but that fact does not give your child license simply to take the item without paying for it. Just because food tastes good does not entitle your child to have it.

Teach your child effective decision-making skills. Help your child develop sound problem-solving and decision-making abilities. Ask leading questions, talk dietary problems through, and avoid giving the whole solution to your child. Your well-meaning solution may not be the best as far as your child is concerned, so be flexible and stay aware of your child's ever-changing needs and wants.

A simple six-step procedure can be quite helpful in guiding your child toward self-improvement in making decisions about resisting the temptation to eat off-limits food. First, help your child identify the problem as one that can be overcome and that involves a mistake in judgment on his part. Second, gather data on your child's thoughts that lead up to the decision to exceed dietary guidelines during moments of temptation. Third, discuss alternatives that can help your child avoid a dietary breech. Fourth, discuss the alternatives and consider their consequences, so that your child understands how helpful some of them can be. Fifth, come to agreement with your child on changes in routines, meal preparation, or other arrangements in order to help him resist temptations to exceed the dietary guidelines. Sixth, re-evaluate the results several days later and explore refined alternatives if your child has continued to eat off-limits food. This highly effective procedure is illustrated in detail in Table 1.

Analyze deviations. If your child is in a consistent pattern of deviating from the guidelines, he should analyze why he keeps making unwise food choices. He needs to change key aspects of the temptation situations so that he can follow the diet better. After a deviation, help your child begin again toward the goal of following the diet. Patience is needed as you guide him to progressively greater self-control. He should be concerned about the self-hurt generated by any deviation, but excessive wallowing in guilt will not be helpful. Build on the positive, encourage your child in self-forgiveness, offer to help eliminate temptation moments, and reassure him that the frequency of deviations will decrease.

Be aware of the discouragement cycle or the complacency cycle if either is occurring. Help everyone in your family to get involved in recognizing the pattern and doing everything possible to deliver your child from it.

Gradually train your child to be alert to the beginning of the chain of events that leads to deviations. If the discouragement cycle seems to be occurring, help your child find other ways to pamper himself when he is feeling down. If the complacency cycle seems to be occurring, reinforce for your child the importance of constant alertness and diligence for maintaining the prescribed food choices. Make sure your child under-

Table 1 How To Teach Dietary Decision-Making Skills

Decision-Making process	Ineffective Method	Effective Method
Identify the problem	Vague, accusatory: "You're not paying attention anymore to your diet. You must not care about your health."	Specific, countable: "Three times this last week you have eaten something off-limits."
Gather Data	Assume you already know all there is to know: "I know what you were thinking, and I don't want any of your excuses."	Find out the facts; search out child's logic and feelings. "Have there been more instances that I'm not aware of? Do you agree that all three were off-limits? What thoughts were going through your head at the times you decided to eat those items?"
Discuss Alternatives	Preach, give no choices; child listens and you do all the talking: "From now on, I'm never letting you stay home alone, and you'll never be allowed to have any . . ."	Encourage child to think of solutions; give choices: "What can we change so that you will be less tempted next time? How else can I help you with this problem? What other things could you do instead of eating at those temptation times?"

Consider Consequences of Alternatives	Assume that your decision is the best one; demand obedience: "If you ever do this again, you're going to get it! There's no point in trying to talk to me about it."	Explore pros and cons of each alternative; suggest possibilities, use "if ..then...": "If I remove that type of food from the kitchen, then our family will need to find a substitute. If your chore time is altered, then you might be less hungry. What do you think about each of these alternatives?"
Decide What to Do	Decide instantly while angry; offer no discussion: "You're grounded for a week; the topic is closed."	Give child credit for creative solutions; compromise; base decisions on needs of entire family: "Let's reach the best solution that meets your needs and protects you—and protects us—from any more of these types of mistakes. You write down our decisions so you'll be sure to know them in the future. We'll discuss them at the next family council."
Reevaluate	No communication with child about the issue until another dietary deviation occurs; no arrangement to check on results of alternative chosen.	Discuss results at a prearranged time, usually several days after incident; allow changes in arrangements. At next family council or PPI meeting: "Do you think that our plan is working? Is there anything about it that you think should be changed?"

stands that his chief error occurs when he is starting to feel better. Teach him to change his attitude to "When I start to feel better, I should be even more diligent about staying on the diet that brought me to that point."

Provide activities for distraction. Give your child something to do in response to stress other than to eat. Suggest exercising, listening to music, communicating about the problem, playing quietly, resting, closing his eyes and relaxing, listening to tapes, reading, going for a walk, doing something special with you, or participating in physically active recreation. Chapter 4 details many types of activities for this purpose.

Teach assertion skills. Teach your child to judge each instance of being offered food on its own merits. He must learn how to refuse inappropriate or unneeded food. The courteous and sensitive host or hostess respects this wish. If this other person displays poor judgment in responding to your child's refusal of off-limits food, the other individual has the problem. The problem is not your child's.

The parents of a six-year-old diet-restricted boy have successfully used the following explanation:

> You know what makes your body feel good and what doesn't. Most people, even your close friends, don't know what is best for you. Everyone has his or her own special body make-up. Some people can't tolerate one type of food, while another person can. Each body is individual and different. You have tuned in to your body and you know how to respect its needs. Just because a person is older and taller doesn't mean that he or she knows better about what you can eat.

Another useful practice to teach your child is simply to leave the situation whenever there is an off-limits food temptation. Instruct your child that the best way to deal with temptations is literally to walk away from them. Give your child a standard statement to make, such as "Excuse me, please, but I have to leave now." Rehearse with your child the types of situations in which he might need to leave and have him actually make the departure statement to you several times for practice. Eventually the simple act of leaving the temptation situations can become automatic for your child.

When leaving the situation is not possible, your child needs to refuse the tempting off-limits food. A suitable standard statement to teach your child is "Thank you, but I'm not allowed to have that type of food. Do you have any . . . (common permitted types of food)?" If no acceptable food is available to your child in a particular situation, teach your child to ask for a glass of water instead, if such a request is within dietary guidelines.

Change your child's exposure to other children or to families who seem to be influencing him to go off the diet. Chapter 7 gives many suggestions for strengthening diet-supporting peer influence.

Discard Ineffective Disciplinary Approaches

When deviations from children's diets occur, many parents think that they must do something to their children immediately to correct the situation and prevent further deviations. It is unrealistic, however, to assume that any disciplinary technique will solve the problem and guarantee no further dietary deviations. The belief that a parent needs to do something to a child immediately to dispose of the problem is more folly than fact.

Stop Punishing

Punishment is often a parent's first choice of action. It is a common myth that punishment teaches children proper behavior and is the best response to misbehavior. Punishments, which are generally given harshly and without being cushioned with love, do not stop dietary deviations.

Punishments are generally more effective the less they are used. Occasional punishment probably does not harm a parent's relationship with a child. The most important danger of punishment is not its occasional use, but its overuse.

Excessive reliance on punishment has several undesirable effects. The child may fail to develop sufficient self-control because punishment is a form of external control. Conscience may be slow to develop; instead, self-centeredness and a "what's in it for me?" attitude sometimes emerge. The child may gradually become more concerned about being caught than about the harmfulness of deviating from the diet. Excessive punishment creates an automatic desire for revenge in the child, a wish to regain a sense of equality with the parent. In a search to get even, the obvious choice is to do the thing that would anger the parent the most—deviate from the diet. To make matters worse, the child may learn to lie in order to escape excessive punishment.

Self-esteem suffers if punishment is used excessively. The child can gradually come to feel deserving of the punishment and of suffering in general. A sense of defeatism and of always doing things incorrectly may develop along with a belief that there is no point in trying to improve self-discipline over dietary matters. Gradually the child may feel less loved, less appreciated, and less wanted than his siblings. Deliberate deviations from the diet can then become an inviting way to attain status and a special place in the family—if the child cannot be best, at least he can become the "best" worst! Excessive punishment, therefore, tends to create the very problems that parents wish to prevent.

Stop Ignoring

Ignoring deprives the child of awareness of the true social impact of the dietary deviations, breaks off communication, and decreases the parent's ability to supervise the diet. It also implies rejection, brings confusion into the situation, and can allow dietary deviations to occur without limits for an extended period of time. Do not ignore dietary deviations; instead, address them as issues to work on with your child.

Stop Scolding

Blame demonstrates that the child cannot make wise choices: "You will never be able to stay on your diet because you are too careless!" Such a belief undermines the entire approach of trying to help the child feel confident with regard to the diet. Instead, the child may become convinced of personal deficiency. The child who is blamed severely is likely to feel like a careless eater who is uncooperative, stubborn, and doomed to further deviations. It comes as no surprise that he is then likely to try to live out that self-concept through his actions.

Scolding tends more to train the child in the bad habit of earning the scoldings than to train in the good habit of following the diet. Scolding, instead of disarming resistance, tends to create and strengthen it. "How many times do I have to tell you!" lectures simply enrage and energize the child to fight back. The child's most potent weapon is to continue to deviate from the diet.

Table 2 illustrates contrasting discouraging and encouraging messages that some parents of diet-restricted children try to use when confronting about dietary deviations. An occasional

Table 2 How to Confront Your Child About Dietary Deviations

Ineffective—Discouraging to Your Child	Effective—Encouraging to Your Child
"Give up. You obviously can't stay on this diet anyway."	"Don't let yourself be discouraged by one mistake."
"You've never been good at staying on this diet, and this proves it."	"You've made a few mistakes about food choices, but you're making fewer as time goes on."
"You're still goofing the diet up. Can't you ever get it straight?"	"You are making fewer of these types of mistaken decisions about your diet."
"You're not watching your diet as well as Lori watches hers. Don't you want to do at least as well as she does?"	"Never mind how Lori is doing. Compare yourself with your own progress—you're making fewer of these types of food mistakes, and that's what is important."
"You'll never be able to do this, apparently."	"You will gradually make fewer of these types of mistakes in food choice as you get more practice with the diet."
"Next time I suppose you will forget again and take the wrong food."	"Maybe next time can be better, because you'll know better what to do."
"There is no excuse for deviating from the guidelines like that."	"Let's see what is causing you the trouble in those kinds of food choice situations."
"You shouldn't be making any kind of mistake now about your diet. You should maintain it perfectly by now."	"We all make mistakes from time to time, dear; that's why pencils have erasers."
"This kind of deviation is terrible."	"The world won't come to an end because of this, but we'd better change something so it doesn't keep happening."
"This deviation makes for a big waste of your time and mine."	"Let's not waste this experience. What can we learn from it so that next time will be better?"
"You should always be able to make these kinds of decisions for yourself."	"Never be afraid to ask me if you are in doubt about a food choice."

review of that table will help you keep the proper mindset for remaining effective and encouraging when discussing dietary temptations with your child.

Use Effective Disciplinary Approaches

Be willing to surrender the need to control. Allow your child to develop his own unique style of doing things, including observing the diet. As long as he is not jeopardizing his psychological and physical welfare, not violating others' rights, not ignoring a principle necessary for maintaining order in your family, and not hindering his personal health, there is little need for a discipline technique.

Good discipline does not involve the frequent use of many disciplinary techniques. Instead, it involves rare use of them with a heavy emphasis on frequent, open, loving flexible communication and mutual need-meeting between parent and child.

Side-step Power Struggles

Insofar as possible, consult your child about the diet during private discussions at calm times, not at moments of deviation or any other crisis points. PPI meetings are excellent for this purpose, as discussed in Chapter 5. Don't let your child draw you into arguments and power struggles. There is no point in arguing with your child about the benefits of the diet. You have made a reasonable choice because it is the best available option. You can be firm without guilt because you know that a well-devised nutritional program is good for your child. If your child disagrees about its potential effectiveness, discuss the matter calmly at another time.

Arguments and power struggles are often reflections of other psychological processes. Deal with the underlying issues rather than debate the merits of the diet. Be empathic, and place yourself in your child's position, but guard against overidentification. The answer does not lie in abandoning the diet.

Sometimes small children crave adult leadership and privately admit that they are more likely to cooperate if someone makes them do something. They actually seek firmness and the reassurance of adult guidance, and they expect parental reminders from time to time. This tendency is a reflection of the natural dependency that small children feel toward loving authority figures. Firmly state your intentions to arrange the diet and your expectation that your young child can follow it cooperatively.

Here are twelve suggestons for avoiding power struggles about the diet that have proven most effective:

1. Isolate the conversation; ask for a "huddle": "I have something special I want to discuss with you, dear."
2. Acknowledge your lack of complete control over the child: "I can't control you and I don't want to." "I'm not handcuffed to you." "I have too much respect for you to try to make you. . ."
3. Express your desire to help: "What can we (parents) do so that you will want to . . . (cooperate, for example)?"
4. Set limits and restrictions, controlling what you will do or won't do: "This is what I will do from now on, and why I will do it. . . ." "I will not do your chores for you if you get sick because of eating off-limits food."
5. Express your want as a hope or wish, not an order: "From now on, I hope that you will be more careful about resisting those kinds of temptations."
6. Give advice if the child agrees to listen: "Since you want my advice, I'll give it to you. My advice is that from now on, you . . ."
7. Avoid the three booby traps:
    a. Vague threat: "You'll be sorry."
    b. Dire prediction: "You'll end up in an early grave."
    c. Ridiculous threat: "Never darken this doorway again."
8. Search for answers together; explore the issue: "Let's learn more about why these foods are bad for you."
9. Remind your child that you are always available: "I'm always willing to talk with you about these kinds of problems, dear."
10. Strengthen your love bond as much as possible: "Let's do something for fun together this weekend—just you and me."
11. Encourage legitimate avenues for the child to express personal uniqueness and preferences: "You may decorate your room any way you want."
12. Refuse to argue: "I'm not going to debate or argue with you about this."

Use Natural Consequences

One of the most powerful ways of teaching the importance of following dietary guidelines is to allow your child to experience the natural consequences of deviations. Natural consequences are the more or less automatic sequence of events occurring after your child misbehaves. They do not involve intervention by other people and are not manufactured by you; instead, you simply allow them to occur. The natural consequence of your child's eating off-limits food is the risk of symptom flare-ups.

When applied as a corrective approach for your child's deviations from the diet, natural consequences can be powerful teachers. It is important that your child recognize them as natural, not as contrived by you. Temporarily separate yourself from the situation as much as possible, avoid intervening, and be quiet. If your child brings up the dietary deviation for discussion, express the expectation that he can change his actions in some way so that next time things will work out more pleasantly.

With natural consequences, there must be limits that guard health and safety. Decide ahead of time whether it is safe to allow the natural consequence to occur as the teaching method. Your child can then learn based on an honest experience with the real and undeniable consequences of the dietary deviation.

Review the experience later with your child. Don't give "I told you so" speeches. Treat the incident as you would any other mistake—an opportunity for your child to learn and improve. This aspect of your attitude is very important for your child's self-esteem. Summarize what he can do so that next time those consequences will not happen: "I am sorry this happened for you. What have you learned from this?" and "What can you do next time so that these things won't happen again?" are appropriate ways to review the event with your child.

Use Logical Consequences

In some instances a natural consequence might not be the most efficient learning method. It might take too long to materialize, or, more importantly, it might simply be inappropriate because of the nature of your child's diet and health situation.

Sometimes overriding concerns call for quicker, more direct intervention. In these circumstances, a logical consequence is the best choice. When it seems inappropriate to permit a natural consequence, intervene in a loving and sensitive way with consequences that are logically related to the nature of the dietary deviation.

In general, try to train your child to assume these four responsibilities:

1. Adherence to the diet
2. Cooperation with your attempts to make diet-appropriate food more available and more palatable
3. Compensation, quickly and completely, for any dietary deviations by eating appropriate nutritional food
4. Changes in decision-making so that similar deviations occur less often in the future

A cardinal characteristic of logical consequences is that you plan them ahead of time. Establish a few good basic rules and guidelines. Everyone should know what will happen if deviations occur. Because you have established and explained the rules prior to the deviation, the disciplinary action is a consequence rather than an emotional reaction. The child thus experiences the consequence as logical in nature. Explain to him the actions you will take in response to any deviation. After your initial explanation, there is no need for additional reminders.

By eating carefully selected nutritional food, your child is to compensate for any nutrient imbalance caused by a dietary deviation. He also needs to compensate for any inconveniences to others caused by symptom flare-ups that were triggered by dietary deviations. The simplest way is to do favors for others.

Logical consequences usually involve moving people or objects. If the child dawdles over food, the parent removes his plate. If the child is being inappropriate, rude, or hurtful to siblings, he must go to his room.

When using logical consequences, put the effort into controlling yourself, not into controlling your child. Control what you will give to your child, do for him, or permit for him. Temporarily withdraw any privilege that is abused. You may want to restrict dietary freedom, and even personal freedom as to where your child may go, in order to monitor him more closely after an irresponsible dietary choice on his part. Withdraw the privilege and give your child a chance to regain it when he shows that he is ready to assume personal responsibility again. If, for example, your child deviates from dietary guidelines while visiting a friend's house, prevent such visits for a few days.

Let the consequences do the teaching. Do not insist that your child display any particular type of attitude or accept the consequence in any special style. Your child may react in a variety of ways—anger, quietness, pouting, or resignation, for example. The benefits can be lost if you become emotionally involved in your child's style of accepting the consequence.

It is important to avoid being too lenient as well as too harsh when choosing a disciplinary action. Effective discipline usually involves discussing the issue later with the child. Table 3 illustrates methods that are too lenient, too harsh, and appropriately firm. Occasional review of that table will help keep your disciplinary actions at the best level of kindness and firmness for maximum impact and corrective power.

Enforce the consequence firmly, dramatically, calmly, quietly, and quickly. There is no need to feel guilty or sorry for your child because the consequence is fair, humane, known by your child ahead of time, justified, and not delivered with vengeance.

Your child should not receive a second chance or an opportunity to maneuver out of facing the consequence. Sometimes this policy takes unusual strength on the part of parents, but it acts as an effective teaching tool. When a similar situation occurs in the future, your child will have the opportunity to choose a better course of action. "Next time you will have another chance" is sufficient response to any plea for a second chance.

When you administer the consequence, you are not retaliating; you are merely following through with what your child already knows will happen. You need not be impatient, angry, or revengeful. Just as with natural consequences, there is no need to rub things in with "I told you this would happen" speeches. There is no necessity for labeling your child as bad and no reason to withhold love from your child.

Even the most effective logical consequence can deteriorate into an aborted disciplinary attempt if misapplied. Coaxing, threatening, giving constant reminders, trying to force a situation, or not having a prior discussion about the consequence can destroy its effectiveness. Your attitude should be one of mild

Table 3 Discipline After Dietary Deviations

Dietary Deviation	Ineffective Method (Too Lenient)	Ineffective Method (Too Harsh)	Effective Method
Child dawdles unnecessarily at meals, fights eating correct food.	Let child eat nothing but tasty off-limits or unhelpful food; agree with child that he should not have to eat prescribed food; remind and coax him to eat.	Criticize; blame; take plate away at first indication of dawdling; dismiss child from table; spak; threaten with future poor health.	Remove plate when rest of family are done eating; say nothing about dawdling; discuss and make changes at next PPI meeting with child.
Child eats tasty off-limits food as an unnecessary snack when parents gone on errand.	Do nothing; remind not to do it again; pity child for not being able to have tasty snacks.	Spank; ground child for one week; scold; criticize, call him a pig.	Take child with you next time; deny fun food at next opportunity; discuss at next PPI meeting with child; remove off-limits food from kitchen.
Child becomes nauseated, feels ill after eating off-limits food.	Pity and soothe child; encourage him to lie down; wait on him; do his chores for him that day; remind him not to do it again.	Tell him he is getting what he deserves; blame; criticize; make him do normal chores and activities.	Briefly acknowledge his misery; require that chores and responsibilities be done but allow him to wait until he feels able, or double chores next day; remove off-limits food from kitchen; require compensatory food at the next meal; discuss at next PPI meeting with child.

111

regret that your child has chosen the dietary deviation that led to the consequence. Make him aware that you do not enjoy the discomfort that he is experiencing and show empathy for his feelings of dismay. Your child must "own" his choice, however, and not simply blame others for his dietary indiscretion.

If you are already deeply involved in power struggles with your child over the diet, a statement of your intended logical consequences can expand the struggle rather than decrease it. For this reason, don't try to use a logical consequence in that circumstance. Instead, side-step and withdraw from the power struggle, following the recommendations discussed earlier.

Work toward a team approach to the diet within your family. Understand the reasons why your child might oppose the diet, and be alert for any dietary deviation cycles that may be occurring. Win your child over to dietary cooperation by the methods suggested in this chapter. Discard ineffective disciplinary approaches and rely on natural and logical consequences in addition to discussions with your child later on. Strengthen your child's dietary decision-making skills, and confront him supportively as you help him decide on better courses of action at temptation moments. In these ways, your efforts at dietary discipline will bring about rapid, consistent improvement in your child's cooperation on the diet.

7. Get Help from Siblings and Other Children

This chapter highlights some of the most likely diet-disrupting stresses than can occur in your child's relationships with other children who live, study, and play with her. You can do much to foster support for your child's dietary effort among these children.

Acting in a spirit of shared problem solving, the children in your family can be of mutual help to one another. Although sibling problems can occur, siblings can bring in friends and interests from the outside world and encourage your child to develop social skills. Siblings become partners for sharing emotion and are sources of affection. Older siblings provide help and care for younger ones and are available for games or company. Most importantly, they dilute the intensity of parents' concentrated dietary efforts on behalf of the diet-restricted child.

Siblings Benefit by Being Involved

There are few better ways to alert children to nutrition than by having them witness close up the day-to-day mechanics of a carefully monitored dietary program. The presence of a diet can bring your family to a higher than average level of attention toward food and food preparation. This opportunity provides a great advantage over other children whose families' eating styles reflect little nutrition awareness.

There are opportunities for serving and helping. These opportunities train siblings in the art of loving others, for love is service. Patience, perseverance, kindness, willingness to experience temporary inconvenience for the sake of a sibling, and similar traits can blossom under the gentle and constant stimulation of rising to these challenges. The siblings can develop a protective, nurturing attitude toward your child, even if your child is older than they are.

The shifts in family responsibilities and the atmosphere of unpredictability are challenges that encourage emotional growth. Helping with home chores instills a sense a responsibility and self-reliance, which in turn increases self-esteem. Under the stimulation of helping the family cope with the diet, siblings can become emotionally mature earlier and less dependent on others than peers who are raised in families without the opportunity to share such responsibilities.

Because it provides a mix of positive as well as negative elements for the siblings to adjust to, helping to maintain the diet within the family is an excellent arena for learning how to sift for what is enjoyable in any situation. Having experienced inconvenience or difficulties because of accommodating to your child's dietary needs, siblings can learn to focus on what is good and pleasurable under any circumstance. This ability to perceive positive aspects in difficult situations is an important lesson in life.

Faced with the possibility of symptom flare-ups in your child as well as with the various adjustments made by family members in support of the diet, siblings can learn patience about minor inconveniences. The siblings of some diet-restricted children are in a unique situation of dealing with very deep issues like life and death, sickness and health. By facing these types of issues, they may come to realize the importance of making the best of each day.

Siblings might need to forfeit certain foods for snacks or meals to avoid tempting your child. In doing so, they can experience in a small way some of the emotional strength your child must display in many social situations. They can develop a respect for your child and for all that she must endure. Their love for your child can grow increasingly strong over time and can buoy the siblings against the inconveniences of dealing with the child's symptoms as well as with the dietary program. In general, the siblings can learn to be supportive of anybody who is handicapped or who requires special attention or services.

Sharing in the family project of assisting your child on the diet, siblings can learn about family unity. They can learn to feel important and helpful as family members. They can learn to recognize that very meaningful relationships exist between themselves and your child, and they can be invited to make every effort to keep those relationships strong.

Your child interacts with and influences every member of your family, and in doing so effects changes in how all family members act. These changed relationships in turn will influence your child. As any changes occur in the diet over time, there are corresponding changes in your child's social system: relationships with siblings and friends, school adjustment, and relationships with significant adults who come in contact with her. One of your responsibilities is to oversee these relationships and guard against their deterioration.

Siblings may assume new roles and responsibilities, including cooking, cleaning, food shopping, reading food labels, running errands, and supervising younger children. They might have to rearrange their own plans and sacrifice some of their other activities to cope with these extended responsibilities. They might also face the possibility of unexpected separation from you, your child, and even from home.

Changes in your child's medical condition can bring considerable stress. If symptoms are not readily visible, additional stresses can occur from the ambiguity and uncertainty of identifying changes in symptoms. Your child should feel free to suggest potentially helpful changes in family routines. Sometimes you may want to decide such matters on your own. Be willing to make compromises in order to maintain customary routines to keep life as normal as possible.

How to Break the News About Your Child's Diagnosis

The siblings should learn as much about the disorder from you as they are old enough to comprehend, as early as possible in the course of helping your child. They should be trained to recognize indications of symptom flare-ups and should become familiar with the dietary program. These kinds of awarenesses allow them to feel more involved and give them a better opportunity to participate in the shared experience of helping.

Beware of a conspiracy of silence in your family pertaining to the disorder or the diet. Unless opportunity is made for private, meaningful conversations, siblings can bury their worries and carry a burden of resentments, anxieties, and misinformation. It is essential that siblings know that they can always talk with you about their concerns. Let their questions be your guide and answer as honestly as possible. Reassure siblings that you have the situation under control by giving answers that are informative. Explore the meanings behind their questions. If indicated, ask: "What do you think about this?" or "Do you have any other concerns?" Take time to address the issues completely and as calmly as possible. Postpone answering a question that you are unable to answer factually; then get professional advice or consult written resources for the answer. Your role as information giver is important and leads to smoother relationships among the children in your family.

You may have a hard time deciding what to tell the siblings. Your first reaction might be to cushion the blow by delaying communication, oversimplifying, or withholding information. Denying the siblings needed information about the seriousness of your child's disorder or about the necessity and mechanics of the diet can result, however, in more problems than it solves. The siblings may be surprisingly receptive to frank, factual information. Although you may hesitate to verbalize your feelings and concerns, the siblings can perceive from your behavior any attempt at cover-up.

It does not harm your children to know that you have feelings, and no parent has ever dissolved from having tears. A moment of shared sorrow can be one of special and tender closeness. You are also showing your children that it is all right for them to express feelings. Prolonged, intense, uncontrolled expression of your grief, however, could be quite burdening to the siblings. Therefore, it might be best to postpone a thorough discussion of diagnosis with the siblings until after you have been able to talk it over with your spouse, another trusted person, or a relevant helping professional.

You might want to begin the conversation with the simple statement that the physician has told you that your child has a disorder. Discuss symptoms and point out that now there is an explanation for why they have occurred. Establish a climate of trust. Do not force excessive information on the siblings, and be willing to answer their questions. Use the same approach when explaining the need for the diet, its mechanics, and its goals.

As the siblings get older, their attitudes and ideas change, and their ability to absorb increasingly complex information improves. Simultaneously, your child's condition, needs, and dietary program probably also evolve.

The most difficult questions tend to be about the possibility of death. The name of the disorder might also be familiar to the siblings and give its own frightening connotations. If you cannot be absolutely certain of your answers, say so. If the issue arises, state the current degree of medical knowledge about the condition and the various treatment options, including the dietary program.

Emotional Reactions to Watch Out For

Siblings who are well behaved, contented, and well adjusted are usually experiencing a stress level that is not significantly uncomfortable and therefore quite manageable. They have a reasonably sure feeling of being loved, guided, and protected within the family setting. They probably do not feel unfairly infringed upon by inconveniences associated with the maintaining of your child's long-term diet.

If your child's disorder or dietary requirements are extremely emotionally stressful for the siblings, they might experience any number of emotional states. Whenever an individual suffers a great personal loss, such as a severe illness or death of a loved one, the five emotional states commonly recognized as the stages of grief can occur: denial, bitterness and anger, bargaining, depression, and acceptance. When siblings first learn of a child's severe illness, they sometimes experience one or more of these grief stages. If they are adolescent, there is also the likelihood of rebellion associated with some of these stages. All siblings do not proceed through these stages at the same rate. Deterioration in personal habits, arguing, lowered self-concepts, power struggles, or misbehavior by the siblings tend to reflect the total stress that your family is under.

Here are some of the most common emotional trouble spots for siblings of diet-restricted children:

Worry and overconcern. Anxiety can cause nightmares, consistent complaints of headache or abdominal pains, bizarre eating patterns, or a preoccupation with reading about the disorder. A sibling may become overprotective, carefully studying everything that your child wants to eat. The sibling may seem obsessed with monitoring any changes in your child's symptoms. A tattletale situation may arise from this overconcern.

Guilt. A sibling might entertain the thought that he could have been responsible for your child's disorder. Several painful questions may seem extremely urgent. Whether or not they are put into words, the following questions can occupy the thoughts of a sibling and provoke feelings of guilt: "Is it my fault?" "Did I do something to make this disorder happen?" "Am I accidentally doing something to keep the disorder active?" "Did my awful thoughts about having a new brother or sister make my sibling sick?"

If siblings have a limited understanding of the connections between cause and effect, they may try to apply their own theories. They may imagine their own thoughts or wishes to be powerful, as if their wishing something could make it happen. They might then wonder whether their angry thoughts toward your child, for some incidental event, could have contributed to the disorder.

Guilt is among the most tormenting of emotions. Children who feel guilty tend to try to atone, such as by arranging to be punished in some way. They may misbehave repeatedly, take obvious physical risks, have frequent accidents, do poorly in school, withdraw from friends and activities that formerly had been enjoyed, or in other ways seek to suffer.

Siblings might feel guilty about being embarrassed at times because of your child's differentness from peers. The siblings may have felt embarrassed because of awkwardness created by dietary concerns in social situations where eating was involved.

Anger and resentment are eventually likely to give way to shame and guilt. Some children feel guilty about thinking "bad" thoughts about their siblings. Your child's siblings might also feel guilty about the ways in which they have treated her at times. Sometimes siblings of diet-restricted children even feel guilty about feeling healthy!

Fears. Siblings may have a fear of catching the disorder. Because of close attachment to your child, lack of understanding of the cause of the disorder or an expectation of being punished for hostile thoughts, they may wonder if the same fate will occur to them. They may express this concern by asking, "Could it happen to me?" or "By the way, what makes a person have this disorder?" This kind of tormenting question might also lead to their heightened concern about their own body parts, functions, and sensations.

Puzzlement and anxiety may occur because the siblings do not understand what is happening to your child. They may not know what to do for her. They might wonder if she ever will be rid of the disorder, how she can continue on the diet (especially if it is very restrictive), and whether they might have to go through the same dietary efforts. They might also be concerned about how to explain to their friends what is happening to your child, to them, and to your family.

Siblings may appear to be indifferent or uncaring, or they may look saddened or worried. They may experience frequent bed-wetting, headaches, poor school performance, severe separation anxiety, or persistent abdominal pains. They may seem emotionally withdrawn as a reflection of their fears. Of course, any of these tendencies might reflect difficulties other than grief or depression, so you should have appropriate helping professionals investigate any of these reactions.

Feeling abandoned. Siblings may conclude that there simply is not enough love to go around and that any attention given to your child means less for them. They might feel somewhat rejected in the face of your apparent preoccupation with your child and the associated dietary matters.

Trouble may develop if your child has to be separated from siblings for an extended period of time. This situation can be worse if you have to be with your child in a hospital or treatment center for several days or weeks. Siblings who do not get to visit are likely to remain uninformed or misinformed, and they run the risk of feeling rejected, overlooked, or abandoned.

Having concluded that they are no longer lovable, siblings may openly ask, "Don't you care about me?" They may act babyish, become ill, or misbehave in order to make you pay more attention to them. They may be very concerned about receiving equal treatment and equal attention. It may be hard for them to wait very long for promised favors or to hold onto the hope that you will pay attention to them in the future. They may resent the apparently privileged status of your child and the periodic lapses in attention shown to their needs. Even though sympathizing somewhat with your child, they may believe that you are neglecting them.

Resentment. Your child's siblings probably have a strong desire to be considered normal and to be just like their friends. This desire may result in their expressing concern that your family not appear different, even if little more than because of your child's special diet.

Siblings who are overburdened by having to take too great a share of the care of your child may want to leave home early and begin life on their own. Hasty or unkind supervision by an older sibling of a smaller child indicates resentment. Siblings may be torn between loyalty to your child and the desire to be rid of the stigma of having a sibling who has prominent dietary restrictions. Gaining independence from the family would then become an extremely important issue, particularly if your child's disorder is severe and of a long-standing nature.

Your child's siblings may at times seem to resent the financial stresses caused by the disorder and its treatment. There may be resentment toward you for spending so much time with your child. Siblings might even be angry with you for "allowing" your child to develop the disorder in the first place.

When social situations involving food become awkward because of your child's dietary restrictions, siblings may be embarrassed. They may also resent the real or imagined burdens on the family that accompany the dietary program, pointing out problems that have occurred when your family tried to take a vacation or tried to go somewhere special for even one day. They may resent limitations on their own lives to accommodate to the disorder and to flare-ups of symptoms. Teasing and intense interaction between the children can sometimes result from this type of resentment.

Siblings can resent any of your actions that they consider to be overprotective or overindulgent of your child. They may conclude that you have catered to your child, that you have overprotected your child, and that she has remained undisciplined because of the tendency for symptoms to flare up.

You are likely not to be the only recipient of the siblings' anger. Rivalry among siblings and between siblings and your child may increase as the disorder continues. The result can sometimes be intense jealousy, exaggerated competition, and even physical hostility.

Your child may capitalize on this situation by trying to manipulate things to gain more special favors from you. Any successes in this effort give more causes for siblings' resentment. A cycle of privileges leading to sibling resentment can occur.

How to Keep Siblings Appropriately Involved

In evaluating your child's relationships with siblings, consider what she does with them and how she feels toward them. Assess how they are functioning, how they view her, and how they view themselves within the family. Some parents of diet-restricted children do this assessment during regular PPI meetings.

It may be wise to encourage an older sibling to be your special helper in monitoring the dietary treatment or other aspects of care for your child. It is important, however, not to overdo the responsibilities given to an older sibling. He must not conclude that the welfare of the child is solely his responsibility.

Help the siblings adapt to the inconveniences of more elaborate food preparation, altered meal schedules, and any other arrangements necessitated by the dietary program. Empathize with the siblings' frustrations and restate and clarify their wishes. Point out that at other times they are more aware of their deep underlying love for your child.

Discuss any of the siblings' feelings of guilt and wrongdoing as soon as they emerge. Tell the siblings in no uncertain terms that they are not responsible for the disorder. Even after reassurance that your child's condition wasn't the result of their own wishes, thoughts, or deeds, siblings may still feel guilty about their resentments toward her. Siblings will find it comforting and supportive to hear you explain that you understand their resentments and that it is all right for them to feel somewhat resentful at times. Of course, take actions that are likely to reduce their resentments as soon as possible.

Any overinvolvement with them on your part would increase the siblings' sense of vulnerability. Give them realistic assurance about themselves and their capabilities for independent functioning.

Play, children's natural medium for self-expression, provides a means of coping with body-related fears. If therapy is indicated, siblings can convey their concerns in drawings or by supervised role-playing of doctors and nurses in play therapy with a mental health professional.

Special tests can rule out inherited disorders. If brothers or sisters carry a genetic trait that might result in an inherited disorder's being passed, they can receive genetic education and counseling during adolescence.

Avoid the mistake of trying to keep everything absolutely equal among the children. When a parent makes a big point about one child's receiving no more and no less than any other child, children tend to become even more jealous and demanding. Give differing gifts or privileges, based on each child's uniqueness and readiness. Explain to each child that you provide different and special things for the various members of the family. This explanation can decrease demands that you "owe" privileges, attention, gifts, or food items to siblings every time one child receives any.

Try to wean the siblings away from blaming people for the inconveniences that they experience in life. Help them understand that tolerating inconveniences is one way of contributing to the family good and is an opportunity for personal growth. Teach them that life is never exactly the way they want it to be. Instead of grumbling about the inconveniences, siblings can and should learn to accept them without blaming anything or anybody. They can learn to trace the reasons for these inconveniences without adding blame during the process.

Help them understand the difficulties faced by your child. Emphasize the importance of the diet. They can learn to become appropriately protective of your child and join you in a united effort. Think together with them about how they can help each other. Use the "if we all work together" attitude as your guide.

Facing these challenges provides an opportunity to learn the real meaning of family and of caring for one another. They can be reassured that they too can receive some special attention when they need it. Emphasize your separate and unique love for each of your children. Explain that your attention to your child in various instances is warranted and does not reflect any diminishing of love for the siblings. Tell the siblings as soon as possible of any likely intensive, temporary preoccupation with your child. This notice can alert them to your limited time and energy without bringing on their resentment.

Teaching the siblings how to deal with their anger is an important and challenging responsibility for you. Siblings can learn that their anger is not caused so much by your child as by the inconveniences of the diet and the symptoms of the disorder. These inconveniences act like a wall, preventing the siblings from enjoying and making full contact with your child. The source of the frustration is the wall that blocks them from contacting your child—not your child.

Help the siblings understand that their anger is self-generated. By allowing themselves to become resentful, they give the disorder and the diet undue power and influence over their lives. Encourage them to be flexible in their needs concerning your child. Your child's symptoms or dietary restrictions should not ruin the siblings' lives.

To break a privilege-resentment cycle, intervene at any point with constructive approaches that block the children's misbehavior. Don't give your child the special undeserved privilege for which she has been manipulating. Take the steps indicated in this chapter to reduce the siblings' feelings of jealousy and resentment. Discourage retaliatory actions by any children in your family and let them know that you do not approve of such actions. Do not go along with manipulative tattling by your child and avoid automatically assuming that the siblings are at fault. Don't enter a situation with an automatic intent to protect and rescue your child from the siblings. Check out the situation thoroughly without jumping to any conclusions.

Make sure that the siblings have enough opportunity to talk with you. Also make plans to spend time with them and do things that interest them. Their sense of belonging in your family is more a reflection of the security they feel in relationship to you than a reflection of their bonds with other children within the family. It is the direct personal connection with each parent that sustains most of each child's sense of belonging.

The siblings' attitudes are very influential. Your child may express a desire to break the diet at mealtime because siblings are eating diet-inappropriate food that is very tempting. If siblings dramatically indicate dislike for your child's required food or dietary restrictions, she may feel supported in opposing the diet. Siblings might also feel guilty that they are helping to make your child feel too separate by not eating food in common with her.

As much as possible, try to serve dishes that are acceptable to every person in your family. At a minimum, try to make the evening meal a time for overlapping food choices so that there is little difference between what your child eats and what the siblings eat.

Your child must respect the siblings' desires. They may be forgoing some of their food pleasures so that she can follow the diet without being tempted by off-limits food that they would otherwise eat. In return, they deserve the opportunity to eat some of their favorite foods now and then. Many parents of diet-restricted children have found it helpful each week to arrange a meal so that each family member can eat anything desired.

Give siblings an opportunity to express their feelings and allow them to talk with involved helping professionals. It may be unrealistic for you to shoulder the entire psychological burden posed by the siblings' reactions to your child. The physician, the dietitian, or other helping professionals can meet with them. Involved helping professionals can, by contact with the siblings, learn more about your family's characteristics and coping methods. Many parents of diet-restricted children have found that face-to-face interviews with a dietitian or a physician help siblings come around to much greater understanding and cooperation. If the issues are not directly nutritional or medical but psychological, a mental health professional may be a better choice.

If appropriate, siblings should be invited along on hospital and clinic visits. They can gain some insight into the diagnostic and treatment procedures that your child must experience in addition to dietary adjustments. This information can strengthen their understanding and enthusiasm about supporting the diet.

A local parent support group may have programs for siblings of diet-restricted children. Adolescent siblings can particularly benefit from this kind of support. Parents, teachers, and organized youth groups can also provide reassurance.

Siblings have a need for a safe and effective arena in which to negotiate roles and expectations. Routine meetings are very helpful. These meetings can increase their assurance that you are attending to their needs. Listen respectfully to their concerns about family processes, particularly those pertaining to food preparation and dietary management for your child. During a weekly PPI meeting, review aspects of daily functioning, paying attention to anything in the sibling's life that decreases happiness or that could be changed by your intervention.

The importance of family council meetings. In contrast to PPI meetings, which should be individual, family council meetings involve the entire family as a group. Hearing the concerns of others articulated calmly and in the spirit of negotiation is a very helpful way for siblings to understand their role in supporting your child's dietary efforts.

The basic idea is simple—regular meetings of the entire family to discuss issues, make plans, voice concerns, solve problems, agree on solutions, and celebrate their love for one another. The family council is essentially a method of allowing your children a voice in the affairs of your family while at the same time providing you with an avenue for exercising your leadership.

In addition to a review of schedules and activities of various family members, the family council involves a discussion of chores and routines. Any family member can make suggestions for changing the routines that are necessary to keep the family functioning. In most families, many daily and weekly routines center on food shopping, storage, preparation, serving, and cleanup. Discussion can include any areas of routine functioning, however, such as clothing, housework, lawn care, planning for family outings, pet care, allowances, car care, and room cleaning.

Concerns and negotiations form an important part of a family council meeting. Discussion can occur about difficulties or conflicts experienced by any family member. Various solutions are proposed, and an agreement is reached on which solution to try, sometimes for an experimental period of one week until the next family council meeting. This open, accepting atmosphere encourages free discussion of the issues pertaining to your child's special diet.

One person takes on the secretarial duty of reviewing and recording the agreements and plans made. This record helps to prevent future misunderstandings among family members. It can be written or tape-recorded. A good way to close a family council meeting is to have a celebration involving games, singing, story telling, refreshments, or a similar experience. With a little bit of advance planning, the family council celebration can become the basis for regular togetherness between parents and children, including preparing and cooking the refreshments.

An important aspect of your leadership during a family council meeting is guarding each child's rights to express genuine concerns and opinions. The children can learn that they have impact on the family's decisions and that the other members of the family value their opinions. Gradually they tend to put more thought into their opinions, and their suggestions become more useful. The family council can quickly eliminate potential problems that might otherwise occur with regard to food selection, shopping, preparation, serving, or storage.

A useful procedure to streamline family council meetings is to have family members write down topics for the family council on slips of paper and put them into a "discussion box." A problem is anything for which a child wants helpful action. For example, the sibling may write down that he has a problem identifying when the diet-restricted child is having a flare-up of certain physical symptoms. Concerns can also be irritating things that happen to family members—called "bugs." For example, the diet-restricted child might write down that she is bugged because an older sibling hovers too closely and monitors her food intake excessively. Things that happen in the family that are confusing to the children and about which they want more information are called "puzzles." For example, the diet-restricted child might want to know why she can't eat this or that food item.

The children can write down problems, bugs, and puzzles on separate slips of paper. Each week the family discusses the items submitted to the discussion box at the family council meeting. This method is an excellent one for facilitating family awareness of dietary issues. It even allows younger children to contribute—by having someone write down for them a few key words as a problem, bug, or puzzle to be put into the discussion box.

Peers Can Affect Your Child's Cooperation

Eating with others is a part of normal social life. Dietary restrictions need not be a significant handicap, however, to normal peer relationships for your child.

Peers' reactions to your child's differentness are unavoidable. Peers tend to notice dietary restrictions and, because of their own strenuous attempts to be accepted and conform, may be embarrassed or appear unsympathetic. Be careful about the complete concealment of symptoms or of dietary restrictions because such efforts reinforce the belief that the condition and the diet are somehow shameful.

Almost every child wants to be similar to other children, to be accepted by peers, and to develop a sense of membership with a peer group. Feedback received from peers can have a powerful influence on your child's self-image. Her judgment may be challenged for the sake of peer acceptance, as when handling dietary temptations within a social group. She may have moments of self-doubt and may fear deviating from group expectations. Such feelings can lead to deviation from the dietary restrictions at the same time.

Playmates are likely to have normal interests in body functions and be curious about your child's special characteristics. They might make strange comments, tease her, ask probing questions, or behave in unusual ways to mask their anxiety about their own changing and developing bodies.

Restrictions on your child's activities may affect relationships with peers. Because of a close identification with one another and lack of understanding of the disorder, they may wonder whether they can catch it.

Additional dietary issues in helping your child with peer relationships are whether and how much to tell about the illness or about the disorder, how to manage the diet and any medications outside the home, how best to participate in sleepovers and extended visits, and how to respond to questions.

How to Teach Your Child What to Say

Accurate information reduces your child's anxiety and uncertainty and provides a sense of influence over difficult situations involving peers. Knowledge arms your child against difficult questions that peers may ask. It also gives her strength to respond to caustic remarks or pressure from peers to deviate from the diet.

Rehearse and role-play how your child can discuss medical and dietary information with her friends. Consider the range of reactions that friends are likely to have so that your child is not caught by surprise by any embarrassing or hostile questions that may come up.

When appropriate, refer peers' questions to your child rather than answer them yourself. Say, for example: "My child is right here; would you like to visit and ask her your questions?" Or "Would you like to talk with her about your concerns?"

When friends ask "How are you?" your child has several options. Help her clarify these options and decide which ones to use in different circumstances. They are given here in a format similar to that which you would use when explaining them to her:

1. "With a pleasant tone, give information related to your condition first; then add information about other areas. For example: 'I have experienced a lot of nausea lately, but otherwise things are going okay.' "
2. "Give only pleasant information not related to the condition and leave information about the symptoms unspoken. For example (even though you may have nausea): 'Energy-wise I feel up today.' "
3. "Ask your friends not to discuss your status and not to inquire about physical status. Talk to them at a pleasant time when they will listen. For example: 'I'd appreciate it if you would simply not keep asking me how I'm feeling. I will let you know about any big changes.' "
4. "In most cases when people say 'How are you?' they really mean 'Hello.' Explain to your friends that you will interpret 'How are you?' as indicating that they really want to know your current health status. Request them ahead of time to restate their greeting in the future by saying 'Hello' rather than saying 'How are you?' Simply return the greeting without assuming that they want a complete account of your current symptoms."

How to Strengthen Your Child's Friendships

Encourage your child to reach out to friends. Especially if the disorder means prolonged dependence, peer support is very important. Peers relate better to a child who contributes admired qualities to the group. Encourage your child's characteristics, skills, and talents that add a sense of accomplishment and facilitate wholesome experiences with peers. Playing a musical instrument, having a hobby or collection, having interesting toys, hosting friends for an overnight visit, or having access to videotaped movies to watch with friends are examples of tools that can help your child reach out to form effective friendships.

Having a few very special friends will help. Many of the fears and frustrations experienced in larger peer groups can be effectively solved in the intimacy of individual friendships.

Good friends may recognize early the signs of symptom flare-ups and may even become somewhat protective of your child. Decide whether certain individual friendships are worth cultivating or whether your child needs to drop them and find better substitutes. Then guide your child in the indicated direction.

To guide your child away from an undesirable friendship, strengthen the competition. Make more desirable friends available for your child. Do everything in your power to encourage friendships with kind, emotionally sensitive children. Encourage your child to have them over as guests, have parties with them, play table games with them, and have them accompany your family on outings and to social events.

Peer relationships can perform many supportive functions if carefully watched and nurtured. To help develop good friendships with peers, encourage your child to follow these guidelines:

- Talk to potential friends rather than remain silent.
- Say pleasing things.
- Ask questions rather than give statements.
- Invite potential friends to do things with you.
- Talk about the potential friend rather than yourself.
- Give occasional gifts and do favors within reason.
- Smile and be pleasant to be around.

Give siblings an understandable explanation of their roles in supporting your child's dietary effort. By keeping siblings informed and listening attentively to their concerns, you can facilitate their wholehearted involvement. Maintain orderly family routines that strengthen all of the love bonds within your family. In these ways, you can help make your child's dietary program a focal point that strengthens unity within your family.

8. Choose the Best Professional Help

The needs arising in your family are the same as those in other families of diet-restricted children in some ways and different in others. Any of these needs might require professional help.

Medical practice concentrates great power in the hands of physicians, sometimes creating helplessness and a sense of loss of control in patients. Many parents of children under treatment feel stripped of important resources such as self-esteem, assertiveness, and a sense of contribution. Active participation in your child's dietary program allows you to relieve feelings of helplessness and reestablishes your role as the primary care giver for your child. Inclusion of brothers and sisters enables them to remain in the mainstream of family life and sustains sibling relationships with your diet-restricted child.

You may have a degree of knowledge and information that is very valuable to share with any helping professional. You are directly involved in getting your child's cooperation, maintaining the dietary procedures, defining the food choices within the diet, and monitoring the results.

Stay Informed

You can probably develop a level of knowledge about your child's condition that is nearly equal to that of helping professionals. There is nothing magical about nutritional, medical, or psychological knowledge. Be confident of your ability to learn whatever is necessary to find the best possible care and the most appropriate dietary measures for your child. Be well informed about your child's health, respect your own understanding of your child, and remain clearheaded about decisions involving the dietary program. Don't be afraid to keep on asking questions until you understand what your child's situation is. An adequate information base increases your sense of personal control, effectiveness, and impact. It also maximizes the likelihood that dietary treatment will be effective. It is important that your child understand the functions of each helping professional who is involved in diagnosing the disorder, maintaining the diet, and caring for other family needs.

Dietitians, physicians, and other helping professionals as well as health agencies, pharmaceutical firms, and other organizations have prepared many books and pamphlets pertaining to dietary concerns. Written materials, while never a substitute for guidance from skilled professionals personally acquainted with your family, can provide an effective backdrop for your approach to your child's diet.

Decide on Which Professionals Can Best Help

Do not expect the physician to meet all your child's needs. Seek out other relevant helping professionals if needed and urge the physician to do the same. Sustaining a child's long-term diet often involves the services of professionals from a variety of disciplines. You should help select and oversee helping professionals in order to modify the services needed. The types of professionals most often involved in helping diet-restricted children include the following:

> *Nutritional:* Nutritionists, dietitians
> *Medical:* Physicians, physical therapists, dentists, pharmacists
> *Nursing:* Clinic, hospital, public health, school
> *Educational:* Teachers, counselors, aides
> *Mental health:* Psychiatrists, psychologists, social workers, clergy, family counselors, rehabilitation counselors.

Nutritionists and Dietitians

Nutritionists are persons with knowledge about dietary and nutritional matters. Dietitians are individuals who have received specialized training and credentials in these areas.

Care must be exercised in the selection of nutritional counseling. The more dramatic nutritional claims often lack scientific backing. Nutritional credentials that sound impressive but that involve little or no academic effort to gain them are available to anyone who seeks to pursue them. The safest method of finding skilled nutritional counseling is to search for solid credentials that accurately reflect the individual's educational experiences. Although many poorly trained food faddists, vitamin sales personnel, "health food" promoters, and others claim nutritional knowledge, the initials "R. D." (registered dietitian) are indicators of formal nutritional training. The American Dietetic Association grants this degree to people who have a bachelor's degree in food and nutrition from a four-year college program and have met clinical training standards in addition to passing a competency exam.

Most medical schools give limited training in nutrition. Some physician-nutritionists have passed a test given by the American Board of Nutrition. They have initials "C. N." (clinical nutritionist) after their "M. D." designation. Most M. D.'s who are not clinical nutritionists work closely with a dietitian when the treatment of a child's disorder calls for prescribed dietary measures.

You may find the best arrangement to be joint services by both types of professionals. The physician might prefer to have the dietitian advise you on specific foods, while the dietitian will want to know the overall dietary treatment plan.

Various dietitians may advocate slightly differing variations in dietary approach for your child, but there should be few major differences in the services offered by any two dietitians. The field of dietetics is constantly changing as scientific understanding of nutrition evolves. Dietitians, like all other professionals, vary widely in their firsthand experiences. Try to select a dietitian who has had direct experience with your child's particular type of diet. If in doubt, ask the dietitian to provide current authoritative written materials on the diet. The ability of the dietitian to do so is good indication that you are receiving complete, up-to-date and accurate nutritional guidance. If the "nutritional consultant" offers what seems to be a magical cure, find someone else. When a dietitian gives straightforward, sensible information, even if it sounds obvious, you probably have found a safe guide for your child's dietary planning.

As early as possible, the dietitian should learn of your child's diagnosis, other disease processes that may be occurring and that might affect nutritional status, and any current medications that may influence appetite or dietary planning. The dietitian can assist you and your child in solving a variety of diet-related difficulties. She can increase your child's understanding of the diet and eagerness to follow it. Specifically, the dietitian

- Assesses the child's dietary needs.
- Suggests foods that are acceptable within dietary guidelines.
- Defines off-limits food.
- Recommends additional nutrition supplements, if needed.
- Provides accurate nutritional information and refutes unfounded nutritional claims.
- Helps you identify any troublesome ingredients or foods by use of a diet diary.
- Helps your child adapt eating habits for better nutrition.
- Instructs in preparing, storing, and serving diet-appropriate food.
- Assists in weight monitoring.
- Counsels for weight maintenance.
- Provides support and encouragement for your child.

The dietitian should take a dietary history, which can involve most or all of these aspects of nutritional concern:

Food budgeting: kinds of fruits, vegetables, and meats purchased; sources of budget information

Menu planning: food preferences, intolerances, sensitivities, food likes and dislikes, allergies

Food preparation: by whom, cooking or food-processing equipment needed, methods of food storage

Meals at home: where eaten, when eaten, with whom, meals skipped—which and how often

Meals away from home: which, how often, facilities—lunch counter, cafeteria, restaurant, school lunch, vending machines

Previous dietary restrictions: reasons for, how long, types, child's response to modified diet

Snacks: types, amounts, how often, circumstances when eaten

Sources of nutrition information: use of advertising, popular publications, books, reliable versus unreliable sources, other professional consultations

Supplements: types of vitamins and minerals taken, how often, reasons for use

Typical day's meals: meals eaten during previous twenty-four hours, frequency of the use of important food groups during an average week.

In taking a dietary history, the dietitian is especially interested in any comments that your child makes about food. The interview is likely to be most successful when the dietitian first assesses your child's willingness to talk about the diet. If your child is fatigued or uncomfortable, family members may want to supply some of the information. The dietitian should use a conversational, casual approach. In order to prevent incomplete or poorly thought out answers, the dietitian should encourage your child to take time to think through each answer. The interview should be flexible, although the dietitian might use a written form to guide the interview.

The dietitian might coordinate individual instruction with visual aids such as leaflets, posters, food models, videotapes, or a motion picture to help your child understand and follow the diet. Another service from dietitians is instruction through classes for families of diet-restricted children. In these group sessions, members participate with persons from several other families. The dietitian provides nutritional guidance in a way that allows each family to share progress made on behalf of their children with other families in the group. Each participant can help others by giving suggestions, exchanging recipes and ideas about food preparation or meal planning, and discussing ways to make their diets more effective.

Physicians

Your family physician or pediatrician should take these roles in relation to your child's program:

Be familiar with your child. Having the advantage of continual contact with your child during the years of growth and development, the primary physician is familiar with her characteristics and those of your family. No specialist who becomes involved at any particular time and who must rely upon sudden acquaintance with your child can substitute for that knowledge. Because the primary physician can relate to your child as an individual, he is in a good position to help get her to follow the diet.

Your child's age and physical status are constantly changing, and symptoms are also changing over time. There are changes in relationships between the physician and each family member. A physician who has long-term familiarity with your family can understand these various types of changes and tailor the dietary recommendations to fit your child's most current needs.

Assess the disorder. The physician should gather detailed information about the history and the course of your child's disorder and should conduct a complete physical examination from time to time.

Assume primary responsibility. The physician should coordinate your child's care among any other involved helping professionals, send her to specialists when indicated, receive reports from those specialists, and help you make the best choices from among dietary or other treatment options.

The physician should continue routine health care, including well-child checkups, supervision of general health, immunizations, and the care of minor illnesses that occur from time to time.

Advise about treatments. The best arrangement is a shared management approach in which the primary physician provides routine care and obtains specialty consultation when needed in areas of medical and dietary concern. The primary-care physician might arrange for a specialist to see your child in consultation while continuing to manage the medical problem.

The physician should interpret the results of laboratory tests and the recommendations of specialists to you and, when appropriate, directly to your child.

Arrange follow-up care. Try to arrange periodic contact among all involved helping professionals to coordinate their services. The primary physician might be able to help arrange this coordination. Phone conferences sometimes work well. Sometimes it is the parent who ends up being the catalyst to arrange this periodic contact, with the aid of the primary physician in monitoring the carrying out of plans that are developed.

During follow-up care, the physician may be instrumental in assuring your child's cooperation. For example, he can talk with her about the importance of nutrition, the dietary guidelines, or the health consequences of deviating from those guidelines.

The physician can also authorize aspects of follow-up care, such as prescriptions, recommendations for special educational programs, or requests for physical therapy for your child.

Nurses

A clinical nurse specialist has added expertise in a particular nursing area and can help your family understand treatment plans. This nurse might also be able to explain the dietary program to your child and help you express your questions and concerns to the primary physician. She might also plan and implement get-acquainted visits with your child at a clinic or other facility.

Being partly responsible for your child's health care within the school system, a school nurse can talk with school personnel and encourage them to keep in touch with the dietitian and physician about any dietary problems occurring at school.

The public health nurse or homemaker's service can be of great help if your child's condition requires home-bound nursing care. Public health nurses often work with families of chronically ill children. A broad nursing background equips the public health nurse to promote home nursing service and teach needed nursing techniques to families with home-bound children. The nurse can provide direct nursing care, help your child cope with the condition, and give supportive instruction. The nurse may also supervise and coordinate other health-care services, including supervision and monitoring of dietary programs.

For many diet-restricted children, the only contact with nurses is in a hospital. Nurses perform very important functions for any hospitalized child. Information on the roles of nurses while your child is hospitalized appears in Chapter 12.

Physical Therapists

The physical therapist is an integral part of both the medical and educational teams. Physical therapy is defined by the American Physical Therapy Association as "a health profession concerned with providing services to individuals that prevent or minimize disability, relieve pain, develop and improve motor function, control postural deviations, and establish and maintain maximum performance within the individual's capabilities."

The physical therapist assists in the management of the physically impaired or developmentally disabled child. The purpose of physical therapy is the rehabilitation of children who are disabled by injury, illness, or birth defects to develop the total body motor function to its maximum.

A physical therapist must have graduated from a four-year college program approved by the American Physical Therapy Association and must complete a period of internship training. Most physical therapists working in educational settings have additional pediatric training.

The types of disabilities that a physical therapist may be involved with include cerebral palsy, spina bifida, muscular dystrophy, learning disabilities, amputations, asthma, cystic fibrosis, congenital heart disease, and mental retardation in addition to other orthopedic and neurological conditions.

Mental Health Professionals

Following a restricted diet is stressful. A mental health professional can help your family deal with these stresses. His role is neither to replace other forms of health care nor to explain away your child's symptoms through social or psychological causes. Instead, the primary goal is to help your family counter the effects of wrestling with the stresses involved in maintaining the diet.

The milder your child's symptoms, the less the likelihood of emotional difficulties. If your child has many obvious symptoms, the need for mental health intervention is more likely. As with most conditions, professional help is more effective if you seek it early. Mental health services are sometimes needed to help diet-restricted children cope emotionally, although the majority of chronically ill children do not need this type of assistance.

A mental health professional usually starts by gathering information on the psychological consequences of the disorder and the diet. The mental health professional may need to meet with family members for a couple of interviews before he can gain a completely clear overview of the psychological stresses your child and family are experiencing. Needed information includes these areas:

Personal development: Personal growth; tasks of daily living accomplished by your child; muscle and coordination skills; emotional maturity; ages at which milestones of development have occurred.

Relationships with parents and siblings: Key areas of conflict; power struggles; competitiveness; and areas of appreciation and strength in family relationships.

Activities outside the home: School performance; friendships; hobbies; talents; community involvement.

Response to the disorder: Understanding of it; participation in self-care; emotional reactions to it; the degree of emotional acceptance of it.

Your relationship to your child: Your views of and behaviors toward your child; your emotional reactions; your state of emotional acceptance of the need for the diet; your participation in the diet and other treatments.

Other areas of parental functioning: How each parent functions as an individual; the nature of the marital relationship; strengths and weaknesses of each parent's relationship to each of the siblings; other life stresses that each parent is facing.

Siblings' reactions to the disorder: Their overall adjustment; their feelings about your child; their involvement in supporting the dietary effort.

Support systems needed: The types of community resources available to your family; the ways in which helping professionals can provide additional support to your family.

In addition to other services, mental health professionals may provide psychotherapy or counseling. Counseling involves exploring options and is essentially a face-to-face discussion. Psychotherapy involves experiencing deeper feelings not ordinarily expressed in day-to-day interactions except through symptoms. A psychotherapy procedure might involve hitting a pillow, developing a make-believe conversation with family members, or using the powers of fantasy and imagination through play or art activities to relieve emotional pressures.

Group counseling. With the mental health professional's help, participants in group counseling come to understand their painful feelings and worrisome thoughts better. Reassured that they share similar challenges in common with others, members gain support from the group. They become stronger in acting as their children's agents for obtaining medical and dietary care. Realizing that they are not unnatural and not alone helps parents develop a greater willingness to examine and articulate their experiences. Through this kind of group counseling, they can develop greater emotional acceptance of their children's dietary situations.

Mental health professionals are generally prepared to deliver services to children as well as to adults. Therefore, services may be provided for any member of your family or any combination of members, depending on your family's needs. The mental health professional might be able to accomplish much more through a few sessions with you, for example, than through the same number of sessions with your child because you control your child's world.

Psychiatrists. Psychiatrists have the M. D. degree and are physicians. After earning their degree, they receive training from social workers, psychologists, and other psychiatrists in mental health skills. In addition to diagnostic, counseling, and psychotherapy skills, they prescribe various medications to improve behavior and the handling of emotions. Psychiatric training is very thorough, with much direct clinical experience required before the psychiatrist is allowed to practice independently.

Psychologists. The doctorate reflects the accepted level of training for psychologists. Psychologists have earned their degree by completing an extensive program of academic study, usually eight years, and supervised clinical experience. Fully qualified psychologists are usually certified or licensed, unless working in a medical or mental health agency.

Services of a psychologist can include testing to provide information about your child's intelligence, academic performance, emotional state, or personality traits that can be related to behavioral problems or dietary difficulties that your child may be showing. The pyschologist can work with your child, consult with other involved professionals, evaluate your child for transitory or long-standing emotional problems, and work to prevent or treat expected or current emotional or behavioral problems.

Social workers. The term "social worker" is often used ambiguously. When not designating a person with extensive, formal training, the term may refer to untrained assistance workers, welfare department caseworkers, or volunteers. Every trained social worker has completed a program of formal academic study, usually six years, and has had supervised clinical experience. A master's degree indicates the generally accepted level of professional training for social workers.

For a social worker who is employed in a medical facility, contacts may continue throughout the course of a child's treatment, including periods of hospitalization and recuperation at home. The social worker can provide empathy, support, counsel, and help your family obtain tangible services such as financial aid.

Clergymen. There are no uniform standards for the licensing of clergymen and no uniform methods of indicating their competence as providers of mental health services. The training given them today in most denominations includes clinical pastoral education.

Theological students are usually assigned to an institution to work with mentally ill persons, children with various kinds of handicaps, or those who may be acutely ill in long-term care. Some theological students are assigned to general hospitals. Some seminary students receive additional training in counseling, psychology, or other behavioral sciences.

Some clergy members have had clinical experience with chronically ill children, but most have not. The theological framework from which a clergyman operates may be of more significance to your family than his counseling skills.

Clergymen are appropriate and needed segments of the health team, but they are often insufficiently utilized by parents of diet-restricted children. There is an obvious religious component to many of the issues faced in maintaining a long-term diet for a child. Feelings of great guilt, fear of divine punishment, expectations of possible miracles, wrestling with the issues of life and death, straining to find meaning in the suffering that may be occurring, and similar stresses can raise spiritual questions in parents and children.

The unique contribution of members of the clergy is to put things in religious perspective in accordance with the belief systems to which they are aligned. The clergyman can explore the following types of questions: Is this punishment? How could God allow this to happen? What can we learn from all of this? How can I deal with my anger? How can I deal with my doubts about God's love or involvement with our family? How can I release my feelings to God? How do I feel toward God after all that has happened?

If there is a struggle over the meaning of the disorder and religious questions have been raised, ideally the clergyman can listen and help. The interpretation of spiritual issues should help all family members cope with the stresses of the disorder and its treatment. Guidance received from members of the clergy should allow your family to operate within its own religious foundation.

Church and synagogue members may be thought of as an extended family who can lend support. Many churches and synagogues take family life very seriously by reaching out into the community with activities for various age groups; therefore, they have members who are used to working with children. These members could be especially helpful to any family trying to work through difficult health and dietary issues.

Develop a Professional Team

You may have researched everything about your child's disorder, while separate professional disciplines may deal extensively with only a single phase of your child's situation. You should be able to develop a spirit of unity with the helping professionals and consider them as partners in a joint effort. Seldom can an individual professional meet any family's entire collection of needs or monitor the ever-changing needs of one individual.

One of the advantages of arranging a combination of professionls to work together as a team is that each professional has access to additional information and skills for the child's benefit. This availability of a wide range of helpful knowledge and services is the hallmark of the team approach.

The team approach allows an automatic insurance about any possible gaps in knowledge from one helping professional to another. When a physician, for example, is aware of a particular diet but has only a superficial familiarity with it, the dietitian can work out the details. Overlapping consequences of the child's disorder might escape full notice, as when a physician prescribes medication for a minor illness without caution about hidden ingredients that may have a dietary impact. The team approach counterbalances these types of potential difficulties in maintaining a dietary program.

To gain the best outcome from the professionals' efforts, use an organized planning approach involving four steps:

1. Define team members. Picking the right professionals who adopt certain policies and have the qualifications listed further on in this chapter prevents many potential problems. The professionals need to define their respective areas of responsibility to one another and to you. There should be close cooperation so that each professional understands the precise role that every other one is to play. They should understand clearly who is responsible for explaining things to your child and to you so that your child is not shifted from one specialist to another without receiving thorough answers to questions or concerns.

2. Define jobs of each member. An effective team approach involves respect for the contribution of each professional as well as acceptance of each team member's fair share of the load. The professionals should know one another's limits, know the limits of their own expertise, and respect one another's expertise.

Try to choose professionals who are familiar with referral services. They should know what is available in your community for any specialized types of help that your child or family may need.

Your choice of physician is essential to the overall quality of care that your child receives. It is important to be satisfied with the physician.

3. Designate a coordinator. Usually the primary physician is the coordinator of the treatment team because he has the greatest familiarity with the child and the family. Parents of diet-restricted children generally discover, however, that they play an important role in assisting the primary physician in guiding the overall care of their children.

4. Set up lines of communication. Urge the involved professionals to communicate clearly and frequently with one another. Avoid fragmentation of medical, dietary, or other services. Check to see that the helping professionals are well informed of one another's actions, and arrange that all involved professionals receive copies of reports and other important information, even if you must perform that service yourself.

Qualifications to Look For When Selecting Helping Professionals

When searching out helping professionals, select those who best fit this description:

Knowledgeable. You want skilled and knowledgeable professionals who have received training in your child's condition and the dietary approach used. In addition to requirements for being licensed or certified to practice within a profession, there are indications of specialized training in various subspecialties, such as diplomate status. Board certification, which is accomplished by passing a written and oral examination in a specialized skill, is one mark of qualification in some fields.

Professionals should inspire your confidence. They should earn your trust. Neither too optimistic nor too pessimistic, they should sustain realistic hopes while not arousing false ones.

Available. The professionals should be realistically available on short notice. Find out ahead of time the circumstances under which they should be contacted. Learn how to reach them in person and by phone, at home and within the professional setting, including at night and on weekends. Find out their arrangements for vacation coverage.

They should meet with you on a regular basis to update their overall understanding of your family's adjustment. During these sessions, they should review your child's progress, discuss changes that have occurred in her functioning, and make any indicated adjustments in treatment.

The professionals should set aside a special time to talk with your child. She should have direct and private access to counsel about the diet from a dietitian or a physician and about any other needs from appropriate professionals. Even though unable to change anything about your child's complaints, helping professionals can be reassuring to her by listening empathically. To your child it will simply feel very good to be understood!

Supportive of referrals. The professionals should help you get needed services for your family. Not all physicians and dietitians, for example, would necessarily treat the same disorder in two different children exactly the same way with exactly the same dietary approach. In the beginning, it may be appropriate to require second opinions to help decide on which dietary approach is most effective.

In some instances, a physician can make a referral in anticipation of a difficulty. Early referrals prevent a scramble for assistance in a crisis or after family members feel overwhelmed, helpless, or angry. Community health departments are often key resources for referrals. Professionals should be aware of the limits to their knowledge and instructive ability, and they should refer you to appropriate other resources, including written materials. If you sense this kind of limitation in a helping professional who is involved with your child, even though the professional may not be aware of his deficient knowledge, you may need to seek other resources. A gastroenterologist, for example, may easily diagnose a disorder of digestive enzymes but, beyond telling your child to avoid certain food products, might not be of much assistance in some other aspects of dietary treatment. In this case, you would hope for a referral to a dietitian or seek out a dietitian yourself.

Professionals should send reports quickly, seek to prevent misinformation and misunderstanding, and see that you and your family receive prompt and efficient professional services.

The professionals should be your child's advocate and help you sort out treatment approaches that may be needed to help you supplement the dietary program. At your request, they should be able to direct you to needed services. They should link you with resources to help during any transitions in care.

The professionals should help by using their credentials to facilitate services. They should help implement your choices at times when you are taking a position that may seem unpopular to others who do not understand your child's situation.

Communicative. The professionals should indicate respect for your opinion by asking questions like "How have you been dealing with this issue?" or "What do you think is the cause of this difficulty?" They should explore what is happening and be willing to consider alternatives. The physician or dietitian, for example, should discuss with you any relevant information about a diet that you may have read in a magazine or a book. The helping professionals should share in decision-making with you. They should be your partners in monitoring the dietary effort.

Medical terms can sometimes be confusing and hamper your understanding of what is happening to your child. Although they should use scientific terms when indicated, the professionals should also speak in common language. They should clarify any kind of dietary or medical concept at your request. Professionals should respond to your questions in a dignified and thoughtful way in a setting that protects confidentiality and privacy.

The professionals should individualize care. They should have a framework flexible enough to remain aware of your child's unique needs. They should know how and when to generalize their knowledge that has been gained from their training and experience. Knowledge of dietary treatment, for example, should be paired with skill in personalizing and adapting general nutritional information to your child's specific situation.

The professionals should be sensitive to your child's capacity to accept medical and nutritional information. By noting her knowledge of nutrition, for example, a dietitian can partially gauge your child's ability to adapt to the diet. Instructing a five-year-old to "be sure to eat one thing from each of the four food groups each day" rarely is as helpful as handing the child a picture of the four food groups and having her check off each time she eats an item from each group, with the check-off list reviewed daily by the parent.

Encouraging. Understanding the impact of chronic disorders and long-term dietary restrictions on families requires a great deal of time, patience, and training. Relationships among you and various helping professionals can become prolonged and intense. For best results, professionals should show sincere interest in your child by taking time and listening attentively.

Select empathic dietitians, physicians, and other professionals who understand the difficulties involved with starting and maintaining children's long-term diets. They tend to ask sensitive questions, listen to your concerns, and respond empathically to questions from you and your child. You can feel increasingly comfortable with the care that they are providing for your child. Empathy by the professionals helps pave the way for high quality communication.

Effective professionals tend to affirm your success as the prime mover behind your child's dietary efforts. They should be encouraging when things are difficult as well as when you are managing the diet smoothly. They should have especially good things to say when you are able to establish the diet with increasing efficiency. They should give compliments and thank your child for cooperating.

The professionals should be supportive if you are having trouble maintaining your child's dietary restrictions completely. Without faultfinding, they should empathize with your concerns and search for practical ways of improving the management of the diet.

Courteous professionals will ensure that elective medical procedures occur at times that are the least disruptive to you and your child. If they don't make such an effort, assert to reschedule those procedures.

Instructive. Professionals should take a few moments to explain concepts and ideas or to explore options. The most effective helping professionals are good teachers who take an instructive role whenever indicated. For self-applied or home-applied remedial programs, such as dietary treatment, this aspect of professional care is especially important. They should give you anticipatory guidance, outlining the expected developments in your child's disorder. They should recommend how various difficulties can be managed as they occur in the future.

Professionals should be willing to deal with uncertainty. Sometimes there is no single, correct answer or definite way to determine ahead of time the most appropriate diet. From time to time, they should check to see whether there is any need to adjust treatments, including dietary recommendations.

They should balance the hope of cure against your child's current medical status. They should also help you and your family enhance the quality of life for your child. They should portray for you the point beyond which therapy is not likely to give meaningful assistance to your child, weigh the benefits and risks of different therapy options, and offer advice about any unconventional or unproven approaches.

Professionals should want to teach your child every useful principle that she is ready to understand and apply. They should, of course, adapt to her capacity, while presenting information at a level neither too complicated nor too simple.

Strengthen Your Partnerships with Helping Professionals

Take responsibility for encouraging clear communication and establishing an effective partnership with each professional. Ideally, consultation with helping professionals involves both parents. When feasible, all other relevant family members should attend at least one session with each helping professional.

In preparation for conferences, expect to give a detailed picture of your child's daily routines. Take along a notebook with her personal history if needed. During your first visit with each one, state the identities of other helping professionals involved in the past as well as currently. Mention any medication that your child is taking and report any outstanding emotional difficulties she may be having.

During any subsequent appointments, bring notes, journal records, or observations about your child's symptoms and a list of dietary issues, if any need to be reviewed.

Don't camouflage stress. Beware of the temptation to hide the negative impacts of your child's disorder from the helping professionals. The office of any helping professional is not the place to hide trouble.

Have your questions written down. Be prepared to provide answers to those questions that the helping professionals are likely to have for you. A list helps you provide orderly information and think ahead of time about the concerns that should be discussed. If your child accompanies you to appointments, your written notes are even more important as you juggle the distractions caused by your child's presence.

Take notes. You are receiving important information; be prepared to write it down. The professionals may try to give you a flood of new information. Because of the complicated and emotionally charged circumstances often surrounding such conversations, however, you may not be able to absorb, understand, or use all of the information immediately. If you have little opportunity to ask questions and are not able to formulate useful questions during the initial session, arrange for a follow-up session.

Don't be afraid to reveal that you do not understand something or that you need more time for explanation of some principle, idea, or procedure. Offer feedback on the adequacy of the information you have received. From time to time, check to make sure that you and the helping professionals have approximately the same understanding of your child's progress. For example, say "This is my understanding of what you have been telling me. Am I understanding you correctly?"

You may want to ask for a written summary of what has been discussed, in addition to the notes you have taken. This kind of summary from the professional is especially helpful if the information given to you has been particularly complicated.

Ask about any ingredients in prescription medications. If your child experiences any reactions to medications, report them immediately. Inquire specifically about when your child should take medications rather than rely solely on what the pharmacist places on the label.

The helping professionals need to learn about your skills as an observer and your accuracy as a reporter. You, in turn, need to learn how to monitor symptom flare-ups as indications that the diet may need adjustment or that your child needs some additional professional services. Develop trust in your own observations and judgments and learn the expectations of the helping professionals. Be forthright about what you can and cannot do in terms of supporting the diet and assisting the helping professionals.

Your role as facilitator for sources of help for your child can be difficult, especially if some of the involved helping professionals do not understand how knowledgeable you are. Be assertive without being offensive, insistent without being pushy, and confident without being overbearing.

The helping professionals want to exercise their skills for the benefit of your child and family, and you must give them the freedom to do just that. On the other hand, it is important that you get truly effective combinations of helping resources. Use caution in the selection procedure and be willing to keep hunting until you find professionals with whom you feel comfortable. If at any point you are not able to play out the correct balance between assertion and cooperativeness, the world hasn't come to an end. Learn from your error and improve your relationship with the next helping professional involved.

Don't endow helping professionals with magical or godlike powers. Don't assume that if they work hard and if you apply the dietary efforts, good health for your child is guaranteed. Don't expect helping professionals to be universal in their knowledge, either about one specific area or many areas. Be thoughtful about what you ask professionals to do for your child. Understand what you can do better than they can, what they can do better than you can, and what risks there are for harm.

Some of what the helping professionals arrange or recommend for your child may be of uncertain benefit or may even be at risk, so make sure that you remain informed. Learn about the diagnosis and the reasons for that diagnosis and know which treatments are being contemplated along with the advantages and disadvantages of each. Stay in the company of your child, if possible, and insist that the helping professionals inform you about new treatment advances, laboratory tests, and results from physical examinations. Go to your helping professional's supervisor or director of the facility if you are not fully satisfied. Remove your child from care if you believe that the methods being used might be unnecessarily hazardous or if you are not sufficiently informed in the matters listed here.

Be alert to any conflicting claims or other inconsistencies among the helping professionals. Such inconsistencies cause uncertainty over whose advice to follow and which sources are the most reliable.

Know your rights and retain control. Appear straightforward, even if you secretly don't feel that way. Beware of seeking professional advice in a pathetic, self-critical way. Avoid searching for a naive, oversimplified guarantee by professionals that all is well.

One of your functions is to use your ever-expanding knowledge about your child to help prevent mistakes that helping professionals would otherwise make. Persistent, assertive behavior gets the best results. Be calm and confident in your desire to help your child and in the knowledge that you are gaining, but avoid a know-it-all attitude. Instead, adopt an "I know a lot and am learning more" attitude. Have faith in your ability to learn more about the disorder and the needed dietary measures.

Try to control your emotions. Most helping professionals understand your initial shock and other reactions. Subsequent interactions are more profitable, however, if you are in control of your emotions.

An amiable attitude goes a long way with everyone. Express your frustrations without seeming to question the integrity or competence of the helping professionals. The helping professionals may understand misdirected anger dumped on them, yet they might react with some anger toward you. Focusing on the helping professionals' limitations or expressing disenchantment with their work does not help your child. In supervising your child's care, remember instead the intentions of the professionals to help and the constraints on their talents.

Remember that you and the helping professionals may have similar feelings at the time you are communicating with each other. They may be just as frustrated, upset, unprepared, or burdened as you. The cluster of emotions that they experience in dealing with your family and your child may simply be the flip side of the same coin representing your feelings. Look for the common ground. Express empathy for the professionals' frustrations now and then.

The professionals have just as great a need for reliable help and information from you as you do from them. In dealing with them, your honesty, courtesy, punctuality, responsibility for maintaining treatment, financial responsibility, and other important aspects of being a partner in care with them are crucial to establishing a consistent treatment approach for your child.

Express appreciation for the care they have given to your child, for specific acts that they have performed, and for suggestions that have worked well. Compliment them for showing any little courtesies. When they are exceptionally thoughtful, give prompt attention, provide a full explanation, require a minimum of paperwork, or present an especially helpful communication directed toward your child, show your appreciation. This kind of feedback not only strengthens your relationship but also provides the professionals with information about the types of office procedures and therapeutic recommendations that are most effective for diet-restricted children in general.

In any established relationship, especially one in which people in different roles are mutually dependent, conflicts may arise. They occur naturally in families and among departments of medical organizations, and they can occur between you and some of the helping professionals. Your child runs some risks, such as inattention by a too-busy professional or excessive demands from an insensitive one. It is, however, difficult to change habits of busy professionals when your child is under their care. Expect a negative reaction at first if you try to encourage a change in philosophy or policy within any organization, hospital, or clinic. Modifying the services of professionals is a difficult uphill battle.

If a continuing personality clash occurs, say something like "I respect your knowledge and experience, but I am afraid that I don't understand why you are using these approaches toward my child." This confrontation statement leads you either to more understanding and a successful partnership or to a mutual decision to arrange for a different helping professional. Your anger should subside if you recognize sufficient concern and competence. If the helping professional does not have enough of the desired traits listed in this chapter, arrange for another.

Telltale signs that it is time to renegotiate your relationship with any helping professional include these:

- You are afraid to call the professional.
- The professional is too busy to see you or your child.
- You do not feel comfortable to air your problems and concerns with the professional.
- The professional gives your child the brush-off, makes fun of your child, or unnecessarily takes away your child's dignity.
- The professional has certain habits or mannerisms that significantly aggravate you or your child.
- A basic philosophical difference exists between you and the professional, and the professional insists that you adopt his values.
- There is insufficient trust that the professional will improve with increased contact.

If you are not satisfied with any of the helping professionals involved with your child, ask one of the other helping professionals for referral elsewhere. Let the professional you are continuing contact with know of the qualities you are looking for in a replacement person.

Helping professionals ideally are sensitive to your child's feelings and attitudes, empathic, and aware of psychological factors. They ask careful questions and listen skillfully for clues about problems that may be interfering with the diet. They work closely and cooperatively with you and other professionals in a united effort to make the diet work for your child. You have the responsibility to oversee the professional care your child and family receive and may need to facilitate communication between the helping professionals from time to time. This effort can be a successful and rewarding one if you are sufficiently assertive and have confidence in your familiarity with your child's needs.

9. Join or Start a Support Group

A parent support group can be an important source of help for your family in easing many of the potential difficulties of maintaining the diet. In addition to the exchange of menu ideas, recipes, and methods of simplifying shopping for specialized food items, the group can provide much emotional support and strengthening of community resources for helping your child.

Depending on bureaucracies to provide services can sometimes be a frustrating process. A highly effective way to overcome that frustration is to work together with other parents to bring about changes in community services, health care services, school programs, the supply of needed food items, nutritional awareness, and other kinds of services.

If an existing parent support group does not meet your needs, or if no support group exists in your community, you may want to organize one. Parents organized as a group can accomplish much more than individuals working separately. Support groups develop power by bringing many parents together for common goals.

An effective support group meets regularly, usually in the evening. The meetings can be conducted by parents, a team of parents and helping professionals, or professionals. Meetings usually take the form of lecture, demonstration, question-and-answer, or informal discussion periods. Professionals may offer informational presentations, or parents may give a practical care-giving demonstration. Parents are the primary conductors of the type of support group discussed in this chapter.

154

Decide on Goals and Services

The goals and services of an efficient parent support group are almost limitless. Here are some of the more common ones among successful support groups involving parents of diet-restricted children:

Contact with others. Members can learn from other families' successes and can receive and share emotional support. Especially in time of crisis, support groups can play an important role in decreasing stresses that parents experience. It is comforting for parents to be in touch with others who have walked a similar path. Parents often develop friendships and continue their associations informally.

An important goal is to acquaint parents with what others have experienced. This type of sharing helps them recognize that their feelings and reactions are appropriate. It reduces their concern about being different or unnatural and helps them identify and communicate their needs to others. It also reassures them that resolving difficult diet-related problems is indeed possible.

A support group can be especially helpful to a single parent or the parent who must arrange the diet without help from a spouse. The "you are not alone" feeling is an important asset.

Instruction of parents. The group can provide parents with opportunities to hear from qualified persons about the nature of their children's problems. Educational group meetings have the additional advantage of allowing parents to absorb significant information slowly by hearing it discussed frequently, from a variety of points of view. They ensure the ready availability of medical, dietary, and psychological information to all members. These types of programs offer options and specific suggestions for managing children's diets and portray techniques to make children's diets more workable. They should be based on what member parents indicate they would like to know. Instructional programs should involve a variety of teaching methods so that interest level remains high.

Parents or dietitians who share specific cooking, menu, or holiday planning ideas, for example, can encourage both the new and the ongoing members. Cooking demonstrations with tasting opportunities bring hope and new zeal for any parents who are bored or frustrated with a limited diet. Suggestions on organizing the kitchen as a workplace, developing menus, streamlining shopping procedures, reading food labels, increasing overall nutrition awareness, using leftovers, developing food storage and rotation methods, and home-preserving of food are almost always highly successful programs in parent support groups involving diet-restricted children. Programs focusing on the psychological components of maintaining prescribed diets for children are also very popular because getting consistent cooperation from the children is crucial to the success of any dietary approach.

Learning about dietary and related treatment methods can be complex. Brief discussions with physicians or dietitians may not equip member parents completely for the responsibilities of dealing with their children's dietary and medical needs. Written instructions about implementing the diet and comprehensive listings of acceptable foods are significant assets in getting parents off to a good start. Providing these kinds of supplementary educational materials for its members is a key function for an effective parent support group. The group must be accurate and professional, however, in the information format and contents. Presenters should avoid any claims of quick cures and should not maintain that everyone's experimentations are justified just because one child showed improvement by eating in a certain way.

Becoming involved in a support group is one way a parent can increase understanding of the specific dietary program that a child must follow. Individual members of the group can subscribe to relevant medical or dietetic journals. The leaders of the group can provide this information to the members through meetings or a newsletter.

Instruction of children. Some very successful support groups routinely sponsor children's educational and social opportunities. These events improve children's understanding of their own diets, provide emotional support, and openly identify others who eat in similar ways. Children's educational programs teach about specific topic areas and coping skills such as relaxation, nutrition, food preparation, food shopping, self-monitoring of food choices, and the use of self-applied diet diaries.

Camps. Camping programs for diet-restricted or medically limited youngsters sponsored by the parent support group aid personal growth and teach about diet and health. The learning environment of the camp is in sharp contrast to the more sterile, drab environments that these children frequently confront—hospitals, clinics, or professional offices. Camps allow these children to enjoy all the experiences of group recreational camps for children without dietary restrictions. They also provide opportunities for the children to succeed in a supportive, consistent environment as well as opportunities to develop meaningful new friendships.

If separate camps of this nature are not possible, the parent support group can conduct a survey of which other camping programs nearby are inclined to incorporate diet-restricted children. The group can then share helpful menu ideas with the camp cooks so that members' children can safely and comfortably participate in those programs.

Respite care. Parents may need temporary child care away from their home or family on occasion. Their options for suitable child care may be distant and hosted by friends or relatives inadequately trained to meet the complex nutritional or medical needs of their diet-restricted children. The group can train interested volunteers or act as a clearinghouse for providers or potential clients for these kinds of respite services.

Research. Because a large number of parents and children with a certain type of disorder or dietary restriction are available for study, a parent support group can assist in research. The focus of the research does not necessarily need to be medical or dietetic. It can have to do with psychological issues, financial concerns, food-processing techniques, or any other aspects that member families have in common. Members of the support group can participate in research by contacting universities, knowing researchers in relevant fields, and through referrals by a national support organization.

Community awareness. Leaders of the parent support group can become acquainted with their local newspaper food editor, medical reporter, or other key personnel. Other media sources, such as television and radio talk programs, may be interested in having a representative of the group participate occasionally.

Sometimes a family may be dealing with a child's symptoms but with no clear-cut diagnosis or treatment plan. By reading or hearing about another such child, through the efforts of the support group, the parents could at least become alerted to question medical consultants about any correlation to their own child. Typically at the onset of diagnosis and treatment, some families feel isolated and misunderstood. As the parent support group makes community members aware of the symptoms and treatments of diet-restricted children through its efforts, the families of these children can experience much greater understanding.

An effective parent support group helps parents combine their skills and resources for the common good. The group can organize food purchasing co-ops and arrange for hard-to-find items, such as special meat or dairy products, from a supplier in a nearby community. It can make nonprocesed or other specialized food more conveniently available at lower costs.

The managers of food outlets are more likely to stock specialty items after the leaders of the parent support group assure them that there is truly a market for those products. Knowing of a support group in the community and being informed of the families involved greatly increases the grocer's or purchasing agent's willingness to stock items of interest to the group.

The parent support group can help develop a community garden. The group could also arrange classes to teach gardening skills for those members who would prefer to grow some of the foods needed for their children's special diets.

Targeting. Targeting means identifying individual or family needs and appropriate resources in the community to meet those needs. Once the support group has identified the needs of member families and their children and has prioritized those needs, the group's united effort can be called into play. For most support groups of families with diet-restricted children, the identified needs include diagnostic, dietary, medical, nursing, behavioral management, social and emotional, educational, recreational, legal, and financial services.

Advocacy. Supplying of advocates and advice-givers to members is another important function of a parent support group. Basic advocacy services include finding out what the parents want or need, outlining their options, assessing their chances of reaching the goals, and advising on courses of action for the parents to take. The advocates should be familiar with the bureaucracy or the system so they can supply extra support to the parents. Parents must be prepared in order to influence helping professionals and programs. An experienced friend or advocate helps member parents increase awareness among professionals, schools, and agencies of services needed by the diet-restricted children and their families. Acting in concert with others of the same interest allows a parent to avoid the appearance of being an outspoken leader of a splinter-group movement.

Rules exist in most health care, nutritional service, and related programs and agencies to assure equal treatment for all. However, some children receive better service than others. They do so primarily because their parents and advocates are more effective in influencing the people who administer and deliver the services.

Parents make not only effective advocates but also the best types of advocates. They have the sense of urgency needed to modify existing services or create new ones, keep going when things get rough, and overcome obstacles that appear along the way.

To be most effective in advocacy, a parent support group should inform parents of their rights and provide them with as much knowledge as possible to help obtain effective services for their diet-restricted children. The group should not replace individual effort, and it should encourage parents to do as much as possible for themselves and for their children. It should train parents, step by step, to be their own advocates. The group should intercede on behalf of an individual parent only if it is clear that the parent is personally unable to obtain rightful services for the child.

A parent support group can influence individual professionals and the leaders of community resources to adopt desired approaches for helping member families. It can help parents determine their legal rights, and it can help them prepare documentation to support requests for services on behalf of their children. It can also help parents identify application and appeals processes of various services within the community.

Parents and professionals can work together for improved understanding of the needs of diet-restricted children and for increasing the availability of specialized food items. A combined follow-up strategy can sometimes be more effective than an individual effort. An outstanding example of this strength of a parent support group occurred this way:

> A bakery provided so-called gluten-free breads to its customers. Families whose children needed to be on gluten-free diets began noticing symptom flare-ups in their children. As individuals, several parents attempted to assess where the dietary breakdown was occurring. Each parent separately inquired of the bakery regarding the bread and was given confirmation that the ingredients were acceptable.
>
> Symptom flare-ups continued in their children. It happened that a support group was just being established. These members of the brand new group began to share notes about the bread from the bakery. As its very first project, the group sent a committee to the bakery and questioned the employees. The personnel at the bakery were indifferent and continued their claim that the bread was acceptable. The group then contacted the U.S. Food and Drug Administration, which investigated the bakery on behalf of the group. The investigation revealed that indeed the bread contained gluten, which was the cause of the symptom flare-ups that had been reported among member families.

This group had no history behind it—no reputation to add to its clout. Simply unifying the efforts of its members gave it great effectiveness at helping the children with their diets. An individual usually does not have the ability or power to have this kind of influence. A parent support group representing numerous individuals and families offers greater consumer power and back-up resources for the needed accountability.

When a community resource has agreed to modify its services on behalf of member families, the group can monitor whether that organization has indeed met the specifications stated in the early negotiations.

The support group can investigate grievances about current services for the children of member families and monitor to make sure that the grievances are heard and complied with, as in the bakery example. The group can also assist parents in going to court if other avenues fail to get results.

A support group can sponsor legislation to aid member families. Lobbying to get the legislation passed and then implemented are additional ways that a support group can remain involved.

How To Start a Parent Support Group

Formation of a parent support group requires a great amount of time and energy. To be effective, the support group must develop leadership, goals, agreed-upon procedures, and routines for smooth decision making. To maintain itself, a parent support group must continually use the energy and resources of its members. It may need assistance at first from a "mother" organization, such as a church, public agency, private foundation, or local government groups. Some local groups can be chartered or accredited by a national organization. A list of concerned parents provided by a physician or dietitian has formed the basis for launching some successful support groups.

The Coordinating Council for Handicapped Children (see Appendix II) recommends a three-meeting procedure for launching a parent support group. Of course, all these ideas need to be adapted to your particular situation.

Meeting number one: The organizational meeting. Establish a core group to help you organize. Place an ad in your local paper, write a letter to the editor, or write a letter to all parents at your child's school, asking that interested parents contact you. Explain the types of concerns that the group will address. Approach television and radio stations about doing a public service announcement to publicize the meeting.

Invite any interested parents to come to the organizational meeting at a specified time and place. Include a name, address, and phone number for inquiries. Call relevant agencies, services, and programs within the community and request each one to send a representative.

The purpose of the organizational meeting is to make plans for a larger, more public meeting that will reach additional parents of diet-restricted children. Parents who cannot come to the organizational meeting but are interested in the group can come to the public meeting.

Meeting number two: The public meeting. The format for the public meeting can be a panel discussion, a guest speaker, or a selection of workshops. Promotional announcements should indicate in a clear and catchy way the meeting format, date, time, and place. At the meeting, get the names and addresses of all who attend. Be sure to announce the date of the third meeting—the follow-up working meeting.

After the public meeting, send thank-you notes to everyone who participated in the program. Set up appointments for personal visits with representatives of relevant agencies and services. Encourage their reactions and cooperation toward the proposed goals and activities of your parent support group. While visiting, personally thank those who attended the program from those particular agencies and services. When they realize you are monitoring their participation and are reinviting them, the supervisors and directors of the agencies and services will be more inclined to lend their support to your group.

Meeting number three: The working meeting. At the first working meeting, elect temporary officers and a nominating committee to select first-term officers. The group should assign committee chairpersons temporarily.

In addition to developing a goals statement, the group should make deliberate plans toward the preparation of bylaws, state charter, incorporation, and tax-exempt status. Your group may want to consider affiliating with local or national organizations or becoming a chapter group under the auspicies of a national organization. Have information from these organizations available at the meeting so that the group will know what the national organization requires for accreditation of a new local chapter. The group should carefully evaluate positive and negative aspects of potential affiliations before deciding about them.

Side-stepping these mundane and cumbersome tasks can seriously hamper your future work in certain circumstances. Leaders of support groups frequently comment that certain benefits, such as access to a bulk-rate mailing permit, make these early procedures very worthwhile despite their apparently time-consuming nature.

How To Keep Your Group Going

In order to work effectively, your parent support group needs efficient help in these areas:

Adequate resources. A parent support group often consists of little more than a core group of volunteers with others occasionally involved. Most groups are not able to support an office and a secretary. They function in minimal facilities and through services that members and leaders donate on a catch-as-catch-can basis—an hour here, an hour there.

Ideally there should be adequate assistance in terms of supplies, information, funds, and services from other groups. The parent support group should have as large an annual budget as possible, with several effective fund-raising approaches. At first, however, most support groups proceed ahead with minimal leadership and finances. Stay alert for your support group's eligibility for local, state, or federal grants or outright gifts from philanthropic organizations.

The fund-raising ideas that parent support groups use are endless and would require another entire book to detail. The best procedure is to establish a fund-raising task force or committee under strong leadership. Develop a service that the group can count on for sustained income on a yearly basis and something that the community learns to count on from the group. This type of fund-raising not only adds consistency and predictability to the group's accounting procedures and financial strength, but it also provides a boost in public exposure and respect among the helping professionals toward the parent support group.

Skilled leaders. Effective leaders have real dedication to the group's goals and demonstrate the ability to motivate members to become stronger in their commitment. They are able to work with people in an encouraging, energizing style. Leaders need to be positive and friendly communicators who maintain contact with the membership and other officers in the group through monthly reports, frequent open meetings, and a newsletter.

Leadership responsibilities include recruiting members, building team spirit, developing other leaders, and supporting fund-raising activities. It is important for those in leadership roles to know their own strengths and weaknesses and plan accordingly. The group should choose leaders on the basis of their ability to lead, devotion to the group and its goals, and willingness to assert themselves for the needs of the group. The group should confirm as temporary leaders those who are already showing dedication by having helped the group since its inception.

Leaders should be open-minded and entertain others' ideas rather than push their own pet projects through. They should be able to take the hard knocks of leadership, asserting for the group's goals to the professional, educational, and medical leaders in the community. Leaders should be able to take a stand that may seem unpopular to certain other groups in the community in order to reach the group's goals. They should be able to see problems through to their solution.

Decision-making processes should be democratic so that all members feel important and committees or task forces rather than one or two individuals make decisions. The leaders should present ideas about the group's potential goals and tactics to members for a vote. Bylaws should satisfy a formal structure, with officers elected for relatively short periods, one year being the standard time for most parent support groups.

Interesting tasks for members. Leaders must recognize that others may not be involved as deeply as they are. The leaders should still find ways to accept the contributions of members to whatever extent the members wish to be involved.

The leaders should be continually aware of the group's goals. Cooperative ventures with affiliated organizations, emphasis on growth of the parent support group, and fund-raising concerns should never progress to the point that the organization becomes an end in itself. The leaders should be concerned with pacing the group's activities to avoid burn-out of themselves and the membership. Effective leaders delegate responsibilities, even if they could do the tasks more quickly and easily.

It is important to guard against giving too many duties to one faithful volunteer while others withdraw from the group because they have too little to do. Members should receive responsibilities appropriate to their skills and talents, and the leaders should find an efficient use for all the talent available within the membership.

Members should have meaningful projects to do and should

graphically understand how their efforts fit into the group's overall purposes. Members get involved because of personal satisfaction and the desire to make a contribution and develop changes on behalf of their diet-restricted children. Members should sense progress and fulfillment and enjoy their membership commitment. The group should address its members' needs directly and also relate to the larger community.

The phenomenon of a continual volunteer turnover occurs in almost all parent support groups. This pattern does not signify that the group leaders are doing anything wrong. The people who are involved come from all walks of life and may have little or nothing in common except the illnesses or dietary restrictions of their children.

The leaders should look for talent within the parent support group before seeking it elsewhere. The membership may be able to provide the entire range of services needed to keep the group going.

The leaders should consider developing a questionnaire that lists the various skills that members are willing to donate. At meetings they should ask for volunteers and ask the members for names of others who have special talents or skills. They should advertise for someone to do specific tasks or fill a well-defined position of leadership through a special mailing or a newsletter to all members. Personal contact remains the most powerful motivator, however, for finding a particular volunteer for a particular task.

Leaders should be sure to ask volunteers for their ideas on how to improve the group's functioning. Innovation and new approaches should always be noted and complimented, especially when an enthusiastic person tackles a difficult task. Leaders should be willing to assign an important project to an inexperienced parent who indicates a real interest in the task. An experienced person might also be assigned as a partner in the task.

Committees and leaders should make assignments, particularly long-term appointments, very carefully. They should not make an appointment simply because the person was the only one willing at first to fill a slot.

Leaders should constantly monitor to make sure that all

volunteers are satisfied. If a task is simply too humdrum or insufficiently stimulating, the volunteer might withdraw services in a short while. Volunteers should not get tired of or bored with the service being donated. Contented volunteers make for a healthy, vital support group.

It is important that the volunteers sense that their efforts and the services they donate are very worthwhile. Leaders should tell them that the group really appreciates the job they are doing. The support group should acknowledge and honor volunteers publicly whenever possible, perhaps by designating them "volunteer of the month" or "volunteer of the year" in the group's announcements and newsletters. This expression may be the only thanks that the volunteers receive because there are no significant tangible means of rewarding their efforts. Symbolic rewards such as certificates, plaques, years-of-service jewelry, and similar items are also important.

In addition to focusing on parents of diet-restricted children, the group should direct its efforts toward recruiting volunteers among handicapped children or adults, senior citizens, college or high school students, or others who might have the time and interest to assist. These individuals would not necessarily become members, but they could become volunteers to assist in a specific task or aspect of day-to-day functioning of the parent support group.

Expanding membership. The membership must be large enough to get the jobs done through skills and contacts of the group's members. Leaders who have links with community organizations, school districts, food sources, and health care systems are of great help.

People are motivated to join a parent support group by the same things that motivate them in other areas of their lives. No one factor can be defined that is always guaranteed to get and then keep people involved.

There is no substitute for a strong and active membership committee. The committee should invite individual memberships for the group as well as encourage participation in the group by community agencies. Referrals of individual parents to the group from physicians, dietitians, or other helping professionals are vital sources for expanding the membership.

A carefully planned and modest dues structure should be considered. Regularly published, high-quality newsletters can provide the much-needed regular contact with each member. Individuals on the membership committee should also solicit through personal contacts. Visits and mailed announcements can make your group known to other organizations within the same geographic area: social service organizations; public agencies; private agencies; hospitals and clinics; educational organizations; service clubs; federal, state, and local government agencies; and special schools in the community.

A small, precise brochure outlining the purposes of the parent support group and including a membership application helps attract new members. Make available some interesting information to illustrate the benefits of belonging to the support group and include this material along with the membership application.

An effective parent support group locates or develops handbooks, recipe guides, nutrition charts, diet diary record sheets, and other materials for more in-depth servicing of the dietary needs of member families. Selling such materials to the general public increases exposure and strengthens the group's finances.

The support group should distribute large quantities of free materials at conventions, conferences, and meetings within the community. A speaker's bureau for use by community service clubs and other organizations would be glad to register your support group and a spokesperson for future reference.

Professionals can make significant contributions to any parent support group. Those who are interested but have very limited time available can nevertheless contribute in an advisory capacity. Professionals generally are interested in lessening parents' struggles and frustrations and the occasional complications and inadequacies of dietary, medical, and related services.

The leaders should encourage member parents and professionals to communicate with and learn from one another. The leaders should encourage those professionals who have the time and energy to participate in the group's purpose to become active officers and policy makers. By including professionals in your support group, a major goal is achieved—providing an opportunity for professionals to understand better the day-to-day issues that parents wrestle with while engineering therapeutic diets for their children.

Decisive action. Through its activities, the support group should produce more than good feelings among its members. The group must meet its initial goals and establish a good track record of accomplishing what it sets out to do. The community must see that the support group has specific attainable goals. Parents tend to stay active in parent support groups as long as their involvement is exciting.

Complaints should become springboards for action. Specific individuals, task forces, or committees should emerge from the group to investigate complaints, and the group should find the best way to establish its role with regard to following up on the complaint.

Most members are struggling at best, especially when first starting their endeavors to keep their children on a prescribed diet. Most need the support offered from the group before being able to give to the group. It is wise to have a task force specifically for helping new members so that they can receive the full impact of the group's helpfulness. These new members can evolve later into contributors to the group on a volunteer basis.

Always direct meetings toward accommodating the group's needs, so that members maintain a strong belief that the group is effective and purposeful. Accomplishing significant goals is satisfying for all members and keeps parents involved, because sufficient benefits trickle down to their families. Group solutions are necessary for group problems. Leaders should ask for members' participation when a particular situation or problem is shared by several member families.

The focus of the parent support group should be on goals. Other activities should be in support of goals, never in opposition to them. The group should avoid draining away energy and resources through trivial activities like parties, picnics, and trips. An occasional such project certainly has its benefits, but the primary focus of such events should be on attracting new members and reestablishing friendships among member families.

It is important to differentiate between goals and objectives: The objectives are the stepping stones toward the goals. Objectives are very specific—a certain person will do a certain thing by a certain time. Committees should continually evaluate and revise goals and should define new objectives toward each new goal.

Sometimes when a parent support group has just been organized and accomplishes one or two initial goals, apathy sets in. Interest in the group declines, and the group folds. A surge of work, time, and funds may be needed to give the group that second wind to carry it on to further accomplishments and sustained growth. A few committed and single-minded members must invest time and energy to keep the group going. The leaders should develop outside assistance, such as from other community helpers or organizations, as early as possible in the organization process.

The guidelines given in this chapter represent the combined experiences of leaders and members of support groups in a variety of settings and involving a great variety of funding, membership size, and focussing of activities. A strong, vital parent support group can flourish in your community, and the information presented here can strengthen that growth if it is applied consistently.

10. Get Cooperation at School

School can be an important source of guidance and information for many of the difficulties you and your family face. School personnel may be able to help by working directly with your child, collaborating with you, or referring your family to community resources. Even when things don't go smoothly, dealing with the school can be a strengthening experience for you. It can become an arena for developing your assertiveness in order to obtain appropriate services for your child.

Parents of children with chronic medical needs are now more fully involved with planning and reviewing school programs than ever before. They are an essential part of the planning team, with a specific area of knowledge equal in importance to that of teachers, other specialists, and school administrators.

Maintaining your child in the same school during elementary years is beneficial. The teachers get to know his needs and can foster his social adjustment more easily than if he is shifted from school to school.

Help Obtain Any Needed Specialized Educational Services

Many of the childhood disease conditions calling for long-term diets also require special measures at school. If dietary concerns are involved, schools are obligated to help with any special dietary arrangements that would qualify under Public Law 94–142.

Public Law 94–142, a landmark civil rights act, is intended to guarantee a fair and equal education for every child. All school districts in the United States are required to develop Individualized Education Programs (IEPs) for every special-needs child and to provide any necessary services within the "least restrictive environment."

Special-needs children are being integrated into regular classrooms in most cases. This process, called "mainstreaming," capitalizes on each child's strengths and addresses his educational needs in a setting that does not cause him to feel isolated or socially undesirable. It saves time, money, and resources. The materials and support needed for special-needs children in a regular classroom cost less than providing special classrooms, special staff, and learning activities outside the mainstreamed situation. The reduction in social and emotional problems that result from mainstreaming is, of course, of great benefit, not only to the children but to society as a whole.

Mainstreaming brings many benefits to the other students. They learn to accept differences and interact successfully with children who have special needs, such as dietary restrictions. By helping their fellow students with special needs, they learn to overcome prejudices or prevent them from developing.

The regular classroom might not be the appropriate setting for every special-needs child. Some do fine there, but others function better in a regular classroom only part of the time or only for school-sponsored social activities.

There are three stages in the process of obtaining specialized services for your child: identification, evaluation, and placement. During the identification phase, qualified professionals observe your child and hold a meeting to decide whether he fulfills the criteria specified in the law. During the evaluation phase, professionals under school auspices do specific testing in order to determine the exact nature of your child's educational needs as well as what special educational services are indicated. During the placement phase, the school staff meets with you to decide on educational placement and draw up an individualized educational program (IEP). When the IEP is finished, your child can begin receiving special services.

If your child can be classified under any covered categories because of the disorder, the school must provide special services. The school personnel must take into account any aspects of your child's disorder, including the need for a special diet, that would otherwise impede your child's academic progress.

Back up your requests for services as much as possible with diagnostic reports, observations, and statements from professionals such as a dietitian or a physician.

The categories of special needs recognized by Public Law 94-142 as requiring special services in the schools are these: deaf, hard of hearing; health impaired in other ways; mentally retarded; multi-handicapped; orthopedically impaired; seriously emotionally disturbed; specific learning disabled; speech/language impaired; and visually impaired.

Conditions that impair academic performance and qualify a child for consideration under this law include chronic or acute health problems such as a heart condition, tuberculosis, rheumatic fever, cystic fibrosis, nephritis, asthma, sickle cell anemia, hemophilia, cerebral palsy, spina bifida, muscular dystrophy, epilepsy, lead poisoning, leukemia, and diabetes.

Feel free to contact the school even if your child is not yet of school age. The law provides incentives for the education of children who are between the ages of three and five. Your public school officials should be able to help you find appropriate services and may offer some direct services immediately. Inform the principal or other qualified personnel that your child has special needs. Indicate all aspects of your child's disorder that might allow Public Law 94-142 to apply for his benefit.

Local school systems and states vary in their definitions of the chronic illnesses serious enough to impede progress in a regular education program. There is no uniform definition of how to determine the severity level to make a child eligible for special services. It is generally agreed that the vast majority of children with chronic diseases, with or without special dietary needs, benefit most by placement in a regular classroom.

An important item in the IEP is the "specific related and supportive services." Typical services provided by school districts include these: audiology services; Braillists, typists, and interpreters; consultative services; counseling and psychological services; medical services for evaluation and diagnostic purposes; occupational therapy; ordinary physical examinations by physicians; parent counseling and training; physical therapy; resource centers; school health nurse services; social work services; special readers; speech and language services; transportation; and visual examinations.

The school also is responsible for providing appropriate nonacademic and extracurricular services for your child. They include adaptive physical education if needed, home economics, music, art, and other nonacademic subjects, and recreational opportunities available to other children.

Assist the Support Services

Academic success for your child may require ongoing collaboration between you, helping professionals such as the dietitian or physician, and school personnel. The physician or dietitian in an office or clinic and the teacher in the classroom each can make valid and accurate observations within one particular setting. Each can also enlarge the view of the other. Close contact by school personnel with each other about various aspects of managing your child's school experience also helps.

Give school employees realistic expectations about your child. Left without adequate information, the school staff are likely to make their own interpretations, which could lead to unrealistic approaches. Become aware of what each staff person does with your child.

The school health nurses might be involved with your child. Sometimes the administrative staff of school health services at the district level is not located at the same place as special education and as pupil personnel services, such as counselors, social workers, and psychologists. There may be communication and policy problems, and services might not be coordinated well. You might need to assist various school-related professionals as they address your child's academic, social, emotional, medical, and dietary needs at school.

Another responsibility of school health services is the administration of medical treatments and medications. There is wide variation among school districts as to how those responsibilities are implemented. Find out the particulars in your child's school district if the administration of medications is an issue for your child at school.

Having your child carry medicine or nutritional supplements to school brings the risk of their loss, theft, or sale. A better method is to leave a supply of medication under appropriate adult supervision at school. If necessary, ask the physician to help make this arrangement. This kind of coordination prevents many problems.

Arrange for School Lunches and Snacks

Snacks brought to the classroom by other children can represent a difficult situation for your child. Work out the details with the teacher. If possible, arrange for her to inform you ahead of time before anyone brings treats to school. Give your child an alternative to take along as a substitute for that day.

The teacher won't always know ahead of time about snacks in the classroom. It is best to have several diet-appropriate treats in the teacher's closet or the school's freezer.

Because you are not there to supervise, the temptation for your child to trade with others may be great. The best insurance is to pack your child's lunch with desirable items that fulfill dietary guidelines. Do whatever you can to help make your child's lunch and snacks seem like the other children's food. If your child has a sufficient quantity and variety of food, he is less likely to trade lunches with other children.

There are many ways to increase the attractiveness of your child's lunch if carried from home. Try varying the type of bread. Cut fruits, vegetables, or other foods into small pieces or different shapes, such as curls, sticks, or roses. Put a surprise in your child's lunch sack or box. Personalize some items with his name. Tuck in a note, comic, joke list, puzzle, set of plastic utensils, or special treat in addition to condiments. Also try enclosing some items that your child can share with friends. A decorative container or a fancy napkin makes the lunch a fun experience.

Help Your Child with the
Challenges of Physical Education

If the sustained energy drain and the exertions of ordinary physical education classes are inadvisable, see that the school makes suitable alternative arrangements. The physical education program can be modified to avoid stresses beyond your child's physical capacities. Adaptations in physical education programs for special-needs children most often employed by schools include changes in equipment, facilities, rules, instruction techniques, and the physical activities required.

The intense spirit of competition that occasionally occurs during physical education activities might also be a burden for any child who is in less than maximum physical condition. On the other hand, sitting out the physical education class may bring ridicule and feelings of isolation. In general, don't exempt your child from the challenges of physical education classes. Make sure, though, that the challenges do not exceed your child's physical capabilities or readiness.

Be Alert for Problem Situations

Any of several difficulties can contribute to poor adjustment or underachievement in school. Repeated absences because of complications from the disorder can interfere with school progress by contributing to underachievement and poor academic performance. To make matters worse, an occasional school employee might misinterpret the chain of events leading to your child's problems. Your child's diet can come under fire by frustrated school personnel. They might mistakenly conclude that your attempts to involve your child in dietary measures are your way of pretending to do something about your child's ongoing behavior problems that actually have other causes. They might try to blame you for the apparent emotional or behavioral problems that your child shows, and those problems might be blamed for your child's school problems. The difficulties that diet-restricted children most often encounter at school include these major categories:

Limited alertness and stamina. Difficulty in concentrating for long periods of time and fatigue lessen the ability to function.

Side effects from medication. Some medications cause side effects such as anxiety, irritability, inattentiveness, or drowsiness. Many side effects are nutrition-related and can affect a child's ability to maintain a prescribed diet at school (see Appendix I).

Diet-maintenance problems. Party snacks, foods used in teaching, and school lunches are the most likely potential sources of dietary disruption. The child may be tempted to eat or drink substances that exceed dietary guidelines. If the child needs extra food in the form of snacks or supplements, he may be embarrassed or even uncooperative. If your child refuses served foods, classmates might tease him. Your child should have a comfortable place and time for eating at school without drawing attention to the special dietary requirements.

Emotional and social maladjustment. There are numerous issues affecting school performance that the diet-restricted child has in common with classmates. Concerns about physical appearance, acceptance among friends, academic achievement, athletic ability, and similar issues can simply be magnified by the child's condition. The added burden of being physically different, being restricted in activity, requiring special educational input or altered social experiences, taking medication, or being on a special diet can increase the child's stress even more. Faltering self-esteem can further lower the child's expectations to perform.

Anxiety over the future or over health can influence motivation and can contribute to a discouraged "why bother?" attitude about performing at school. The child may begin to feel inferior or different and may increasingly dislike school as the medical condition progresses. There may be various excuses to avoid doing homework. Peer relationships, school loyalties, recognition among classmates, and extracurricular activities might not develop in a natural fashion. When the child repeatedly does poorly at school, discouragement and emotional problems become almost unavoidable.

Excessive school absence. Missing school for two or three days at a time disrupts the flow of assignments. The child runs the risk of trying to catch up with peers after missed instruction. Lower grades on tests may occur because of missed classes.

The child may show distress through symptoms. A child who needs to avoid school is likely to complain of headache or an upset stomach, which genuinely occurs at the time. If the child repeats such complaints, especially in the early morning, a school phobia may be occurring. The child might also suffer a flare-up of symptoms related to the disorder.

The more prolonged the avoidance of school, the more apprehensive the child is likely to be about returning. School avoidance is a psychological emergency. Close and prompt collaboration with relevant helping professionals and school personnel should begin at the earliest possible time.

Understand the Teacher's Role

The vast majority of teachers are very interested in making school a successful experience for your diet-restricted child. The teacher's role involves these major areas of responsibility:

Accepting your child's condition. The concerned teacher's attitude is one that conceives of your child as a precious human being, with the same lovability and needs as others. She is a firm and kind person who understands children and enjoys learning about them. She tries to display warmth and friendliness toward your child.

She regards your child's educational needs as a challenge and an opportunity to expand her teaching skills. It is a fulfilling experience for a teacher to meet the academic considerations of a special-needs child and to incorporate that child into the overall school experience.

If your child lacks stamina, additional time between classes would be helpful. A frequent need for the bathroom requires arrangements for leaving the classroom quietly and without creating undue attention. Arrangements may also need to be made for unobtrusive but supervised taking of medication.

Helping at transition times. Any switch in schools can be difficult for your child because of the flood of new situations and new people. Transition is even more difficult when the style of class scheduling is different between the two schools. The child who transfers from a quiet, small elementary school to a junior high or middle school with hundreds of other students is put under severe stress. Because of the many new faces, complicated class rotation schedules, abundant rules, confusing lunchtime procedures, and a host of other pressures, such a transition can be difficult for a child with special dietary needs.

To aid at these times, your child may need a personal relationship with a guide-teacher, a counselor, a principal, or another adult in the school building. Being with a caring adult can help him focus on ways of improving adjustment, including managing the diet while at school.

Learning more about your child. The alert teacher probably wants to obtain a brief history from you about your child's interests, favorite activities, special talents, and other personal bits of information. The types of situations that tend to trigger any symptoms in your child are especially important for her. The teacher should be interested in reading any pamphlets or books that you might share with her that describe your child's condition, dietary needs, or desirable educational approaches.

The teacher should want to learn about your child's styles of dealing with potentially stressful tasks, in order to find the best way to stimulate wholehearted participation in class. If your child lacks self-confidence, gives up quickly, or hesitates at challenging tasks, the teacher would be particularly interested in any methods that other teachers have found effective.

Compensating for absences. The concerned teacher wants to plan with you ahead of time for anticipated extended absences so that your child can keep his assignments current. For especially lengthy absences, the teacher may be able to arrange a home-bound education program. Some school districts assign a home-bound instruction tutor after a student has missed a certain number of school days or is unable to attend for a predictable period of time in the immediate future. The teacher may recommend qualified instructors in the community who can tutor on a fee-for-service basis. A local college or university might be able to recruit students who are interested in private tutoring either for pay or as volunteers. Even classmates or older siblings can help. The concerned teacher wants to make sure that your child receives whatever ongoing services he needs so that reentry after the period of absence goes smoothly.

The process of resuming daily attendance after a period of absence is a difficult one that has many social and psychological barriers. It represents a special challenge for the teacher as well as your child. Work together with the school staff after any extended absence to make sure that your child's reentry into day-to-day school activities goes as smoothly as possible.

Make the Most of Teacher Conferences

Personal conferences provide the most effective way to set up appropriate expectations and inform the teacher about your child's dietary concerns. Various management issues may arise in the school setting. Your child may need some sort of special consideration by school personnel as a result. Questions from the following categories are likely to come up during the first conference each year:

Restrictions. Does your child's present condition involve any specific restrictions authorized by a physician? Can your child participate in physical education classes without restriction? What alternative physical education procedures should be allowed for your child? Are there any physical activities that are inappropriate for your child? Can your child participate on any sports team without restriction? To what extent should the school provide rest periods, and what type of rest should be made available for your child?

Information about the disorder. Is your child's disorder improving, worsening, stabilized, or fluctuating? What considerations need to be discussed for future academic planning? Does your child's disorder require any specific approaches or cautions by school personnel? What kinds of ongoing support activities should the teacher conduct? What is your child's understanding of the disorder and its treatments? What explanations of the disorder should the teacher give to the classmates? What procedures should she follow in a medical emergency?

Medications. Is your child presently taking medication? How does your child's medication affect behavior? Has the medication dosage been adjusted recently? How often are medication dosages adjusted? What are the side effects of the medication? Does your child need any special protective or orthopedic equipment? What procedure should the teacher follow if your child arrives at school without having taken medication? What kinds of adult supervision are necessary when your child takes medication during the school day? Should any medication be kept at school for your child? At what times of day does your child take medication?

Dietary matters. Does your child's condition require any modification of the school lunch program? Is supervision of your child during lunch necessary to ensure diet observance? Should there be any special coordination about snacks that may be brought to school? What treats or snacks can you leave at school for your child during class parties? Should any special food be stored in a refrigerator or freezer at the school?

Support services. Does your child need physical, occupational, or speech therapy? Does your child need assistance in personal hygiene? Does your child require other support services, such as those provided by a counselor, social worker, or other professional outside the classroom?

Academic pressure. Is there any need to shorten or modify your child's school day? Should your child have special seating? How should the teacher individualize your child's homework or classroom work?

During the school year, the teacher should review information about your child's performance in school, with special attention to indicators of problems such as absenteeism, low grades, or misbehavior.

Assist the Teacher

Of all the available support systems, the classroom teacher is the key figure in determining your child's school success. Get to know her. Meet with her individually, and if necessary, invite her to your home. Everything you can do to develop a positive, trusting relationship with the teacher is beneficial. If you work together, you may be able to make discoveries about how best to help your child that you would not be able to do individually.

The first few moments of teacher conferences are crucial. Make your warmth and friendliness toward the teacher apparent to set the tone for a cooperative relationship.

Let the teacher know your ideas about your child, the things that your child does well, and the ways your child learns best. Don't hesitate also to express your concerns when you think that things are not going as well as they could. When differences of opinion arise, talk them out. Look for ways to reach a compromise, keeping in mind your child's overall physical and emotional needs. Share your valuable insight and information about your child's learning processes with the teacher. You know better than the teacher what stimulates and what bores your child.

Be alert to nonessential communicating with the teacher. A reasonably frequent flow of communication helps the teacher understand your child and manage any dietary concerns. An excess of letters, conferences, and phone calls, however, can cause harmful attitudes to develop. The teacher may start thinking of you as an overprotective parent, more to be avoided than to be heeded.

Acknowledge the good job that the teacher is doing with your child. Point out the strengths and thank her for special favors given and for the effort and concern she shows. Empathize with her challenges in trying to integrate your child's dietary arrangements into the daily classroom routines and activities.

The teacher may feel inadequate in dealing with your child because she does not fully understand the medical and dietary issues involved. Most teachers have very little training or experience in helping diet-restricted children. Your child may represent a special challenge for the teacher, so be patient and tolerant.

The teacher should learn about the developmental and educational implications of your child's medical condition. The teacher doesn't automatically know whether your child's unusual or disruptive behavior is the result of the condition, a dietary deviation, or some unrelated problem. Give as much guidance as possible to help her understand the causes of any problem behaviors that may develop at school.

An occasional teacher not willing to accept instruction from a parent may accept it from an authoritative written source. The goal is to see that the teacher becomes familiar with your child's disorder in general and with your child's dietary and other needs in particular. Supply written materials, if the teacher appears likely to respond well to such an approach.

Don't assume that school personnel keep the files up-to-date or review all of them regularly. Sometimes a school's in-service training program can include discussion of conditions requiring special dietary procedures. Parents may be allowed to recommend topics for in-service school training, including possible speakers on the topic of procedures for diet-restricted children at school.

In maintaining the delicate balance between your firmness and understanding of the teacher's frustrations, show an awareness of the rights of the other students in the class. Help the teacher balance your child's individualized needs against the requirements of the larger group of children in the classroom.

If extreme conflict arises with the teacher, basic issues must be resolved before progress can be made. If the teacher makes excuses to side-step the obligation to deal appropriately with your child's dietary needs, then an even more serious situation exists.

It is important to avoid an apologetic "I'm sure you know best" attitude toward the teacher. State clearly and strongly what you expect her to do for your child and be sure that she understands your expectation. She is more likely to respect you and cooperate if you are polite, self-assured, and firm. Make clear your intentions to assist the teacher in every way possible.

A nonthreatening approach is an absolute must. Disarm the teacher by showing empathy and understanding of her frustrations. Acknowledge in a matter-of-fact tone that you are aware that your child creates some special challenges. Further indicate that it appears as if no matter what is tried, there are no solutions. In time, the teacher may show increased appreciation and understanding of the difficult task of meeting your child's dietary and other needs at school. From that point on, you may find the teacher to be an understanding ally because both of you are facing similar challenges.

Do not automatically interpret hesitancy on the teacher's part as an effort to avoid helping your child. If you approach the school and the teacher as adversaries, they are likely to become adversaries in return. If you approach them as potential allies at first, you will usually find them to be a cooperative team.

11. Make Arrangements for Holidays and Away-From-Home Times

In the life of almost any child, there are times when other adults—neighbors, relatives or friends—take over and temporarily supervise aspects of child care, including the providing of food. This temporary supervision can be for a few hours, or it may last as long as several weeks. Usually the supervising adults have the disadvantage of not being thoroughly familiar with your child's medical and nutritional needs, and they come into the situation with their own preconceived notions, biases, and feelings about nutritional matters.

Additional well-meaning helpers such as school volunteers, scout leaders, school-homeroom "mothers," or youth group advisors might also be responsible for the temporary care of your child from time to time.

How to Maintain the Diet When Other Adults Care for Your Child

Some adults are not able to respond emotionally to your child's situation. They may not understand the medical condition or the impact of dietary requirements because of their own personal views. Sometimes the help that these adults may try to give is restricted by their own lack of experience, resulting in destructive or inappropriate interactions with your child. One example would be encouraging your child to ignore her dietary restrictions in an attempt to show kindness to her.

It is common for compassionate adults to be indulgent as a way of showing love. Well-meaning, caring adults may have no idea that an ingredient in a juice or a treat may cause a dangerous symptom or reaction in your child.

Adults supervising your child may be unwilling to maintain dietary restrictions. This tendency is especially likely if the off-limits food items are commonly regarded as healthful for most people. "How can milk possibly hurt any child!" and "How is it that wheat can give your daughter trouble when it is a healthful grain?" are typical indications of this kind of disbelief.

Adult care givers may have inappropriate expectations. They might expect you to appear constantly depressed or grief-stricken. They might be surprised that you dare have a break in your worry. They might also expect to see immediate improvement in your child because of the perceived strictness of the dietary guidelines and then disapprove of the dietary effort if immediate improvement is not obvious to them.

Adults temporarily charged with the care of your child can stir up or intensify your underlying concerns about the overall effectiveness of the dietary efforts. They may express strong doubts or long-lasting disbelief about your child's disorder or the treatment methods being used and sometimes might even deny that your child could possibly need the diet. They might disagree with some aspects of the way you are administering the diet. They may aggravate sibling rivalry by trying to pity or spoil your child. On the other hand, they might discriminate against or avoid your child.

To prevent these types of difficulties when your child must be temporarily under the care of other adults, be clear and firm in stating the importance of following the dietary guidelines. People usually respect your strength if you display firmness cushioned with courtesy. Communicate to care-giving adults that your child's diet involves certain absolute standards. Certain basics are to be followed, and certain foods are not allowed in any quantity.

Try to get them to understand what helps your child the most. Give guidelines that make the diet easy to follow. Don't give so much information that they may worry, fear caring for your child, or feel excessively responsible.

Assure them of the diet's credibility, which increases the longer your child has been on the diet. Gradually, care-giving adults can adapt to the need for maintaining your child's diet on a long-term basis. If necessary, refer them to authoritative written sources about the need for the diet.

Lists of acceptable foods are sometimes easier and more effective than lists of off-limits foods. People tend to question the diet less if you simply tell them what to feed your child rather than which foods are not allowed.

Friends and relatives may express their caring in one or both of two different ways: at an emotional level, or through actions and favors. They may express concerns such as "We care, we're there; we feel your pain." Or they may display a more utilitarian approach such as by providing child care or assisting in grocery shopping. You are arbitrarily limiting the love shown if you insist that the concerned adults give only a specific type of care. Instead, try to allow the display that is the most honest and direct expression for them. Of course, reserve the right to have the final say about what type of help you can allow for your child.

Carefully consider the number of details about your child's condition to share. In some circumstances, it is best to make only a vague statement about the diagnosis and the special diet, with no further elaboration. In other circumstances, it might be wise to inform care-giving adults about your child's situation in greater detail. You might want to give a general description of dietary do's and don'ts without arousing alarm. They might want to know what symptoms to expect in case there is an accidental deviation from the dietary requirements.

In the case of an emergency or a question, it would be helpful to leave with the adult care giver the name and phone number of your physician, dietitian, or contact persons in a local support group. If your child frequently visits a certain adult care giver, provide a supply of diet-acceptable food and keep it replenished.

Explaining symptoms that may result from deviating from the dietary guidelines generally helps care-giving adults get the message about the seriousness involved. The more drastic and immediate the physical reaction, the greater the acceptance and understanding people tend to manifest. If the reaction is delayed somewhat from the moment of ingestion, some people tend to find the connection between food intake and the reaction difficult to understand or believe.

Those who have an emotional investment may have occasion for remembering your child in a special way on holidays
or birthdays. Consider offering them a list of acceptable foods
or ingredients. If the dietary guidelines are so restrictive that
you don't want others preparing food for your child, suggest suitable nonfood gifts or privileges that would be appropriate.

Avoid being indignant when someone has attempted to
remember and please your child but in the process has accidentally provided a food that is off-limits. To spare the feelings
of a particular adult, there may be times when you should
graciously accept gift food not in keeping with your child's dietary limitations but simply not allow your child to eat it. Show
appreciation for the time and energy spent by the person and
thank the person for the caring and the concern shown. Focus
your gratitude on the well-meaning intention of the giver, not
on the food. If necessary, politely explain that the food can be
used by the rest of the family or that your child cannot have that
item for medical reasons.

When you leave your child temporarily under the care of
a sitter, you may be especially concerned. One solution is to arrange a child-care co-op among other parents to provide child-
care on a reciprocal basis. This arrangement is frequently the
product of the efforts of parent support groups of diet-restricted
children.

It may be necessary to reduce get-togethers with certain
friends or relatives if they persist in being uncooperative. It is
generally best to set limits in a calm but firm way about your
child's diet adherence when they supervise. Appeal to their
respect for your role as protector of your child.

Another important matter to consider is arranging for a
smooth transfer of dietary care to any other adult who might
permanently care for your child in the event of your death. Maintain a medical and dietary file as well as a recipe notebook or
file box and mention both resources in your will.

When Grandparents Want to Help

Grandparents usually have a strong emotional investment
in nurturing the health of their grandchildren, in part because
they have been so involved in raising the parents of their grandchildren. Love that grandparents extend is often rich, deep, and

consistent. There is no denying that expressions of caring and support from well-balanced, emotionally mature grandparents can be a vital component to family life.

Your child's condition may become the center of attention at family gatherings. Conversation about the condition may occur in her presence, sometimes insensitively, as if she weren't even there. Grandparents may begin to shower extra attention, gifts, or special treats, even to the extent of inviting her to deviate from the dietary restrictions on special occasions. During visits, they sometimes may try to express love by bringing out a tray of goodies baked especially for your family. In this way, they might accidentally be inviting your child to deviate from the diet unless you are confident that what they are offering is within your child's diet. It helps if you abstain along with your child.

Many grandparents give love in rich and satisfying abundance to their grandchildren. Advancing age, however, can sometimes weaken their adaptive ability. Some parents of diet-restricted children have found that grandparents are not consistently able to provide the necessary level of support for maintaining their children's diets. At the initial time of diagnosis, they may not be able to understand all that you tell them about the child's condition. They may seem overwhelmed, confused, or forget significant facts. They may continue to ask questions many times even though you have previously attempted to supply answers.

The intensity of your distress, the severity of your child's disorder, and the inconveniences of the dietary restrictions may be too great for some grandparents to face directly. They might seem to avoid your child, apparently being somewhat fearful of being responsible for her well-being if she is left under their care. Any decline in stamina or endurance in grandparents takes its toll. Problems related to their advancing age can sometimes leave them with precious little energy left over for supporting your child on a restricted diet.

Faced with their own declining condition, some grandparents may find it difficult to empathize with your need to be flexible or adjust to your child's difficulties. They might not be able to comfort you. On the contrary, you may be the one who is comforting them. At a time when you need courage, strength, or hope, grandparents' display of any distress can further drain your emotional resources.

In deciding how best to arrange for temporary care of your child by grandparents, be sure to capitalize on their strengths and talents. Many grandparents are quite energetic, alert, and flexible about food preparation and dietary care of their grandchildren. The grandparents' love for your child may be bountiful and may motivate them to cooperate fully in maintaining the dietary program while she is under their care.

If they want to cook as a way of showing love, grandparents should also provide diet-acceptable foods for your child along with whatever else they serve. Don't expect the entire meal to be totally compatible with your child's restrictions, however; for some very restrictive diets, the necessary level of scrutiny often can be just too overwhelming for elderly people. Helping to coordinate a menu plan for meals and snacks or actually contributing major acceptable ingredients could be well within their capabilities and might be an excellent way for them to show their love.

While it might be difficult to communicate with some grandparents about your child's dietary needs, inroads can be made. Instead of giving repeated explanations, share a brief and precise pamphlet, portions of a book, or a magazine article.

To emphasize what you have verbally explained, another useful tool is to write down your instructions for applying the diet as the need arises. Define clearly and firmly your wishes for their dietary supervision over your child. If they seem at first unable to adapt to your instructions effectively, seek the services of a helping professional to give the necessary message to them. Consider having them attend a conference with your child's dietitian, physician, or with a contact person in a parent support group.

When grandparents are providing child care for an extended period, written instructions are all the more essential to prevent confusion. Be sure to list acceptable food items, information about meal and snack schedules, and any needed modification of specialized food items. Including a few favorite recipes would be helpful to the cook who truly wants to please your child. Whenever you sense grandparents' apprehension about the total responsibility of caring for your child, reassure them by offering verbal and written directions.

Recognize the limits of the emotional support that your child's grandparents can provide. Do not overtax them or expect too much. Some grandparents respond best if they can help in tangible ways, such as by providing transportation, visiting your child, assisting with household routines, going shopping, preparing food you provided the ingredients for, or giving occasional child care.

Another option is to prepare the required foods yourself. Do not assume, however, that you have to bring enough of your child's food to feed everyone present at a special gathering or for ongoing child-care situations.

How to Plan Your Travel and Travel Your Plan

One of the most challenging times to maintain your child's diet is when the family travels for an extended period. Your plans usually become more elaborate than those of families without special dietary considerations.

There are many ways to manage the dietary aspects of extended travel. Whatever the method of transportation, there is no substitute for thorough advance planning, which should include preparations for what to do in case of transportation difficulties, medical emergencies, or unavailability of required food for your child. Once you have developed good plans, stick to them as much as possible.

Consider all aspects of the journey as well as the specifics of meeting your child's special nutritional needs. The method of transportation you use can have significant impact on your ability to maintain the diet. In addition, you must make many decisions about what to take along. Plans should include effective routines for comfort and safety. Make plans also about eating meals in restaurants as opposed to preparing food as you travel.

Consider traveling less and staying longer. Rather than spending most of the time exploring as you travel, it is usually better to spend your vacation time enjoying sights and activities at your destination. It is easier to maintain your child's diet and a regular schedule of meals in one location than when constantly moving to different locations.

After a few well-planned outings, the process of developing your list of take-along items and your family's observance of the various routines can become second nature. Future vacationing and other travel gradually becomes easier to organize and more enjoyable.

Choose Your Destination and Means of Travel Carefully

The choice of destination and the type of lodging en route affect everyone's enjoyment of the trip. Your choice of destination can influence the availability of seasonal food items, such as fresh fruits and vegetables. Climatic factors such as heat and cold, dampness and dryness, and the prevalence of allergens indoors and outdoors also vary from location to location.

Some travel agents specialize in the needs of the disabled and handicapped. Travel guides are available from travel agents, libraries, and bookstores describing the accessibility of various geographic regions, sightseeing attractions, overnight accommodations, transportation facilities, and related information. You can obtain additional information about such special facilities by writing to the local Chamber of Commerce in the area you intend to visit.

In planning for dietary needs, consider writing to medical, dietary, or parent support organizations that might be able to provide food and restaurant resource lists for various parts of the country.

The slower the mode of transportation and the more distant the destination, the greater the dietary challenge posed by the trip. Air travel has the obvious advantage of reaching the destination in hours rather than days; thus there is little cause for worry about dietary needs en route.

Most airlines extend special dietary accommodations. If the timing of meals is crucial, notify the attendant when boarding the plane. Although the airlines personnel who have prepared the meal try to honor your food requests, it is best to check the meal tray thoroughly for any questionable food items. Sometimes an airline may offer a choice of several types of meal categories—sodium-free, sugar-free, vegetarian—so you may have to select a meal that is the most compatible with your child's needs. If notified in advance, the airline may also allow you to bring on board a small cooler of diet-acceptable food.

Bus and train passenger services usually allow you to bring food on board for your child. Because buses and trains need to be boarded quickly, have all your child's food carefully packed for easy portability.

If the mode of transportation is not to be a public conveyance, some parents of diet-restricted children rent a motor home, travel trailer or camper-van. A built-in kitchen, if such an arrangement is available, is sometimes a practical way to facilitate dietary management during a journey.

Arrange Suitable Overnight Lodging

If overnight lodging is necessary, take into account the time involved, the expense, the effort required, the comfort provided, and the ability of the accommodation to suit your child's dietary and medical needs. Motels, the most frequent choice among travelers, vary a great deal in the quality of the accommodations and the expense involved. Outdoor camping saves money but usually involves some loss of convenience, time, and living space within the vehicle to store the camping gear. Sleeping within the vehicle is another option, made easier in recent years by the availability of motor homes, RVs, camper units, and travel trailers. Overnight accommodations may be available at the homes of friends and relatives. Each of these methods has advantages as well as drawbacks. Careful consideration of these factors prior to starting the trip is well worth the effort.

The suitability of the specific motel and the room can greatly influence the success of the overnight stay. Consider making advance lodging reservations using reputable motel chain or travel reference guides. This precaution helps assure consistent cleanliness and adequacy of accommodations. While making reservations, consider checking each motel's rules about cooking and eating in the room. Some motels even offer picnic facilities. Making prior reservations prevents your spending time in a phone booth to locate a motel in the late evening. Under those circumstances, you would probably settle for anything that is available rather than choose lodging in accordance with convenience, price, and suitability for your child.

Bring Diet-Related Items Along

In your planning, include two categories of items: those taken along and those purchased along the way. The decision about what to take depends on the available space for storage and comfortable seating as well as the economy of taking items from home rather than buying supplies en route. Bring no more than you need.

In addition to other medical supplies, include an emergency contact list with names, addresses, and phone numbers of physicians and relatives. Bring medical records such as vaccinations, allergy information and eyeglass prescriptions if the trip involves some hazard or border crossing. Check ahead about what foods are permitted across national or state borders; certain fresh fruits and vegetables and other plants are sometimes prohibited.

Although symptoms may rarely flare up, take medical precautions. Include in your provisions a letter from your child's physician, stating your child's name, explicit instructions regarding the use of any medications, allergy or sensitivity considerations, precise description of the diet, and additional information that would be helpful in a medical emergency. You might want a "To Whom It May Concern" letter from your child's dietitian or physician to help convince motel or restaurant personnel of the appropriateness of any special requests that you need to make.

If your child's nutritional status is especially unstable, find the names of other physicians or dietitians along the route and at the destination who can help in case of a problem. Also take along a list of professional organizations or a parent support group from the area to which you will be traveling and along the route as resources to guide you to medical and dietary services as well as to any specialized food sources.

As an extra precaution, you may want your child to wear a medical bracelet or necklace through Medic-Alert. This service provides, for a fee, an emblem listing your child's name, file number, and an emergency number that any physician can use to get significant medical information in an emergency. For travel abroad, Inter-Medic provides a worldwide directory of physicians and a system of recording special health concerns of children. Your child's physician can help with either of these arrangements.

Plan for Meals

Your family will spend much travel time eating, and the expense of eating is one of the most costly aspects of a lengthy trip. Give careful thought to planning for the appropriate balance of economy, convenience, taste, nutrition, and suitability for your child's dietary needs.

Unless you plan to eat exclusively at restaurants, develop a detailed menu ahead of time. You can make some food items at home; then refrigerate, freeze, or wrap them for the trip. Purchase along the way items that are routinely available from grocery stores.

It may be helpful to take along a list of your child's dietary restrictions, including a list of acceptable foods most likely to be available in restaurants during the trip. In a matter of seconds, you can make a quick comparison between this list and any restaurant's menu in order to narrow the food choices while dining out.

You can easily prepare some types of meals in a motel room. Even the counter space in the bathroom can be adequate for heating soup or cooking a small meal in an electric skillet. You can prepare more elaborate meals with emphasis on heated items if you have brought along the utensils. The morning routine at motels can include a check of food supplies, development of a grocery list, and preparation of sandwiches or boxed lunches for the noon meal.

Preparing your own meals helps keep your child within prescribed dietary limits. If you plan to prepare meals as you travel, consider taking these items:

Container of food-preparation utensils: The exact assortment of utensils for preparing and eating food would depend on your family's meal plans. For most travel situations consider these items: paper cups, eating utensils, plates and bowls, window-groove-mounted beverage cup holders, drinking straws, can opener, bottle opener, tablecloth, sharp knife, large spoon and fork, spatula, thermos, dish soap, hand soap, plastic or foil wrap, and garbage bags.

Container of nonrefrigerated foods: A cardboard box or plastic dishpan can hold dry or boxed foods, condiments, spices, and canned goods.

Electric frying pan: This item is versatile because it can bake, fry, boil, or warm food.

Electric two- or three-cup water pot: This item allows for a choice of beverages and can thaw or heat up stews, soups, or other food.

Ice chest: Make ice ahead of time by filling milk containers with water and putting them into a freezer prior to the trip. If you use juice for this purpose, you can drink it as it thaws. The ice chest can store items like juices, dairy products, meat, and beverages. Insulate unpackaged items from the melting ice by putting them into one-gallon plastic bags and setting them on top of the ice blocks. Store liquids in spill-proof plastic containers.

Mixing bowl: The bowl can be used for mixing, washing dishes, making salads, washing ingredients of food items being prepared, or storing leftovers.

Picnic jug filled with water: In addition to the obvious advantage of having water for drinking, the jug provides a ready source of water for wiping hands and faces, cleaning utensils, wiping spills, and various other purposes.

Pump vacuum container: This device allows family members to obtain any beverage conveniently while traveling.

Prepare for Diet Disruptions

Despite your best efforts, restaurants and grocery stores may not be able to provide for all of your child's dietary needs. To prepare for difficulties in finding suitable food en route, keep at least two days' supply of food that conforms to your child's requirements.

Assign someone to help manage the diet, especially if your child's disorder results in rapid or severe symptoms after deviations from the diet. This person should be sensitive to the onset of any symptoms and should also check that an emergency light snack is always available. Use the snack whenever the eating schedule is slightly off or unexpected events disrupt planned mealtimes. This simple precaution can save an embarrassing situation and can spare everyone from a hungry and out-of-sorts child.

Prepare for Eating in Restaurants

The various stresses of travel make restaurant eating a tempting activity. Depending entirely on restaurants, however, can be risky. A symptomatic reaction to restaurant food could significantly reduce the pleasures of your trip, and not just for your child. In order to maintain the diet, you may need information about food preparation as well as ingredients. This information, however, might be difficult to obtain. The rigors of travel, furthermore, may make you or your child less discriminating and more willing to deviate from dietary guidelines.

One way to select the best restaurants is by advance planning through contact with parent support groups. In some communities local groups develop lists of restaurants that are best able to serve individuals with particular dietary restrictions. If you have access to such information and time allows, use their advice about which restaurants to patronize. Food quality is more consistent in some restaurant chains. Try asking for a list of locations of any chain restaurants that seem particularly suitable for your child's special dietary needs.

Telephone directory advertising may portray specialty products and menu dishes potentially suitable for your child. If you know in advance about your dining-out intentions, call ahead to check about menus and any other relevant aspects of potential restaurants. Cafeteria-style restaurants are probably better choices than other types because they offer a relatively wide variety of food that can be inspected before purchase. Salad bars in many different types of restaurants also allow for inspection of the food and opportunities to make choices from among the items offered.

Once you select a specific restaurant, you need to decide about which foods are acceptable. Menu items that are closest to their natural state have the most predictable content and nutritional value. To maintain the best control over your child's dietary intake, choose simple, individual food items instead of casseroles, meat loaves, chef salads, creamed dishes, sauces, gravies, condiments, breaded fancy meats, and food with coatings of any kind. Frying of food often introduces additional ingredients. Most foods can be prepared in a variety of ways. Whole cuts of meat usually are more predictable than chopped or ground meat, which may contain fillers or breadings. A slice of fresh lemon squeezed onto salads avoids all questions about ingredients in the salad dressings.

Know specifically what your child can and cannot eat and bring a copy of this list if there is any doubt. In some restaurants, it may be best to order a very plain food item, using acceptable condiments and other foods from your own supply to complete the meal for your child.

The convenience and economy of fast-food dining make it an attractive option for some traveling families. If a fast-food meal has nutritional deficits, consider how it will fit into a well-balanced food selection for the whole day. If appropriate for your child's disorder and dietary program, you can compensate for the meal's inadequacies later by snacks or a carefully selected evening meal high in the nutrients that were missing in the questionable fast-food meal.

Obtaining efficient and understanding service is an important part of restaurant dining. If you become frustrated, you won't enjoy your meal. Ask about the ingredients used or the methods of preparation of specific menu items. Your child's health is the most important factor.

Restaurant personnel are likely to cooperate with you if you don't put them on the defensive. Show by your attitude, statements, and actions that you intend to patronize the restaurant, that you plan to enjoy the meal, and that you are assuming that the meal suits your family's needs. Make it clear, however, that you must double-check certain aspects of the menu because of important medical considerations.

State that your child is considering a certain menu item but that you need information about its ingredients and preparation before you can place your order. If you need to give a brief explanation of your child's dietary requirements, use discretion in what you say about the diet. Don't let the necessity for scrutiny about the food and its preparation become a spectacle.

A common error is to use trigger statements that make restaurant personnel defensive. Food-service workers may become so overwhelmed with the term "disease," for example, that they may frantically wonder whether they might catch the disease or whether the disease might contaminate the food in the restaurant. Never use trigger statements such as these:

- "We cannot eat your food."
- "My child is sick."
- "My child has a disease and cannot eat your food."
- "My child might get sick on your food."
- "I want to check out your food before we eat."
- "We are always very careful in restaurants."
- "Before we order we want to make sure your food . . ."

Instead, use statements such as these:

- "My child has special medical needs and is on a special diet."
- "My child has special diet needs."
- "My child has severe allergies to certain foods."
- "My child is sensitive to certain ingredients in food."

Don't expect the person who serves you to know the details about ingredients or cooking procedures. If necessary, talk with the manager, supervisor, or cook. Ask a polite question about the ingredients or preparation: "My child has some allergies and cannot eat any food that contains ____. Can you please tell me whether this menu item has ____ in it?" or "Could you please find out from the cook which cooking method is used on this menu item?" Even though it may not be accurate, the simple statement that your child has "severe allergies" to certain chemicals, ingredients, or foods usually gains the necessary cooperation.

Avoid a domineering, holier-than-thou, or white-glove-inspection attitude. Maintain a spirit of helpful cooperation by smiling as you make the inquiry. A congenial spirit is hard for any restaurant personnel to ignore. Remember also that your courteous handling of restaurant situations helps train your child to develop increased responsibility for self-monitoring of food choices in the future.

How to Enjoy Holidays

Hospitality often includes serving food to guests. Dining and partying together often are ways of celebrating love and friendship of family and friends during holidays. To accept in part or reject someone's food can create misunderstanding and hard feelings. In order to participate gracefully in holiday festivities, your child needs to develop sensitive communication skills.

For holidays, special events, or even just an ordinary day, your child should be committed to following the dietary guidelines. She should have an underlying attitude that a holiday celebration does not give license to test or stretch dietary limits. The commitment must be made in advance of a given event so that she can avoid the temptation to rationalize about eating off-limits food. Your child should make the decision once and for all about what kinds of food to eat on holidays. In this way, she can avoid having to think through each temptation that arises. The excuse of "I've been so careful on my diet the last few months, so just a little cheat won't hurt" leads to far more than just one taste!

Your child's diet may require significant modification in the planning and serving of holiday foods. Perhaps she can select from the food being served, or it may be necessary to eat only specially prepared food within the dietary restrictions. Discuss guidelines about making food selections with your child prior to any special event.

Overeating is a significant temptation during holidays. When your family is invited to someone's home, your child may need to resist the temptation to eat off-limits food as well as the temptation to overeat. If her dietary program allows, you may want to provide a well-balanced meal or significant snack prior to your child's attending the event.

As a holiday approaches, maintain family routines that are customary and secure. Just one stay-up-late night immediately prior to a holiday might affect your child's ability to cope with a variety of stresses, including dietary decisions. To help prevent any unusual cravings, plan simple but nutritious meals to be served at regular times. Avoid delays in mealtimes unless a substantial snack is available.

Planning ahead for special days may differ only slightly from the way things were prior to your child's dietary adjustments. Foresight can allow holidays to remain memorable experiences for your child, as well as for those celebrating with your family. Without proper planning, however, holidays can bring dietary failures, frustrations, embarrassment, and strife.

Despite dietary restrictions, your child can fully participate in the festivities. Maintain a calendar with your family's holiday events and commitments. Identify what types of foods are likely to be served. Clarify in advance with the host, hostess, or sponsoring group how your child prefers to handle the various activities and food situations. Perhaps it would be appropriate to offer bringing particular food items, which she could share with others. It might be helpful for her to take along diet-appropriate food items that are similar to what the other children are eating.

Make a conscientious effort to include your child in the joy of holiday food planning, shopping, and preparation. As you work together in these activities, there are opportunities to stress the importance of observing the diet even when it is difficult to maintain. By doing so, you are equipping your child for the reality of living with dietary measures over an extended period of time. She may even develop a sense of personal pride in her special food as she participates in these types of holiday plans. The goal is to convince your child of the truthfulness of the belief that permits her to say: "I'm special, and I eat special foods to help me feel better. My food is just as special as the holiday food others get to eat."

This is the time to go that extra mile to prepare a favorite food item. Most cookbooks offer tantalizing holiday food ideas that can be altered to accommodate children's dietary guidelines. Locate those rarely used recipes you might have tucked away for special occasions and take the time to prepare them. Traditional family recipes frequently can be adjusted also, and serving a favorite family treasure could be of real encouragement to your child. Prepare most of the items ahead of time and freeze them so that your own holiday celebration time is not monopolized by frenzied food preparation.

Some major holiday treats acceptable for your child's diet may be available in specialty sections, or even regular departments, of grocery stores. It is prudent as a rule to purchase an ample amount so that you have these special treats on hand when your child attends a holiday event. She may wish to share her special treats with other children. This act of sharing something special can help build her feelings of belonging and acceptance.

Prepare your child for the probable event of being offered a food item that is not compatible with her diet. An overly zealous host who constantly encourages guests to indulge in a variety of food selections can present a challenge for even the most staunch dieter. Discuss with your child how this overbearing gesture might be handled. Remind her of the importance of self-control with respect to eating. Encourage your child to relax, eat slowly from acceptable food selections, and enjoy the experience.

"I'm sorry, but I cannot eat ____. Thank you anyway" is an effective way for your child to set limits on an overeager host. Rehearsing various situations by role-playing may prove helpful. An abrupt or defensive "I can't eat that" retort might insult the well-intentioned host. On the other hand, your child may opt to receive the particular food item being offered and then pass it on to an accepting sibling who is not bound by the same dietary restrictions. Under some circumstances, your creative child may wish to receive the food, then negotiate a trade with a sibling or a friend so as to bring an acceptable reward to herself after all.

Be tactful when inquiring about the types of food being served. While you should not feel apologetic for your inquiry, you should anticipate that most people are unaware of your child's need for dietary intervention and specific details related to the diet unless they personally have been involved with your child. Your inquiry is not out of place, an imposition, or an insult. If, however, you sense that the host is offended or feels awkward, immediately reassure that you are not suggesting a change in the entire menu to accommodate your child. Instead, make it clear that you are simply trying to determine how your child can best handle the eating situation. If the host seems determined to offer a questionable food item but you sense that he would be open-minded, suggest that he use a specific brand name or a substitute ingredient of your choosing.

To reduce possible confusion or conflict about food choices, de–emphasize the serving and eating of food. Instead, attempt to focus on other joys of holiday celebrations. Continuing to participate in various meaningful family traditions channels positive thoughts and energies for the entire family.

Instead of focusing attention on typical foods or treats found in an Easter basket, a Valentine heart box, a Christmas stocking, birthday-party favors, or a Halloween sack, concentrate on small gifts or party favors such as balloons, pencils, erasers, tickets, or coloring crayons. The use of riddles or treasure-hunt notes for a gift or a surprise is a success for any age.

Directing thoughts to what your child and others can do for someone else can add long-lasting meaning and significance. Holidays are times for spreading joy and love. Bringing happiness to others and finding ways to be of service to them can become meaningful parts of any holiday celebration. Games and organized sporting events at holiday times might also be an option. One child may want to become the photographer of the special event; another, the make-believe newspaper reporter or announcer.

There are always exciting alternatives to an elaborate dinner or party at someone's home where the primary focus of attention would be on the serving of food. Specifically attempt to plan a particular celebration around a community event, sightseeing excursion, or outdoor activity. Any snacks or meals during the celebration should be low-key.

Tap your child's creative talents for decorations, announcements, or festive setups. Consider having your child help make decorations for the entire area occupied by the party—centerpieces for tables, window displays, individualized name tags or place cards, or even costumes. A small holiday craft item can be a special treasure for guests if your family is entertaining. Supervise occasionally, especially when your child is working with anything hot or likely to stain.

Your child will enjoy the opportunity to experiment, discover, dream, imagine, and express original ideas in a free and open way through arts and crafts. Display the production proudly as an expression of her uniqueness and as a gift of love. It is the process of producing the item—not the quality level of the finished product—that provides the real source of joy at holiday time!

Be aware of potential difficulties in relinquishing dietary supervision to adult care givers for extended periods. Make appropriate preparations ahead of time, provide clear instructions, perhaps prepare some food yourself, and convince the care givers of the importance of upholding the dietary guidelines. During extended travel, carefully select the destination and mode of travel, the items to be brought along, and the restaurants you will patronize. Develop effective methods of getting restaurant personnel to help you find correct food items for your child. During holidays, take advantage of the need to prepare special holiday food, encourage meaningful nonfood traditions, and support crafts projects as substitutes for focusing on food. Prepare your child ahead of time to resist the temptation to overindulge with food. By following these types of procedures, you can help ensure continuous dietary cooperation even under times of disruption in ordinary mealtime routines.

12. Help Your Child at the Hospital

Many of the children's symptom complexes and diseases that involve special diets as part of medical treatment also involve complications that result in hospitalizations of the children. Some diet-restricted children enter hospitals repeatedly, and these experiences can be especially traumatic.

It is important to know how to support your child's dietary effort during the period of hospitalization. Some diet-restricted children can simply go off their diets while in the hospital. Others face rapid and severe medical consequences if they deviate from their diets; for these children, maintaining the long-term diet throughout the hospitalization experience is crucial.

When a diet-restricted child is hospitalized, the prescribed diet might continue despite the hospitalization; or a new set of dietary guidelines might start while the child is in the hospital because of medical procedures involved there. If the physician orders a new, hospital-originated diet for your child, become familiar with it as quickly as possible. Then follow the same procedures you would if you were helping your hospitalized child maintain a previously prescribed but still ongoing diet.

The two circumstances under which your child might be hospitalized would be injury with no chance of preparation ahead of time, or a hospitalization with an opportunity for advance preparation. Hospitalizations for which parents have time to prepare allow the use of more of the suggestions given in this chapter than emergency hospitalizations do.

If your child is having an emergency hospitalization, try to follow as many of these common sense rules as possible:

1. Be available during the first six to eight hours to provide necessary medical information to the hospital staff and to give emotional support to your child.
2. Gather information about the hospital routines and procedures as best you can, and give relevant information to your child in a way that he can understand. It takes hospital personnel days to learn about any particular child's unique way of understanding things in order to make their care effective.
3. Bring a list of your child's exact dietary guidelines if the prescribed diet your child has been observing is other than for a diabetic condition. A list of strong food likes and dislikes also helps.
4. Avoid communicating your anxiety to your child. Most emergency-hospitalized children have no negative preconceptions, but a display of too much parental anxiety can make the experience a tense one.
5. Stay as long as you can with your child, day and night if appropriate and possible.

Preparing Your Child

The recommendations given in this chapter have proven to be useful for diet-related concerns when parents have the opportunity for advance planning prior to their child's hospitalization. There are many additional steps to take to make hospitalization a more pleasant experience for any child; consult your child's physician for specific actions best suited to your child's individual needs.

Ask the physician and hospital staff about procedures that you and your child can anticipate, including where your child will be, visiting restrictions, how you can communicate with the hospital dietitian, persons with whom to coordinate your participation in your child's care, and what items you should bring your child from home.

Be honest and direct in answering your child's questions. If you do not at first know the answers, find out the information from an authoritative source. Children who are going to be hospitalized ask these types of questions most often: Why am I going to the hospital? Is it my fault? Where will Mom and Dad be? Will it hurt? What is going to happen to me? Will I get scars? and When will I get to come home again?

Many books are available for children about hospitalization procedures and the feelings that they have about being in a hospital. Use these books to give simple truthful information about what your child will do, experience, and observe. Explain what occurrences are likely to take place and why your child must be hospitalized. Some hospitals provide a videotape or slide presentation illustrating what your child can expect and orienting him in a way that reduces potential anticipatory anxiety and stress. See Suggestions for Further Reading for a source of information about written materials for helping any child adapt to being hospitalized. Hospitalizations may be more stressful for your child if they are repeated, are for extended periods of time, involve separation from you, or occur when your child is below age five.

You cannot be expected to know all the routines that your child will experience; therefore, it is impossible for you to do a thorough job of preparing your child by yourself. Accompany your child to the hospital for a preadmission visit to become familiar with it and learn what procedures and facilities are involved. Discuss your role in preparation and support of your child with personnel at the hospital. Get the hospital staff to explain their routines and roles to you so that you can then explain them to your child. Orient your child to the room, the nursing unit, and any other areas of the hospital as appropriate. The primary physician can also provide guidance and information about things to expect from hospitalization and what to tell your child.

Your child's cooperativeness at mealtimes during hospitalization can be affected by these fears, which become more significant the longer your child is hospitalized:

Abandonment: Experiencing an intense need for comfort and reassurance because of the pain of separation.

Misery: Worries about feeling sick and being in physical discomfort.

Confusion: Feeling bewildered at the array of intimidating equipment and unfamiliar personnel.

Deformity: Worries about mutilation or deformation of the body as a result of the illness or the treatment procedures.

Loss of privacy: Being a public spectacle; being touched and inspected on body parts that are ordinarily clothed.

Loss of self-determination: Feeling helpless to alter routines established by adults; not being allowed to make significant self-choice decisions.

Loss of identity: Feeling a loss of contact with family members or with favorite clothes and foods.

Reentry: Worries about resuming responsibilities at home and about reestablishing a place socially and emotionally in school and among peers after discharge.

Death: Worries about the possibility of dying while hospitalized or after discharge.

Separation from parents is a major concern for preschoolers and toddlers. Sometimes they think they are being abandoned if they are admitted to a hospital. They may have difficulty understanding the passage of time so that temporary situations seem permanent. They may regress in areas of formerly attained skill, such as drinking from a cup or feeding themselves. Such regression is usually temporary, and the total effects on very young children of separation from parents are less with short stays than with long stays at a hospital.

These five tendencies are the most common types of emotional reactions of children experiencing significant hospitalization stress:

Protesting: Giving outbursts of angry protests or tantrums; refusing to cooperate.

Being insecure: Appearing surprisingly fearful that family members are endangered; imagining them in an accident as they drive to the hospital; appearing extremely anxious.

Forming a shell: Appearing stoic; enduring misery bravely without complaint; denying having any concerns; denying that there is a reason for being hospitalized.

Trying harder: Becoming compliant and docile; seeming to be too good for the situation; becoming too eager to please.

Pulling inward: Losing interest in all procedures; appearing withdrawn; becoming sad, weepy, or apathetic; behaving in babyish ways.

If your efforts to comfort and reassure your child seem insufficient to lessen the intensity of any of these reactions, ask the hospital staff for their suggestions. If any of these reactions persists after discharge, have a qualified mental health professional assist you and your child.

Teaming Up With the Hospital Staff

Insist on being available and taking part in the care of your child whenever possible. The focus on this chapter is on aspects of dietary care, but the principles apply to other aspects of hospital care as well.

Help your child feel connected to home. The less different the hospital seems from home, the more cooperative your child is likely to be about eating. Do what you can to encourage an atmosphere of warmth and acceptance. Write out customary routines and leave the note in the room with your child, taped to the wall if necessary. Make your child's experience as unhospital-like as possible, encouraging your child to sit at a table to eat meals and to wear his own clothes.

Encourage self-care by giving your child food-selection options in a supervised way. Hospitalization often provides opportunity for a child to practice and be rewarded for appropriate food selections.

Be careful with gifts. Favorite foods and special treats within dietary guidelines are preferable to new toys for the diet-restricted hospitalized child. The dietitian may be able to help, and sometimes the hospital can provide special treats.

In sharing the responsibility for your child's dietary care, remember that you know your child's preferences and habits best. You may not be able to alter medical procedures, but you can provide something that none of the staff provide—solid, supportive, loving, reassuring, informed, and sustained parenting of your child. Regard the nursing staff, the physicians, the dietitian, and any other involved personnel as partners in a team effort to help your child. Notice and comment on the actions of hospital professionals that reveal significant competence, concern, and compassion. Don't let the occasional negatives of a busy hospital outweigh the positives.

Nurses. It is important to develop a good working relationship with the nurses. They clearly have a key role in assisting your child with all phases of hospitalization, including dietary matters. Give them your advice about the best approach for your child. Ask for as much information as possible so that your skills and knowledge can be best employed by them.

The nurse as a member of the hospital staff has the most intimate and constant association with your child. The nurse maintains contact between your child and all other helping professionals, gives assistance at mealtime, observes your child's response to meals, and comes the closest to delivering a supplement to parental attention and affection at mealtimes. Attention to nutrition is an important part of nursing care.

The direct nutrition-related service that the nurse gives is usually different from the service given by the physician and the dietitian. In smaller hospitals, however, the nurse may also have added responsibilities, including supervising either a hospital-originated diet or a previously prescribed ongoing diet for a child.

The nurse is involved with providing a pleasant environment conducive to eating, preparing your child for meals, helping your child with self-feeding, and seeing that your child eats prescribed food. The nurse also records the adequacy of food intake and related information for the physician, the dietitian, and other staff members. The nurse can help identify needs for outside assistance and arrange for instructions to you with regard to the post-discharge diet, if originating at the hospital.

Dietitians. The dietitian, under the authority of the physician, is responsible for the nutritional care of your child while he is hospitalized. The dietitian has the responsibility for maintaining any hospital-originated diet for your child as well as continuing any previously prescribed diet for him. For a hospital-originated diet, the dietitian may interpret the physician's order and determine daily meal patterns to be individualized according to your child's habits and modified as your child's nutritional needs evolve.

The dietitian is an important support person who should work closely with the physician and have direct access to your child. The dietitian should encourage your child to maintain a high level of nutrition while in the hospital. Although the dietitian can give your child individualized attention, she is usually responsible for the dietary needs of many patients and may not be able to spend an extensive amount of time doing individual diet teaching. She can give the initial instructions, but often further follow-up is necessary, either by an outpatient dietitian or by referral to children's group classes focusing on nutrition and dietary instructions.

The dietitian in the hospital neither prepares the meals, nor readies the tray for delivery to your child. The dietary department plans the meal and makes every effort to see that the food served to your child fulfills all the requirements of either a previously prescribed or a hospital-originated diet. A dietitian's knowledge about a particular dietary program, however, is still not an absolute guarantee that the various food service personnel involved in delivering food to your child will carry it out. Do not hesitate to question what is being served. You know best what your child can tolerate within the previously prescribed dietary guidelines. If you have any questions about the food being served, be sure to ask about the food selection *before* it is presented to your child. It is very difficult to take food away from a child once it has been served.

For hospital-originated diets, the staff may hand you a diet list at discharge that looks quite difficult or contains ingredients that may seem impossible to locate. You may be tempted to surrender to some favorite foods for your child, even though they may have become inappropriate. In such a case, the dietitian may be able to give suggestions as to where to buy, what to buy, and how to find cookbooks that best fit into your family's food habits and budget.

Helping Your Child at Mealtimes

If you are overconcerned about your child's eating, you can accidentally intensify the problem. Trying to force foods on a sick child can trigger nausea and vomiting and can cause a strong negative emotional reaction to being fed. Such a reaction can create all kinds of problems during the convalescent period or later hospitalizations.

If your child experiences a lengthy hospitalization, assist the nurse in monitoring your child's eating habits. Observe what and how your child eats, so hospital personnel can adopt procedures to strengthen your child's appetite. Informing the nurse, for example, that your child eats well with other children but plays with food if left alone allows the nurse to plan for activities to strengthen your child's cooperation at later mealtimes when you might not be present.

Consider having another family member feed your child occasionally. Use familiar eating utensils, such as a favorite plate, cup, fork and spoon set, or novelty straw. Try to arrange that the physicians and nurses avoid any unpleasant medical procedures immediately before or after your child eats, so that he is rested and pain-free at mealtimes.

Serving small frequent meals instead of three large meals or supplementing three meals with appropriate nutritious between-meal snacks can also help. Finger-foods are sometimes more appetizing for hospitalized children than foods that must be eaten with utensils.

The physician's temporary dietary strategy for your child might require new foods. The menu, however, should involve foods that are similar to those which your child is used to eating at home, as much as possible. Your child's hospital confinement is no time to introduce completely new foods unless they are absolutely essential. Talk to the dietitian if menu items are extremely contrary to your child's liking or tolerance.

Even though careful menu planning takes your child's preferences into account, sometimes the portions may be too large and unfamiliar or the hospital food may include variations in flavors or textures that your child is tempted to resist. Do not punish by removing dessert or threatening to leave. Accept your child's refusals, present other food choices, distract him with something else, then reoffer the refused food later.

Good nutrition prior to surgery is especially important. It ensures fewer postoperative complications, better wound healing, and shorter convalescence. After surgery, your child will probably be on a very limited food intake schedule, starting with small sips of water and slowly advancing to a hospital-originated diet ordered by the hospital physician. Following surgery, the need for some nutrients may be greatly increased. A fairly simple operation could involve a moderate deficiency in food intake for several days. Intravenous fluids can supply some nutrients, but your child's full nutritional needs may not be met. Fortunately, these kinds of nutritional losses are usually not serious.

For nonemergency surgery, thoughtful advance planning for your child's dietary needs helps improve your child's preoperative condition, encourages better response during the surgery, and maintains correct nutrition after the operation. The extent to which the physicians decide to delay any surgery in order to improve your child's preoperative nutritional state is a highly individualized matter. Maintaining good nutrition during and after surgery is much easier than trying to strengthen a malnourished child.

Recuperation can be a difficult time that needs preparation. During the recovery period, your child might need reassurance about why dietary restrictions are going to continue or why modifications in those restrictions may have become necessary.

In order to ensure continued nutritional care and improvement, the physician might recommend an organized dietary program and a monitoring system after discharge. There may even be a need to integrate two separate sets of dietary restrictions for a period of time—the previously prescribed diet as well as the hospital-originated discharge diet. The discharge diet is designed to speed recuperation and help strengthen your child's overall medical status in as brief a time period as possible. If your child is nutritionally improved in the hospital but then discharged into a clinic or other medical facility where there is little or no interest in nutrition, be especially watchful. Be alert also to situations in which there is no provision of meeting your child's nutritional needs by a dietitian.

You have important roles at each phase of your child's hospitalization: preparatory, during the hospitalization itself, and during follow-up care. Use the services of hospital personnel wisely, and be present with your child as much as possible. Check your child's tray if necessary. By following the suggestions given in this chapter, you can effectively improve the nutritional care your child receives while in the hospital.

13. Maintain the Diet Despite Marital Stress

Fortunately, the contents of this chapter do not apply to the majority of parents of diet-restricted children. Most marriages are strengthened by the challenge of making the necessary preparations for a child's long-term diet. The spouses work together toward a common goal, communicate frequently, and make joint decisions that lead to improvements in the welfare of the child and the family.

A child's medical condition requiring a long-term diet can, however, exert stresses that are too great for an already weakened marriage to withstand. For a few, it leads to a chain of events that threaten to tax the bonds of family unity.

Emotional and physical fatigue can develop while parents are trying to survive those complicated days prior to diagnosis. An increasing inability to cope can greatly reduce the emotional strength necessary to deal with the diagnosis and the initial adjustments of treatment.

Marital stresses arising from trying to keep a child on a long-term diet differ from family to family. The spouses, too, may have differing reactions to these stresses. Each has to adjust to the other's reaction, the child's symptoms, and the difficulties involved in administering the dietary treatment. As a couple, they have all the usual responsibilities of parenting. They must also resolve their differing reactions to the child and must deal with stresses in relationships among the children in the family.

The necessity for both parents to work outside the home brings with it a cluster of problems that are not easy to overcome. If one parent has a severe emotional problem or a disturbance such as alcoholism, the ripple effects are destructive to the social, emotional, and physical well-being of all family members. If one parent cares for the child's dietary concerns without significant help from the other, additional stresses can occur. Lack of organization in the household can disrupt mealtimes, resulting in catch-as-catch-can eating habits among the children.

How to Recognize Destructive Marital Patterns

Although reading this list may seem discouraging and even frightening, it is important to be aware of potential pitfalls. Many such situations evolve so slowly that the spouses do not realize that the patterns are developing. Few would admit to creating these situations intentionally, yet they occur occasionally among parents of diet-restricted children.

Partial Denial

One spouse denies the need for the diet while the other recognizes it. The denying spouse criticizes the diet-supporting spouse for being too emotional or overprotective. The denying spouse clings blindly to the belief that nothing is wrong with the child. The denying spouse's interest is more in defense of a wounded ego than in the child's welfare.

Joint Denial

The second parent joins the first parent in denying the need for the diet. This pattern is particularly destructive. Never recognizing what they are dealing with, the parents remain ill-equipped to help the child. The child, meanwhile, becomes increasingly worse. Symptoms grow, follow their natural course, and are never addressed by any medical or dietary intervention.

Partial Abuse

Seething with resentment, one parent becomes physically, emotionally, or verbally abusive toward the child. The other parent is not abusive and might react in a variety of ways. The abusing parent may threaten to cease parental functioning if the nonabusive parent complains. The nonabusive parent learns to hide the child's symptoms from the abusive parent, in order to protect the child. Likely reactions of the nonabusive parent include assuming all parental duties, monitoring the child's diet, and becoming overinvolved with the child in matters pertaining to the diet.

Joint Abuse

Both parents become abusive toward the child. Couples who commit child abuse usually manage to find reasons for continuing their actions. When the abuse comes to the attention of social agencies, such couples often move out of the geographic area rather than face the risk of losing their children. A large number of abused children, in fact, have medical conditions requiring extra measures of parental attention and responsibility, such as long-term prescribed diets.

Partial Overinvolvement

One parent becomes overinvolved with the child. This parent develops the habit of running interference to the point of overprotecting, spoiling, overnurturing, nagging, or pitying the child because of the need for dietary restrictions. The other parent may react in any of several ways, including overcompensating in the opposite direction by becoming abusive toward the child.

Joint Overinvolvement

Both parents become overinvolved and deal with the child in a servantlike way, taking on for themselves the entire responsibility for dietary management and many other aspects of self-care that the child should be managing. The result is a demanding child who is unprepared to meet the challenges of life and who is catered to continually by two exhausted and guilt-ridden parents. The excessively dependent relationship with the parents harms the child's emotional development.

Partial Emotional Bankruptcy

One parent declares emotional bankruptcy, forcing the other parent to assume the total responsibility for the diet and other aspects of care. The bankrupt parent becomes neglectful and acts irresponsibly about all aspects of parenting. The parent with all of the burden may become very angry toward the bankrupt parent and the child. The bankrupt parent may feel guilty for creating such a situation but may also be quick to justify the action and blame everything on the child, with an "If it weren't for that child and that diet!" attitude.

Joint Emotional Bankruptcy

Sometimes both parents declare emotional bankruptcy. The second parent joins in an attempt to unload the responsibility for dietary and other aspects of care onto an external source. If the child remains in the home, there may be gross physical and emotional neglect. Another aspect of this pattern is that both parents become too dependent on outside help for advice. They gradually stop making their own decisions and slowly surrender their leadership functions about dietary management as well as other aspects of child rearing to relatives, friends, or social agencies. They literally don't follow through with the needed measures to assure that the child follows the diet.

One-Upmanship

One parent tries to manage the child's diet alone. The second parent seems not to understand the stresses involved. By criticizing the first parent, the second parent eventually feels superior. The first parent feels misunderstood and blamed by the second parent.

Both parents allow the primary dietary responsibilities to remain with the first parent, who suffers not only from the burden of managing the diet but also from the critical attacks of the second parent. If symptoms or other problems occur, the first parent is blamed for not managing the diet correctly. The second parent typically claims that everything would be better if the first parent would improve in how the diet is being managed.

The second parent gains a sense of superiority by labeling the first parent as inferior, inept, uncaring, ignorant, or weak. The motive for the second parent is to escape scrutiny by keeping the spotlight on the supposed shortcomings of the first parent. Meanwhile the second parent undermines any improvement that the first parent tries to make in dietary management.

The first parent is often overburdened. The parent who is in the one-up position is, in fact, more at ease with the child, partly by being underinvolved in the day-to-day tasks of maintaining the dietary program and other aspects of parenting. The one-up parent can claim in self-righteous fashion to know how to handle the child and to have fewer difficulties in managing the diet.

Mutual One-Upmanship

When the first parent counterattacks, the two cannot arrive at mutual decisions about dietary management for the child. They struggle instead for prestige and status, each attempting to feel superior to the other. Each wants to pin the blame on the other for the child's continuing difficulties and symptoms, as well as the continuing problems in managing the diet. Each considers the other weak, incompetent, abusive, and unfit to supervise the child's diet. Each asserts that everything would be all right if the *other* parent would improve.

Divided and Conquered

Primarily through lack of communication with each other, parents can be deceived by the child's manipulations about the diet. The situation can deteriorate so that the child eventually succeeds in dealing with only one parent, rather than both. The child thus first divides, then conquers the parents.

A child might, for example, learn to play one parent against the other by lying. She may ask the more flexible parent for permission to eat off-limits food that the other parent would not allow. Another common manipulation occurs after the first parent denies the child permission to eat a diet-inappropriate food item. The child tells the second parent that the parent who denied permission has granted permission if the second parent agrees: "Dad said I could eat this if it is okay with you, Mom." A similar manipulation is that the child, after receiving a noncommital answer from one parent, tells the other that the first parent has given permission for the off-limits food item.

The child may keep pestering until one parent gives in to end the harassment. Like a bulldozer, the child keeps driving forward, pushing everything, including the parent's resistance, out of the way in order to get what she wants. The child does not go from one parent to the other in this case, but bullies either parent into changing "no" to "yes" about permitting a diet-inappropriate food item.

Sometimes the child's manipulation may involve taking advantage of a conflict that already exists. If the parents cannot agree on whether they should allow the child to have a certain food item, for example, she approaches the more flexible parent for permission to have it.

Overcompensation

The excess of one parental trait in the first parent is responded to by the second parent who develops too much of the opposite tendency. For diets with some discretion involved, the crucial factor is not that the parents differ in their preferred amount of flexibility or rigidity concerning dietary guidelines; it is the extremeness of their approaches that causes the problems.

Instead of being pulled together, the parents drive themselves further and further apart. The flexible parent, for example, becomes increasingly flexible about the diet and avoids all strict and conservative interpretations of dietary guidelines. The strict parent, on the other hand, feels no obligation to give in to an occasional questionable food item. The more flexible parent is already allowing the child to stretch the limits of the diet. Each time the child is treated softly, the firm parent becomes more firm. Each time the child is treated firmly, the soft parent becomes more soft and flexible with regard to dietary enforcement. At any specific moment, the child is treated too rigidly or too flexibly about which foods are allowed, depending upon which of the two parents is supervising at the time.

How to Prevent and Reduce These Patterns

The first step in shielding your marital relationship from these patterns is to recognize them. Spot the patterns that seem to be most likely to develop in your own marriage. Awareness opens the door for reversing these trends, and without awareness there is no chance for an effective solution.

If any of these patterns is already occurring, seek assistance from a qualified mental health professional who is knowledgeable in family relationships. Seldom can even the best intentioned of efforts reverse any of these trends without professional guidance.

The greater the amount of stress in your marriage and the longer these patterns have developed, the greater the need for activities that clarify the communication between the two of you and strengthen your marriage. Regardless of how pressured or discouraging the situation, there is always hope for improvement as long as you are aware of what is occurring.

The more confident you are as parents, the more gracefully you can respond to the stresses of your child's diet. Everything you do to increase your parenting skill and knowledge helps.

Also improve your skill as spouses. Study and learn as much as possible about your marital relationship. Attend workshops, seminars, classes, retreats, and similar programs that focus on marriage enrichment, and read constructive materials in this area.

Notice your child's attempts to play one parent against the other about food privileges. Does she bulldoze one parent? Does the child find weak spots because parents differ from each other about whether or not to allow her to have certain food items? Does the child hide behind the more flexible parent and push for questionable food items? Bring any such manipulations to the forefront and deal with them as misbehavior.

Consider the events that have occurred just before you enter the situation. Before criticizing your spouse, be willing to consider an instant replay of the preceding moments. Find out what has been happening with your child and with your spouse during the last few hours prior to a moment of conflict over dietary observance

Accept the fact that you are both trying to do what is best for your child. Even if your approach to a particular dietary question may be different, support your spouse's effort. Even though the two of you may disagree, one person's solution may not be the only effective answer.

Rise above mutual criticism. Don't try to pin blame on each other. Deal with the specifics of the dietary question in the spirit of mutual respect and acceptance. The important question in each situation is "What is the best solution for this dietary question at this time?" rather than "Who is the better parent?" Consult your child's physician or dietitian or approved and authoritative written sources to settle such questions.

The principle of co-parenting is one of the most useful tools for preventing destructive marital patterns. Co-parenting means simply checking with each other before giving an answer to a child's request. The answer is a mutually agreed-upon solution developed by quick negotiation between parents.

The negotiation should take place immediately and in privacy. If you cannot arrange to discuss the matter immediately, arrange a time of day as a deadline for giving the child the answer to a question about dietary observance.

Co-parenting allows you to balance each other in a natural, constructive way. It causes the two approaches to dietary questions to come close together. Both of you can become less extreme, less one-sided, and more flexible in coping with the total needs of the situation. Co-parenting also protects each of you from being canceled out by manipulations. Your child faces two united parents, not two divided parents. Playing one parent against the other in such a circumstance is impossible.

Have regular reviews of the diet. Your family pivots on your marital relationship, and your marital relationship pivots on your love for each other, which must be nurtured by romance and companionship. Having regular parenting meetings allows you to reserve your regular private times together for their intended purpose—romance, not problem solving.

At regular intervals discuss with your spouse the routine decisions that are necessary as part of family leadership, including those pertaining to your child's diet program. This routine problem-solving meeting is one of your most powerful tools for maintaining strong unity with your spouse in supporting the diet. Have these meetings to prepare for the routine PPI meetings during which you discuss with your child her progress on the diet.

How To Meet the Challenges of
Being the Custodial Parent

If you are a single parent who has primary responsibility for your child's long-term diet, some potential problem areas include these:

Overinvolvement. Because of the forced intensity of your relationship, one of the most likely pitfalls is too much emotional dependency by you on your child and by your child on you. The responsibilities of managing the diet may seem magnified because you are without a partner to share them.

The genetic accusation. Occasionally a noncustodial parent criticizes a custodial parent for contributing to the necessity for the long-term diet. The criticism is aimed at your genes and at the idea, whether accurate or not, that the child inherited from you the various tendencies requiring dietary correction. In this sense, the noncustodial parent can express anger by an illegitimate attack on your alleged "contribution" to your child's problem through the genes.

Noncustodial visitation. During visitations, the child is no longer under your direct supervision, and maintenance of the diet is left to the child's own self-control, the noncustodial parent's desires, and to those others with whom your child is left temporarily during the visit.

Child as a weapon. During the last part of a visit, the noncustodial parent might sometimes allow an off-limits food for your child, causing symptoms to flare up. Your child then comes back to you in an unbalanced state. The noncustodial parent uses your child's diet, magnified by deviations, as a way to cause you additional, utterly unnecessary burdens and suffering.

Undercutting the diet. The noncustodial parent might wish to impress your child with how flexible that parent is and how much fun can occur during visits. Or the noncustodial parent may simply not believe in the merits of the diet and attempt to prove the point by purposefully not holding fast to dietary restrictions.

Limited time and energy. Especially as an employed single parent, you may have very little time and energy left after earning an income, doing housework, providing meals, and spending a few moments with your child each day. Any inconveniences that may accompany the child's diet may seem very difficult to overcome.

Fears. A major discouragement as a single custodial parent is the belief that you must have a spouse in order to be happy. A common fear is that you cannot live on your own and that your children cannot possibly be normal in a one-parent household. You may also wonder whether you can ever make realistic arrangements for coping with a child who must be on a special long-term diet.

One of your most important sources of help is the passage of time. Time is needed to discover your whole personhood, beyond your role as parent. You also need sufficient time to develop confidence that you can cope with all that life hands you, including managing your child's diet. The best answers to fears about the difficulties of single parenting are determined efforts to make life work.

The struggles of the single parent of a diet-restricted child are basically the same as those of other single parents, although some difficulties may be magnified. Good child care is important. Take frequent breaks for personal renewal, and develop and refine the art of personal assertion.

Make time-saving arrangements ahead of time. Purchase as many prepared food items as possible, of course being sure to check the ingredients carefully. Contemplate how to minimize your kitchen time. Perhaps a friend or a relative would agree to assist with any necessary baking or other food preparations, if you provide the ingredients and recipes. Identify one or two restaurants where your child can safely order a menu item—especially for those nights when time and energy pressures seem insurmountable.

Avoid becoming distracted by trivial problems. There are so many battles to fight that it makes no sense to become distraught over little problems, imaginary ones, or potential future difficulties that you do not need to tackle currently.

A sense of humor goes a long way toward making things easier to bear. Sometimes the hardest battle for the single parent is to allow for basic humanness. Take one day at a time with as much humor as possible. By taking this step, you can become less bothered by others' mistakes and faults.

Make sure that your child's life is adequately balanced and that your own needs are met in arenas other than child rearing. The best solution for limited time and energy is arranging as balanced and well-rounded a life as possible. Make sure that you get adequate sleep, nutrition, exercise, and mental relief from the intensity of workaday activities. In this way you can ensure against accidentally depending on your child for adult-level emotional support.

The best protection against developing an overinvolved style of parenting is to adopt a "sieve" role—filter and screen the difficulties that life hands your child but avoid unnecessary rescuing from dietary and other challenges.

If the noncustodial parent allows dietary excesses, find out why. If the matter is open to negotiation and if the noncustodial parent listens to your reasons, explain the need for staying within the dietary guidelines for your child's sake. Prepare and send diet-appropriate food along with your child during visits if necessary. This measure, although time consuming, gives the noncustodial parent no remaining excuse for allowing dietary deviations.

If there are hard feelings from the marriage and you are the target of criticisms or other retaliatory antics, consider reducing your communication to the barest minimum. Converse only in a businesslike and superficial manner. Harsh confrontation of a critical noncustodial parent is unlikely to work because it simply reinforces that person's primary intention— to hurt you and cause more upset in your life.

Be like a willow tree in a hurricane. Instead of reacting like an oak tree that opposes the wind and becomes uprooted, let the storm and fury of the noncustodial parent's antics toward you occur without being overcome with them. Bend like the willow and let the impact of the noncustodial parent's action leave your awareness just as rapidly as it comes in. After all, you have apparently done a better job of working through your feelings about the marriage than the noncustodial parent has!

If this type of emotional insulation and reducing of your communication to the noncustodial parent are not sufficient, and if confronting that person is not a suitable option, secure an attorney to explore your legal rights. Just as difficult patterns in a marriage call for professional marriage counseling, destructive patterns toward the diet by the noncustodial parent call for an attorney if direct discussion proves fruitless.

Develop the attitude that "no spouse" is better than "any spouse." Make it clear to anyone you date seriously that you and your family are a "package deal." Any potential future spouse should enjoy the children as much as you do and should be supportive of the diet.

By recognizing potential trouble spots early, seeking to strengthen your marriage constantly, and making diet-supportive decisions in an open-minded spirit of shared leadership, you can lessen the impact of the diet on your marriage. Even after divorce, you can take measures to help ensure that the noncustodial parent continues to cooperate with maintaining the diet. The procedures given in this chapter can go a long way toward smoothing the difficult process of engineering a united dietary effort despite marital difficulties.

A Final Word of Encouragement

This book provides solid, practical guidance and suggestions for preventing or solving the types of situations that parents of diet-restricted children have found to be the most troublesome. We do not want you to feel overwhelmed or intimidated, however, by this elaborate listing of potential problems. Be assured that the vast majority of diet-restricted children are successful in their efforts to attain better health through dietary means. Please select from this sourcebook those suggestions that appear to be most relevant to your situation.

Have confidence that improvement in any dietary situation requiring your directed attention will be relatively easy to attain if you follow the suggestions given in this book. Never let the negatives in your child's situation outweigh your awareness of the positives. Treat dietary efforts as you would any other important aspect of parenting your child. A prescribed diet is serious business, but it can be an interesting and fulfilling project for everyone if treated in the right spirit. Your gift of time, resourcefulness, and commitment is priceless in helping your child achieve health and well-being.

APPENDIX I
Nutrition-Related Effects
of Some Medications
Occasionally Prescribed
for Diet-Restricted Children

Prescribed medicines can have a direct bearing on some children's ability to benefit from long-term diets. Pharmaceutical products have ten key effects relevant to nutrition:

NV – nausea and vomiting
TA – altered sense of taste
DN – decreased absorption of some nutrients
DA – decreased appetite
IA – increased appetite
DE – dental effects, such as mouth sores or swelling of gums
IG – increased glucose absorption
DG – decreased ability to absorb glucose
DI – diarrhea
CO – constipation

These effects are more likely to occur with high-dosage levels and with prolonged use of the medicine. Other effects, some of which may be related to nutrition, can also occur. All these effects will not necessarily occur with each child or each use of any specific pharmaceutical product. The manufacturers of medicines constantly refine and improve their products in an attempt to reduce these kinds of effects.

Table 4 lists the types of nutrition-related effects that are most likely to occur. Medications are given by the generic class of chemical (for example, Cephalosporins), and one example of each class is given by brand name (for example, Duricef is a brand of a Cephalosporin). Within each generic class, several individual products are generally available under various brand names. Each product differs slightly from the others within its class, both as to its chemical composition and its nutrition-related effects. The indicated effects apply to each generic class of chemicals but may not be totally applicable to every brand of product within each class. The brand name given as an example of each generic class in the table was selected randomly. It may or may not have all the indicated characteristics of the general class under which it is given.

To find out whether your child is being affected by any of the indicated nutrition-related effects, consult your pharmacist or physician. In some cases, dietary measures can compensate for many of these effects.

Table 4 Nutrition-Related Effects of Some Medications Occasionally Prescribed for Diet-Restricted Children

Class of Medicine	Generic Chemical Class and Typical Brand of Product	NV	TA	DN	DA	IA	DE	IG	DG	DI	CO
Adrenocortical steroids (anti-inflammatory, allergy symptoms)	Betamethasone (Celestone)							•			
	Dexamethasone (Decadron)							•			
	Methylprednisolone (Medrol)							•			
	Prednisone (Deltasone)	•		•		•		•			
	Triamcinolone (Aristocort)							•			
Analgesics (pain relievers); Antipyretics (fever reducers)	Acetaminophen (Tylenol)	•									
	Aspirin	•	•								
	Codeine, morphine (Demerol)	•		•							•
	Fenoprofen (Nalfon)	•								•	•
	Ibuprofen (Motrin)	•							•	•	•
	Indomethacin (Indocin)	•							•	•	•
	Meclofenamate (Meclomen)	•							•	•	•
	Naproxen (Naprosyn)	•							•	•	•
	Sulindac (Clinoril)	•							•	•	•
	Tolmetin (Tolectin)	•									
Antacids	Aluminum hydroxide (Amphojel)	•		•							•
	Calcium carbonate (Rolaids)	•		•							•

Table 4 (Continued)

Class of Medicine	Generic Chemical Class and Typical Brand of Product	NV	TA	DN	DA	IA	DE	IG	DG	DI	CO
Antacids, continued	Magnesium carbonate (Dolomite)	•								•	
	Sodium bicarbonate	•									
Anti-asthmatics	Theophylline (Theo-Dur)	•			•					•	
Antibiotics	Ampicillin (Amcill)			•			•			•	
	Cephalosporins (Duricef)										
	Chloramphenicol (Chloromycetin)	•		•					•		
	Erythromycin (Ilosone)	•			•					•	
	Penicillins (Pen Vee K)	•		•	•					•	
	Sulfonamides (Septra)	•		•	•					•	
	Tetracyclines (Sumycin)	•		•	•		•		•	•	
Anticonvulsants	Hydantoins (Dilantin)	•		•	•		•			•	
	Barbiturates (Phenobarbital)			•							
Antidepressants	MAO Inhibitors (Nardil)	•		•	•		•			•	•
	Tricyclics (Tofranil)	•	•	•	•	•	•				•
Antihistamines (hay fever symptoms)	(Benadryl, Phenergan)	•					•				•

Category	Drug												
Antimetabolites (anti-cancer)	Fluorouracil (Efudex)	•				•							•
	Mercaptopurine (Purinethol)	•				•				•			
	Methotrexate	•				•				•			
	Thioquanine	•				•				•			
Antituberculars	Cycloserine (Seromycin)					•				•			
	Ethambutol (Myambutol)					•				•			
	Ethionamide (Trecator)	•				•				•			•
	Isoniazid (INH)					•			•	•			
	Paraminosalicylic Acid (PAS)	•				•				•			
	Pyrazinamide (PZA)					•				•			
	Rifampin (Rifamycin)					•				•			
Cough medicines	Codeine	•				•				•		•	
	Decongestants (Sudafed)					•				•		•	
Ganglionic blockers (stomach cramping symptoms)	Atropine-containing (Donnatol)	•				•				•		•	•
	Atropine-free (Pamine)					•				•			
Laxatives	Bisacodyl (Dulcolax)					•				•		•	
	Cascara					•				•		•	
	Mineral oil					•				•			
	Phenolphthalein					•				•		•	

229

Table 4 (Continued)

Class of Medicine	Generic Chemical Class and Typical Brand of Product	NV	TA	DN	DA	IA	DE	IG	DG	DI	CO
Motion sickness medicines	(Dramamine, Tigan)	•					•				•
Stimulants	Dextroamphetamine (Dexedrine)				•						
	Methylphenidate (Ritalin)				•						
	Pemoline sulfate (Cylert)				•						
Tranquilizers, Major	Phenothiazines (Mellaril)	•	•	•		•	•			•	•
Tranquilizers, Minor	Benzodiazepine (Valium)	•	•	•		•	•			•	•
	Meprobamate (Equanil)	•	•		•					•	•
Other medicines	Cholestyramine (Questran)			•							
	Digitalis (Lanoxin)	•									•
	Diuretics (Esidrix)	•		•							•
	Ferrous sulfate (Feosol)	•									•
	Griseofulvin (Fulvicin)	•	•							•	

APPENDIX II
Nutrition-Related Organizations

The following organizations are involved with children's disorders for which nutritional or dietary measures have been claimed to be relevant. These organizations provide various types of information for parents of children who may have special dietary considerations. They give behavior management, medical, bibliographic, state or local affiliation, and other types of information. Some of these organizations provide recipes, cookbooks, and nutritional information. Inclusion in this list does not necessarily imply that the relationship of diet to the indicated disorder is universally accepted by medical or dietetic authorities. Because nutritional knowledge is constantly advancing, these organizations continually alter and improve the services they provide. Inclusion in this list does not necessarily indicate that the authors of the book endorse or recommend all the approaches or information offered at any given time by these organizations.

Please include a self-addressed stamped envelope when writing for information. The organizations are listed alphabetically with primary interest in parentheses.

Allergy Foundation of America (allergy)
801 Second Avenue
New York, NY 10007

American Academy of Allergy & Immunology (allergy)
611 E. Wells St.
Milwaukee, WI 53202

American Allergy Association (allergy)
PO Box 7273
Menlo Park, CA 94026

American Anorexia/Bulimia Association (anorexia nervosa/bulimia)
418 E. 76th St.
New York, NY 10021

American Cancer Society (cancer)
1599 Clifton Rd NE
Atlanta, GA 30329

American Celiac Society (celiac sprue)
58 Musano Ct.
West Orange, NJ 07052

American College of Allergy & Immunology (allergy)
800 E. Northwest Hwy., Ste. 1080
Palatine, IL 60067

American Diabetes Association (diabetes)
2 Reservoir Circle #203
Baltimore, MD 21208

American Heart Association (heart-related disorders)
7272 Greenville Avenue
Dallas, TX 75231

American Juvenile Arthritis Organization (arthritis)
1314 Spring St. NW
Atlanta, GA 30309

American Lupus Society (lupus)
3914 Del Amo Blvd., Ste. 922
Torrance, CA 950503

American Society for Parental & Enteral Nutrition (digestive diseases)
8630 Fenton St. #412
Silver Springs, MD 20910

American Society of Bariatric Physicians (overweight)
5600 S. Quebec Ste. 160-D
Englewood, CO 80111

Arthritis Foundation (arthritis)
1314 Spring St. NW
Atlanta, GA 30309

Overeaters Anonymous (overweight)
PO Box 92870
Los Angeles, CA 90009

Prader-Willi Syndrome Association (Prader-Willi syndrome)
6490 Excelsior Blvd. E-102
Long Lake, MN 55426

Price-Pottenger Nutrition Foundation (nutrition)
PO Box 2614
La Mesa, CA 91944

Spina Bifida Association of America (spina bifida)
4590 MacArthur Blvd. NW, Ste. 250
Washington, DC 20007

Tops Club (overweight)
PO Box 07360
Milwaukee, WI 53207

Tuberous Sclerosis Association of America (tuberous sclerosis)
97 Vernon St.
Middleborough, MA 02346

United Cerebral Palsy Association (cerebral palsy)
7 Penn Plaza, Ste. 804
New York, NY 10001

Weight Watchers International (overweight)
500 N. Broadway
Jericho, NY 11753

National Foundation for Asthma, Inc. (asthma)
PO Box 30069
Tucson, AZ 85751

National Foundation for Ileitis & Colitis (ileitis/colitis)
444 Park Avenue South, 11th floor
New York, NY 10016

National Headache Foundation (headaches)
5252 N. Western Avenue
Chicago, IL 60625

National Hypoglycemia Association (hypoglycemia)
PO Box 120
Ridgewood, NJ 07451

National Information Center for Handicapped Children & Youth
(advocacy)
PO Box 1492
Washington, DC 20013

National Kidney Foundation (kidney disorders)
30 E. 33rd St., Ste. 1100
New York, NY 10016

National Reye's Syndrome Foundation (mental health, nervous
system)
PO Box 829
Bryan, OH 43506

National Tuberous Sclerosis Association (tuberous sclerosis)
8000 Corporate Dr., Ste. 120
Landover, MD 20785

North American Society for Pediatric Gastroenterology & Nutrition
(digestive diseases)
1056 E. 19th Ave.
Denver, CO 80218

Nutrition Education Association (nutrition)
PO Box 20301
3647 Glen Haven
Houston, TX 77225

International Association of Cancer Victors & Friends (cancer)
7740 W. Manchester Avenue #110
Playa del Rey, CA 90293

Juvenile Diabetes Foundation International (diabetes)
432 Park Avenue South
New York, NY 10016

Leukemia Society of America, Inc. (cancer)
733 Third Avenue
New York, NY 10017

Lupus Foundation of America (lupus)
4 Research Pl., Ste. 180
Rockville, MD 20850

Medic Alert Foundation International (medical identification)
2323 Colorado
Turlock, CA 95380

Muscular Dystrophy Association (muscular dystrophy)
3561 E. Sunrise Dr.
Tucson, AZ 85718

National Anorexic Aid Society (anorexia nervosa)
1925 E. Dublin-Granville Rd.
Columbus, OH 43229

National Association for Sickle Cell Disease (sickle cell disease)
3345 Wilshire Blvd., Ste. 1106
Los Angeles, CA 90010

National Association of Anorexia Nervosa & Associated Disorders
(anorexia nervosa)
PO Box 7
Highland Park, IL 60035

National Association of Protection & Advocacy Systems (advocacy)
900 2nd St. NE, Ste. 211
Washington, DC 20002

National Ataxia Foundation (Friedreich's ataxia)
15500 Wayzata Blvd., Ste. 750
Wayzata, MN 55391

Association for Research of Childhood Cancer (cancer)
PO Box 251
Buffalo, NY 14225

Asthma & Allergy Foundation of America (allergy/asthma)
1125 15th St. NW Ste. 502
Washington, DC 20005

Autism Society of America (autism)
8601 Georgia Ave., Ste. 503
Silver Spring, MD 20910

Cancer Care (cancer)
1180 Avenue of Americas
New York, NY 10036

Cancer Information Service (cancer)
Boy Scout Bldg., Rm. 340
9000 Rockville Pike
Bethesda, MD 20205

Candlelight Cancer Foundation (cancer)
1312 18th St. NW #200
Washington, DC 20036

Celiac Sprue Association of the United States (celiac sprue)
PO Box 31700
Omaha, NB 68131

Cystic Fibrosis Foundation (cystic fibrosis)
6931 Arlington Rd. #200
Bethesda, MD 20814

Epilepsy Foundation of America (epilepsy)
4351 Garden City Dr.
Landover, MD 20785

Feingold Association of the United States (sensitivities)
PO Box 6550
Alexandria, VA 22306

Gluten Intolerance Group of North America (celiac sprue, DH)
PO Box 23053
Seattle, WA 98102

Suggestions for Further Reading

Howell, Mary, *Healing at Home: A Guide to Health Care for Children*. Boston: Beacon, 1978.

Kushner, Harold, *When Bad Things Happen to Good People*. New York: Schocken, 1981.

McCollum, Audrey, *The Chronically Ill Child: A Guide for Parents and Professionals*. New Haven, Conn.: Yale University Press, 1981.

Peairs, Lillian and Richard, *What Every Child Needs*. New York: Harper & Row, 1974.

Schmidt, Lois, *Nutrition for Children with Special Needs*. St. Paul, Minn.: United Cerebral Palsy of Minnesota, 1985. (Mailing address: 1821 University Ave., Rm S-233, St. Paul, MN 55104).

Taylor, John, *The Hyperactive Child and the Family: The Complete What-to-Do Handbook*. New York: Dodd, Mead, 1983.

Lorin, Martin, *The Parents' Book of Physical Fitness for Children*. New York: Atheneum, 1978.

Taylor, John, *Helping Hands and Smiling Faces—How to Get Cooperation from Children on Household Chores*. Doylestown, Pa.: MARCO PRODUCTS, 1983. (Mailing address: Box 1052, Doylestown, PA 18901).

Briggs, Dorothy, *Your Child's Self-Esteem*. New York: Doubleday, 1975.

Des Jardins, Charlotte, *How to Organize an Effective Parent/Advocacy Group and Move Bureaucracies*. Chicago: Coordinating Council for Handicapped Children, 1980. (Mailing address: 407 S. Dearborn, Rm 680, Chicago, IL 60605).

Faber, Adele, and Mazlish, Elaine, *How to Talk So Kids Will Listen and Listen So Kids Will Talk*. New York: Avon, 1982.

Losoncy, Louis, *Turning People On: How to Be an Encouraging Person*. Englewood Cliffs, N.J.: Prentice-Hall, Inc., 1977.

Taylor, John, *Dynamic Parenting: How To Establish Parent Education Programs*. Doylestown, Pa.: MARCO PRODUCTS, 1984. (Mailing address: Box 1052, Doylestown, PA 18901).

Education of the Handicapped Act and Regulations. Alexandria, Va.: CRR Publishing Co., 1985. (Mailing address: Box 1905, Alexandria, VA 22313-1905).

Frank Majorie, *I Can Make a Rainbow*. Nashville, Tenn.: Incenive Pub's, 1976. (Mailing address: 2400 Crestmoor Dr., Nashville, TN 37205).

Taylor, John, *Smiles Across the Miles: How to Enjoy Car Travel with Children*. Doylestown, Pa.: MARCO PRODUCTS, 1983. (Mailing address: Box 1052, Doylestown, PA 18901).

(Numerous publications are available to assist in preparing a child for hospitalization from Association for the Care of Children's Health, 3615 Wisconsin, Ave. NW, Washington, DC 20016)

About the Authors

R. Sharon Latta, the mother of two adopted and two foster children, has individually experienced with each of the four children different medical and behavioral symptoms requiring dietary adjustment. Because information for the necessary modification in food preparations is limited, she has researched in depth the implications of gluten-free (wheat, oats, barley, and rye), sucrose-limited, lactose-free, corn-free, yeast-free, salicylate-free, and preservative-free diets. Her thorough data gathering soon became the foundational basis for assisting families with comparable dietary needs. She is also consulted by dietitians and physicians regarding a variety of dietary details. She is frequently called upon to provide emotional support to families during the diagnosis process and as they learn to adjust to new culinary habits. Her expertise about the dynamics of getting a child to accept food limitations and her many years of experience assisting parents to accept the adjustments that they too must make have led her to spearhead the development of two support groups: the Feingold Association of the Northwest and the Willamette Valley Gluten-Intolerance Group, which together have served more than 6,000 families. She participates with each affiliated national organization by contributing organizationally and writing a variety of diet-related articles for their newsletters. While raising four children on special diets and managing a business management career, she responds to parents' inquiries, speaks before high school, university, and mental health groups, and contributes to local parent support groups for diet-restricted children.

John F. Taylor, Ph.D. is a family psychologist in Salem, Oregon who has guided the diagnosis and treatment of many children with specialized dietary needs. He is the author of several books, including *Person to Person: Awareness Techniques for Counselors; Helping Your Hyperactive Child; Diagnostic Interviewing of the Misbehaving Child, Positive Prescriptions for Negative Parenting, The Hyperactive Child and the Family*, and the "Sharpening Your Counseling Skills" column in the journal *Practical Ideas for Counselors*.

Index